Fuzzy Fiction

Stages, volume 21

Fuzzy Fiction

Jean-Louis Hippolyte

UNIVERSITY OF NEBRASKA PRESS • LINCOLN AND LONDON

Acknowledgments

Many people and institutions made this book possible. My greatest debt is to Warren Motte, who not only directed the Ph.D. dissertation that served as the basis for this book but also gave me the inspiration and desire to study a fascinating and enormously important body of work that had received little critical attention.

Several other people have read and commented on the manuscript at the various stages of its composition. I am especially grateful to William Cloonan, whose keen critical eye and warm support helped me through some of the most crucial phases of the writing. I am also indebted to David Bellos, Alexandre Dauge-Roth, Pamela Genova, Van Kelly, Lydie Moudileno, Gerald Prince, Sylvia Sauter, and Peter Schulman for their invaluable intellectual contributions to my project.

Unless otherwise indicated, all translations are mine.

1. Etat des lieux (Introduction)

Inventory

We live in an age of cultural and ideological vacuity. This truism is being repeated ad nauseam from the right and the left, describing in turn the much mediatized death of the ideologies, the McDonaldization of the culture industry, the photos of Robert Mapplethorpe, the novels of Salman Rushdie, those of Barbara Cartland, the homogeneous banality of television, pornography, the Internet, the rise of sects and fundamentalisms, the godlessness of secular societies, censorship, the lack of censorship, and on. Unfortunately this winter of discontent has not spared the field of literature, in France or elsewhere. Indeed, for a number of critics, after centuries of literary progress, stretching from the Ur-novels of Rabelais to the formal deconstructions of the New Novel, the end of French fiction is at hand, as if "a crisis of economic and social structures engendered, *mutatis mutandis*, an analogous crisis in the various domains of aesthetics."[1] Pursuing what Josiane Savigneau called "French detestation," Jean-Marie Domenach, editor of *Esprit*, who heralded the coming of the New Novel in 1958, now warns of an impending doomsday for French literature, of the reign of the useless, the gaudy, and the meaningless.[2] Exeunt *les belles lettres*, enter the postmodern. For his part Maurice Nadeau presents the new generation of French writers in the following terms: "After the terror comes the reaction. Which is to say 'the return to . . .' which seems like a return to freedom. Return to history, return to stories, return to the subject (after the description of so many objects), return to 'creation,' return to the 'oeuvre,' return to characters, to plot, to narrative."[3] Today for Pierre Michon we are witnessing the return of "non-literature on the very turf of the literary,"[4] for the return to plot and subject signals a reactionary attack on the values of the previous avant-garde, and in particular on the theories of the sign and text articulated by Roland Barthes, Philippe Sollers, and Jacques Derrida. This indictment of post-modernism's hedonistic and relativistic tendencies, and subsequent critique of today's perceived individualism and political vacuity, fall within the frame of an overall belief in the messianic nature of art in general and literature in particular. Against the cultural logic of consumer capitalism a familiar rhetoric of art as salvation has yet again flourished in artistic and academic circles, to the right and left of the political spectrum, from Sollers to Pierre Bourdieu, giving a new life to Matthew Arnold's definition of culture as the best that has been thought and known.

Yet for all the prophesying of the naysayers one would be ill advised to judge today's texts by yesterday's standards, blaming their design for our inadequacy of perception, or to overlook the embattled position of the avant-garde in today's cultural institutions. According to François Rosset: "Right now the mass media take up the field and speak *for* literature and *on* literature (the media as part of an economic circuit that includes announcers and distributors and implies notions of immediate economic return, an audience, a preformatted public, etc.). One may denounce the arrogance of the avant-gardes, their histrionics or vacuity, but the powers-that-be, under which literature toils today, are far deadlier."[5] Caught in the nefarious dynamics of the mediatization of literature, writers must now vie for their five minutes of fame on television, without which their books have little chance of existing. But the game is not without risks. In *Sur la télévision* Bourdieu rails that not only does television act as a mediumnic opium for the masses, but it has also gained an almost complete monopoly with regards to deciding the cultural agenda, thus becoming the supreme arbiter in the marketplace of intellectual values. Arguing for the autonomy of the domains of cultural production and against the heteronomy of "made-for-TV" intellectuals and philosophers ("essay writers, journalist-writers, traditionalist novelists"), Bourdieu warns that heteronomy—that is, the crossing-over of spurious scientists, politicians, and writers to the small screen—constitutes nothing less than "collaboration," a grave accusation in the postwar political and cultural environment.[6] Indeed, for Bourdieu the isotopic configurations of this "collaboration" can only turn the intellectual debate into a media circus, a Babel-like maze of discourses that eventually cancel one another out, in the manner of today's political shows, where what seems to matter most is not so much whether issues are being resolved, but that a certain level of noise (both literal and semantic) is generated.

Bourdieu's contention that television is both antidemocratic and culturally insipid is part of a widespread critique of the electronic mass media. In his cynical opus *La télévision* Jean-Philippe Toussaint joins the anti-TV chorus by casting doubt upon TV's greatest claim, that it can accurately represent reality. "If artists represent reality in their works," the narrator muses, "it is to embrace the world and capture its essence, whereas television, if it represents the world, does so by mistake, . . . through mere technical determinism, through incontinence." And yet even if the narrator of *La télévision* is all too aware of the trite illusionist nature of television, of its *incontinence*, as he so eloquently puts it, he cannot help but watch it for hours on end, drifting into a state of apathy and exhaustion.[7] For him, as for the "journalist-philosophers" of Bourdieu, television looms large on the horizon, like a mediational white whale for retinally sensitive Ahabs.

If this were not enough, authors who resist the lure of the small screen—when they don't answer the siren call of the big screen, à la Bernard-Henri Levy—find themselves caught between a rock and a hard place, for the state of publishing seems equally grim. Indeed, today's frantic mercantilization of art has dispelled any illusion as to the immediate future of literature. Small publishing houses more than ever tarry under the pressure of bigger houses, and bookstores that may have carried obscure experimental literature are being ground down by the bookstore chain FNAC and other major groups (e.g., Amazon.fr, BOP.com). Without the moral caution of Canal+ (or the attribution of a major literary prize, like the Goncourt or the Fémina), a book today has very little chance of seeing the light of day or remaining on bookstore shelves more than a few weeks. But even media coverage (should it happen) may not allow authors to be financially self-supporting. The late Jérôme Lindon, founder and former director of Editions de Minuit, put the financial break-even point for authors at ten thousand copies. Below that writers must rely on other sources of income or apply for one of a number of writing fellowships, like the Médicis. In a way today's writers find themselves in a position more similar to that of seventeenth-century artists, whose work was commissioned by the king, than that of their nineteenth-century peers, who were more financially independent. In the face of such pressure, in the absence of more consequential support from critical journals, and due to the plethora of texts that come out each year and the ever-slimmer chances of media coverage, it should not be surprising that writers now favor more adumbrative types of radicalism than did former avant-gardes. Indeed, there were sixty daily or weekly newspapers for every one hundred novels published each year before World War II, compared to a dozen or so newspapers for three to four hundred novels published per year now.[8]

Of course a century ago artists and writers were in a situation not completely unlike this one. As Manet, Flaubert, and Baudelaire were struggling with the predicament of censorship and the misgivings of the general public, the likes of Octave Feuillet and Jacques Offenbach were producing bestsellers and filling theaters to capacity. And yet the avant-garde still went on to revolutionize aesthetics and become a cardinal part of the cultural capital, from academia to the art market. "This will kill that" (Ceci tuera cela), Archdeacon Frollo—who had not read Marshall McLuhan—may have forewarned in *Notre Dame de Paris*, arguing that the new cultural commodity (literature) would replace the old (architecture, and in this case religious architecture). Yet to this day architecture still plays a significant—albeit diminished—role in the elaboration of cultural values, from the modernist Eiffel Tower to the ostentatiously postmodern structures of Disneyland and Las Vegas. Likewise the current fears brought about by the development of the Internet sound like yet further McLuhanian doomsday predictions. But despite the warning signs emanating from some quarters, to this day nothing permits us to say that the computer, or the Internet, or both, will sound the death knell of the Gutenberg galaxy. Rather, the Internet has provided a number of new outlets for young or established artists, some of whom run their own sites (François Bon, for instance) and some of whom are published online, like Michel Houellebecq, Frédéric Beigbeder, and Yann Quéfellec on oohoo.com, or Jacques Séréna, Alina Reyes, and François Bon on the Web site Inventaire/Invention.

Yet another element belies the idea that today's literature has forsaken avant-gardism and fallen into some postmodern consumer zero-consciousness. Throughout the nineteenth century up until the 1970s literary history was defined in Darwinian terms, best illustrated by the *Lagarde & Michard* manual, as the evolution, or progress, of novelistic forms extending from Cervantes to degree-zero writing (Barthes). But today's writers do not necessarily write "after" Robbe-Grillet, or "after" Sollers; they might rather write "like" Cervantes, Faulkner, and Proust, without being concerned by anachrony. For Ursula Heise the postmodern has allowed us "to articulate the past and present not in terms of sequentiality, but in an often deliberately paradoxical and self-contradictory simultaneity."[9] Speaking of the new generation, Paul Otchakovsky-Laurens, director of Editions POL, argues that it has achieved "the project of the previous generation, that of a literature in movement that got rid of its yoke. They [today's writers] no longer must stage their position based on specific intellectual currents." He adds: "They are part of them. The time is about tolerance, about the opening out of individualities, about freedom of form, with the following caveat, whereby 'all things are equal' against which one must fight."[10]

The problem here is one of designation: how does avant-garde literature define itself? For the most part it does not. Most writers today shun association and *embrigadement*, and the few ephemeral movements that surface now and again are the result of promotional campaigns rather than the efforts of authors themselves. Thus when Minuit's editor-in-chief, Jérôme Lindon, launched an advertising campaign around a literature of "impassivity," featuring Minuit writers Jean-Philippe Toussaint, Jean Echenoz, Christian Gailly, and Christian Oster, he did so more with marketability in mind than with the intention of establishing new critical or literary paradigms. (Incidentally, a few decades earlier Lindon and Robbe-Grillet invented the New Novel for much the same reason.) In the same vein it was Editions J'ai Lu that brought readers an unfussy "New Generation" (Nouvelle Génération), and not literary critics, rounding up their own motley collection of young Turks, like the scandalous and mediatic Virginie Despentes, but also the trashy Medhi Belhaj Kacem (better known as MBK) and hopefuls Eric Faye, Eric Holder, Michel Houellebecq, Lorette Nobécourt, and Vincent Ravalec. In 1998, not wanting to be left out, NRF christened its happenstance collection of minimalists the "Less than Nothing" (Moins que rien); the group included Philippe Delerm, Gil Jouanard, Eric Holder, Jean-Pierre Ostende, Pierre Autin-Grenier, and François de Cornière. Michel Houellebecq, the much decried author of *Les particules élémentaires*, found himself expelled from Perpendiculaire, a hyperrealist movement centered around a journal of the same name (created in 1995), which consisted of Nicolas Bourriaud, Christophe Duchatelet, Jean-Yves Jouannais, Jacques-François Marchandise, Laurent Quintreau, and Christophe Kihm. Others, like François Coupry, Patrick Carré, Georges-Olivier Châteaureynaud, Hubert Haddad, Jean Lévi,

Marc Petit, and Frédérick Tristan, found common ground in the investigation of the real via fantasy and mythology in an antirealist school that dubbed itself "The New Fiction" (La Nouvelle Fiction) in the early 1990s. Finally, Pierre Alferi and Olivier Cadiot created the "Revue de Littérature Générale" at POL, eschewing manifestos and grandstanding declarations for a minute investigation of literature's "lyrical mechanic" (mécanique lyrique), of its base materials and processes.[11] All in all, due to the respective needs of authors and publishing houses, the literary field has become more parceled than ever, the emergence and constant reconfiguration of short-lived associations and groups speaking more to the need for writers and their publishers to adapt to an ever-changing environment than to the need for a label.

However, besides the shift in nomenclature, the break from the tradition of "schools" and "movements" is of momentous importance. Instead of testifying to a lack, or to an irreversible decadence, as Jean-Marie Domenach would have us believe, or to what Pierre Brunel calls "a reflux," which he associates with the very idea of "postmodernism," this shift resonates as an affirmation of diversity, of a multifaceted environment in which the individual writer evolves, seeking his or her own intertext. The successes of francophone writers, from Patrick Chamoiseau to Edouard Glissant, the colonization and subversion of traditionally male genres such as the thriller and the erotic story by women writers like Alina Reyes, Marie Redonnet, Virginie Despentes, and others: these testify to the fact that the turbulences agitating the field of French literature are opening up exciting new horizons. Of course the subversive dissemination of discourses and praxes only concerns some happy few, the "disengaged writers" (écrivains dégagés) of whom Julien Gracq spoke,[12] for most of today's novelists still pander to the well-known fictional recipes of Stendhal and the traditional nineteenth-century novel; a quick glimpse around the shelves of today's libraries would unquestionably show that many a marquise still goes out at five. For those "happy few" who choose not to pander to time-honored fictional recipes, only a few publishing venues open themselves, beginning with Editions de Minuit, POL, Seuil, Gallimard, and Actes Sud, all of which mark the last redoubt for a literature of alterity, fuzziness, and ambiguity. Among these happy few one may count, among others, Jean Echenoz, Jean-Philippe Toussaint, François Bon, Lydie Salvayre, Eric Laurrent, Marie NDiaye, Marie Redonnet, Patrick Chamoiseau, Jacques Séréna, Christian Oster, Nina Bouraoui, Hervé Guibert, Antoine Volodine, and Eric Chevillard.

These writers occupy a resolutely exogenous position vis-à-vis the still dominant aesthetics of belles-lettres, against the formal and aesthetic predictability of the Académie Française, while being at the same time more steeped in "cultural information" (le donné culturel)—the expression is Pierre Brunel's—than the textualist experiments of the 1960s and 1970s.[13] If, for the New Novelists, literature inhabited only language, these postmodernists engage the closeness of the self-referential text and explore its symbiotic relationship with culture, or the feedback loop between text and culture, offering, in David Porush's words, dissipative structures for a chaotic environment.[14] The problem here is again one of perception. Postmodernism's critique of the avant-garde—the death of the utopias, the end of the singularity of the self, the demise of the artist-as-hero—has been perceived by antipostmodernists like Fredric Jameson as the negation of what modernism stood for. Yet postmodernism has not turned the page on everything that modernism accomplished, such as the need for art to be engaged in a perpetual revolution, or the importance of fantasy, even if it did undertake a critique of the modernist heritage. John Barth sums up the issue thus: "If the Modernists, carrying the torch of Romanticism, taught us that linearity, rationality, consciousness, cause and effect, naive illusionism, transparent language, innocent anecdote, and middle-class moral conventions are not the whole story, then from the perspective of these closing decades of our century we may appreciate that the contraries of these things are not the whole story either. Disjunction, simultaneity, irrationalism, self-reflexiveness, medium-as-message, political olympianism, . . . these

are not the whole story either."[15] When the New Novel proposed a
renewal of the forms and contents of the traditional novel, the emphasis shifted to the textual, to problems of enunciation rather than
anecdote, to polysemy rather than monosemy, to *écriture* rather
than writing. Bringing the reader's attention to the construction
of meaning justified the antimimetic stance of the New Novel, if
one were to unpack the fallacy of what Barthes called the "effet de
réel," even if the New Novelists readily acknowledged the liminal
work done by predecessors Flaubert, Dostoevsky, Joyce, Faulkner,
and Henry James in engaging the representational tradition.[16] But
if the New Novel was a reaction against the tenets of Balzacian
prose, today's fiction does not present itself as a reactive movement, and this is one of its major idiosyncrasies. Sollers argues
that, since Mallarmé, experimental literature has been considered
an experience of the limits. It is these limits that the new fiction
interrogates, as a series of diverse and frequently contradictory
subversions from within takes place, a multiple cannibalization of
the canon across genres and across periods.

   Hence the much discussed return of the plot—which some view
as a betrayal of textualist praxes—consists rather of a reappraisal
of fiction and its referents, a resurfacing of the plot, for it would be
naive to think that the plot ever disappeared, even at the height of
the literary experimentalism of the 1970s. Rather, it was encoded
differently, fragmented, ill seen or ill said, but never absent, for the
plot has been a constant fixture of narratives since Aristotle, "the
very organizing line, the thread of designs that makes narratives
possible."[17] Likewise the concept of posthistory, for some associated with the idea of the postmodern, which declares that the Enlightenment's notion of progress has come to a screeching halt—as
per Jean-François Lyotard's demise of grand narratives—plays today like an expression of the inertness of the Cold War. The political immobility of the 1950s and the 1960s corresponded with
narratives of repetition and variation, such as Alain Robbe-Grillet's *La jalousie*, Michel Butor's *L'emploi du temps*, and Raymond
Queneau's *Exercices de style*, as opposed to the more open-ended

feeling of contemporary culture, paving the way for "writing after the end" (une écriture d'après le désastre).

Bruno Blanckeman points out that plot and history were not the only features of fictional narratives to stage a comeback in the late 1970s and 1980s. So did "character, . . . verisimilitude, the primacy of ideas, whether conformist or radical." Borrowing from these categories, popularized by Robbe-Grillet in *Pour un nouveau roman*, Blanckeman goes on to show that the fiction of the past twenty years has done two things: "make use of fiction and condemn it as such."[18] Indeed, the reemergence of pleonastic narrative forms in a number of contemporary texts has not heralded a return to canonical categories and genres. Rather, it underscores the "undecidability" of today's narratives, to use Blanckeman's expression. But more importantly Blanckeman here identifies one of the narrative reversions that have provided critics with some of their most rancorous reproaches, namely the return of the subject. For Bernard Fauconnier the New Novel was animated by the desire to rid the narrative of character and dominated by "the need to found a rhetoric of nothing that gave count of the dissolution of the self."[19] Yet New Novelists never put the subject to death, even if the subject became an unknown, an avatar, under erasure, differed. For his part, after the era of suspicion initiated by the New Novel, Léon Roudiez welcomes today's return of what he labels the *gynetext*, writing from the body and of the body, of its "sensations, perceptions, rhythm, physical and nervous peculiarities, flavors, outbursts of sensuality, and so forth."[20] But the body, its sensations, hardly disappeared from discourse, from Sarraute's tropisms to Robbe-Grillet's sadomasochistic games. And it is the New Novelists themselves, and those around them, from Alain Robbe-Grillet to Nathalie Sarraute, Marguerite Duras, Roland Barthes, and Patrick Modiano, who initiated the return to the ego.

From Modernism to Fuzziness

After Proust and Freud the modern self became an "isolated self," speaking through an unreliable narrator, subjective, mystified by the world around and within, anguished, nauseated, attempting to map out shifting territories and dissolving timelines, like the land surveyor of Kafka's *Castle* or the detectives of Butor's *L'emploi du temps* and Robbe-Grillet's *Les gommes*. What compounded modern anguish was the notion that, as modern physics taught us, the individual observer had come to play a singularly important role in determining the nature of physical—and by the same token, psychological—reality. As Margery Arent Safir reports, according to Heisenberg, "the common division of the world into subject and object, inner world and outer world, body and soul is no longer adequate."[21] A sense of weariness and loss began pervading the human condition, from the Absurd of Camus and Ionesco to the melancholy playfulness of Georges Perec.

Out of the modern malaise postmodernity retained the subjective nature of truth-building and elaborated narratives based on self-directed irony and skepticism, encompassing everything, from Lyotard's grand narratives to Barthes's intransitive textualities, creating texts that invited and defeated interpretation. Charting the evolution from modernism to postmodernism, N. Katherine Hayles traces an aesthetic of "denaturing" at play, "not as a mimetic representation of the world of objects but a sign system generating significance internally through a series of relational differences."[22] Foremost in this process of denaturing the denaturing of self has become a process of disassembly and reassembly, an ongoing deconstruction of identity markers, from gender to nationality. What is cardinal to this process of denaturing is the fact that the postmodern novel is marked by a prevalent sense of "vagueness," a vagueness that appears both resilient and pervasive, affecting objects as well as concepts, the observer and the observed, and finally offering a paradoxical coincidence of presence and absence, a ubiquity of being and not-being.

In 1975 genre-breaking experimentalist Claude Ollier published a seminal piece entitled *Fuzzy sets*. A very Mallarmean piece, *Fuzzy sets* was the last book in a cycle of texts that began with *La vie sur Epsilon* (1972) and includes *Enigma* (1973) and *Our, ou vingt ans après* (1974), which saw the gradual fragmentation of the narrative as form and medium: "The text itself [stated] that its primary goal [was] incorporation of 'vagueness'" (le flou [99]), that is, assimilation of fuzziness, uncertainty, ambiguity."[23] If the lacunae of *Fuzzy Sets*, from diacritic dissemination to formal fragmentation, read like a fitting and timely obituary to the textualist experiments of the 1960s, they also spotlighted a new literary and critical paradigm, "fuzziness," which had much bearing on French fiction and theory after the 1970s, from the lipogrammatic dynamics of Perec's *La disparition* to the jazzed-up collages of Jean Echenoz, from Derrida's *Dissémination* to Gilles Deleuze's *Mille plateaux*.

The study of fuzziness (also labeled "vagueness") was initially undertaken by Bertrand Russell a century ago. While working on set theory, Russell attempted to reduce all of mathematics to logic symbols but found, in the words of Bart Kosko, that "the symbols of math did not match well with the concepts of the physical world."[24] This problem, commonly known as the "mismatch problem," accounts for our use of bivalent logic (more specifically binary oppositions) to describe a world of grays, of multivalued quantities, undefined identities, and shifting boundaries. Following upon Russell, Lofti Zadeh then coined the term *fuzzy*, which was popularized by mathematician Kosko in the 1980s. But the mismatch problem was not exactly novel. A few centuries earlier Descartes had already pondered the limits between being and nonbeing, finding the frontier between them quite nebulous. What was groundbreaking was that fuzzy theorists now targeted the language of math rather than the reality described. Much like their fellow deconstructionists in the field of literary and cultural studies, Zadeh and Kosko were concerned with the transitive nature of language, with how semantic and structural lacunae translate into ontological malaise.

"Fuzzy sets" have traditionally allowed theorists to design a practical test of an overall theory by alluding to concepts that are the cornerstones of basic mathematics. A fuzzy set is "a set whose members belong to it to some degree. In contrast a standard or non-fuzzy set contains its members all or none. The set of even numbers has no fuzzy members, each member belongs to it 0% or 100%, [while] the set of big molecules has graded membership: some molecules are bigger than others and so belong to it to greater degree. In the same way most properties like redness or tallness or goodness admit degrees and thus define fuzzy sets."[25] Taking the macroscopic view, Michael Tye contends that "there are no such things as mountains, deserts, and clouds . . . , [that] boundaries are objectively fuzzy."[26] One might even state that objects, like properties and relations, are by and large beset by vagueness. What then distinguishes an object from other objects at the microscopic level, as microparticles interact and commingle, blurring borders? Because of the vagueness of objects, fuzzy theorists contend that identity itself has become problematic, insofar as individual objects and/or beings may no longer exist independently from one another.

If fuzzy sets are permeable and changing, nonfuzzy sets are closed and markedly deterministic, bespeaking a rationalist ethos, pointing to our impulse to trace borders and constitute categories. For Foucault, as for set theorists, we collocate things in a given category because of the need for the category itself; sets are only determined by their members, and these can be chosen at random. Commenting on Borges, Foucault illustrates this point by referring to his use of a "Chinese 'laundry-list,'" which counts out the members of the paradigm of *animals*, including items as different as "(a) belonging to the emperor, (b) stuffed, (c) tamed, (d) suckling pigs, (e) sirens, (f) fantastical, (g) wild dogs, (h) included in the present classification, (j) innumerable, (k) drawn with a fine brush made with camel hair, (l) etc., (m) that just broke the jug, (n) that look like flies from afar."[27] Likewise my own choice of a "set" of writers (Jean-Philippe Toussaint, Marie Redonnet, Eric Chevillard, François Bon, and Antoine Volodine) may seem arbitrary, as an investigation of the use(s) of vagueness in contemporary French literature may well net an entirely different group of writers, including Jean Echenoz, Patrick Deville, Eric Laurrent, and Michel

Houellebecq, to name but a few. But because of the constraints of time and space, and in spite (and because) of the different aesthetics at play in the texts of the five writers I have chosen, I propose to underscore the importance of fuzziness, both figuratively and structurally, in the contemporary novel at large and in forward-thinking and avant-garde fiction in particular.

Narrators as Strange Attractors

Summarizing one of postmodernism's pleonasms, Blanckeman calls postmodern textualities "undecidable": "The notion of un-decidable narrative suggests . . . a text with varying degrees of fictionality, one that subverts traditional literary categories by overwriting their protocol. Rather than opting for unilateral tension, or polarizing concentration, it prefers to explore narrative possibilities, and questions prejudices and wagers—it is a meandering narrative that thrives outside the beaten path, across the margins. Plurality, differences, simultaneities, paradoxes: such are its cultural paradigms. Problematic fictions . . . , identities simultaneously instituted and destituted, through innovative autobiographical prose."[28] Yet if I agree with Blanckeman's description of the postmodern ethos, I take issue with his coining of "undecidability" as its operating concept. These texts are not undecidable; I will contend they are always decidable, but to a certain extent, between 0 and 100 percent. They incorporate fuzziness and must be studied through it. I will argue further that the postmodern self is an undetermined ego, a fuzzy subject, contingent and ephemeral, speaking through a fractal narrator, but one that still functions as a narrative agency, one that indeed takes to task the kaleidoscopic or variable nature of the real. The paradoxical coincidence of order and disorder, the seemingly infinite exploration of narrative options, the principle of undifferentiated identity—all participate in this general poetics of vagueness.

   In the chaotic economy of the text narrators do come to occupy a singularly important position, functioning as strange attractors—that is to say, points toward which the system irreversibly evolves—in an open-ended narrative environment that is permanently recomposing itself. It should come as no surprise then that today's fuzzy fictions cannibalize popular genres like the erotic story or the *roman noir*. Not only are both genres resolutely narrative, story-driven, putting much emphasis on the narrator, but because they deal with issues of consumption and exhaustion—literally and metaphorically—they also allow readers to measure what Hélène Milliex calls "the erosion of being."[29] Articulating such a poetics of erosion, today's fictions ask how one may "lean against nothingness," as Lydie Salvayre puts it in *La puissance des mouches*—or in other words how one constructs a narrative in an unreliable environment and in the absence of privileged frames of reference.[30] "What can one do against fatigue? Wear oneself out," jests Mr. Songe in Robert Pinget's *Taches d'encre*.[31] Assuredly such exhaustion may take different forms and follow different aesthetic paths. If Marie Redonnet's prostrate characters slowly drag themselves to death—and the end of the text—Eric Chevillard's mad Encyclopedist, Furne (think of "furnace"), deploys phenomenal amounts of energy in order to complete his *grand oeuvre* before the end (*Le caoutchouc décidément*). For Jean-Philippe Toussaint's dispassionate heroes the irreversibility of the second law of thermodynamics forces one to engage resolutely on a course toward indecision. Agonizing "on the roadside of the imaginary" (sur les bas-côtés de l'imaginaire), Antoine Volodine's narrator in *Le port intérieur* is a prattler who owes much to Louis René des Forêts's *Le bavard*, but here he speaks to suspend—if only temporarily—the advance of death.[32]

But the world is a building rotten from the inside, argues François Bon, "old world, . . . dying world,"[33] leading today's novelists to implement sets of delaying tactics to slow the passing of time and the deliquescence of the system. Narrative progression finds itself delayed, through the regressive plotting of Eric Chevillard and Marie Redonnet's Bildungsromans, the cyclical narratives of Volodine, and the reticent narratives of Jean-Philippe Toussaint.

Plotting against linear time, today's fiction recalls the delaying tactics of picaresque literature and the general dissemination of baroque aesthetics, where the "accidents" that fracture the linear progression of things prevent the system from secreting its teleology. Yet even if the relation between cause and effect appears destabilized in these fictions, and impermanence impels characters toward extreme and abnormal forms of behavior while hurling them through the endless whirl of undetermined psyches and appearances, the text still remains, paradoxically, the only space where one can begin to make sense of chaos.

Since the 1970s much attention has been given to narration and narrators rather than to textualist praxes. Concurrently many critics have noted the growing importance of autobiographies in twentieth-century literature, from Sartre's *Les mots* to the more experimental variations of late twentieth-century fiction. A short list would include, among many, Robbe-Grillet's autobiographical trilogy, Doubrovsky's autofictions, Jean-Philippe Toussaint's auto-portraits, Annie Ernaux's minimalist pieces, Jean Rouaud's hybrid autonovelistic trilogy, Christine Angot's psychological scrapings, and the convulsive biofictions of Kacem—which look decisively more toward Artaud and Lautréamont than they do toward standard narrator-centered chronological autobiographies. The paradoxical nature of autobiography, Jean-Philippe Miraux suggests, proceeds from the fact that it is a genre torn between two imperatives: truth and the narrating of that truth: "Autobiography is a rebirth, an initiative that allows for an eventual reconquest of oneself, a reconstruction, a reconstitution."[34]

What the works of the five writers I have chosen have in common with the formal and ideological concerns of autobiography (most of them have little or no interest in writing standard auto-biographies) is a shared concern with the construction of identity, with the literary investigating of the self, with probing its questionable homogeneity and exposing the mechanics of its construction. Identity functions first and foremost as a verbal construct here, and the vagaries of toponymy, character development, and narrative focalization all alert the reader to a reading strategy of naming as differing. For these "men without qualities," or with too many of them, there is no difference between self and other, but a *différance*. Medhi Belhaj Kacem calls today's autobiographies "exobiographies"—Derrida prefers "otobiographies," while Bon speaks of "external monologues"—that is, biographies in which the reader activates the context, in which the author writes "in advance the life of each and every one."[35] What these discourses bear out is that, at the end of the twentieth century, the rise of individualism coincides, paradoxically, with the demise of the individual as exemplum, as singular and exemplary, as exobiography takes to task the constitutive paradox of autobiography and the problematic writing of History. As much as the absence of the character, its relentless fragmentation then translates the problematization of the notion of subject, and fuzziness interrogates the dissolution of the self in the multiplication of reflections. This fragmentation of narrative agency is of course translated in representation of time and space, whereby multiple alternative temporalities and spaces create a paradox that is constitutive of much new French fiction.

Yet the alterity of this fuzzy fiction does not entail a treatment of alterity as a topic, though the theme of otherness and difference does surface regularly and there is indeed some degree of focus on the poor and the disenfranchised. Therefore François Bon may evoke the "downtrodden" (les gens de bas estat), but he does not mean so much the poor in economic terms, but those who lack access to the symbolic order. For his part Antoine Volodine makes reference to "strange birds" who don't quite fit in, dissidents who only exist on the margins of the system. Marie Redonnet laments her "flawed women" (femmes mal formées). Eric Chevillard juggles with parasitic "intellectual troublemakers" (des empêcheurs de penser en rond). Considered together, and in spite of their disparities, all these oddballs articulate a general need for an inventory of epistemological categories. And in this gallery of freaks none stands out as quite as odd or indeterminate as Eric Chevillard's fuzzy hero Palafox:

> *At first sight everything may lead to believe that Palafox*
> *is a chick, a simple chick, after his eggshell breaks open,*
> *a baby ostrich like many that are born every day in the*
> *world, with long legs and an elongated neck, a very or-*
> *dinary baby giraffe, with yellow fur and brown spots,*
> *one of these silent and fearsome leopards, ready to eat a*
> *man, a blue shark like all blue sharks, bloodthirsty, all in*
> *all another bothersome mosquito, with its very custom-*
> *ary trunk, an ordinary baby elephant, but one begins to*
> *doubt. Palafox croaks. Palafox licks our face and our*
> *hands. So our certainties vacillate. Let's take a closer*
> *look at Palafox.*[36]

Of course there is nothing normal or customary here, but a fuzzy subject, ever changing, undefined, one whose exact character and uniqueness are constantly reassessed.

If the French fiction of the past two decades seems at first much more accessible and playful than the arcane creations of the New Novel (Sollers's almost unreadable *H* comes to mind), today's novelists suggest we should be Pascalian readers, aware of the substantive divergence of literature when confronted with the reader's gaze. For fuzziness questions the nature and function of fiction after the formal dead ends of the 1960s and underlines its inherent unaccountability, its duplicity, no matter how readable the stuff may now seem. Reading, like writing, must at this point be approached "as a challenge," warns François Bon, and a transgression.[37] Thus the typology of fuzzy characters ranges far and wide in today's fiction, from the transient pairings of Redonnet to the recycled figures of Volodine, through the ubiquitous and metamorphic heroes of Chevillard, the dispassionate characterless protagonists of Toussaint, and the multilayered polyphonic ensembles of Bon.[38] But in spite of their differences all these figures end up sharing the same epistemological uncertainty and are permeated by the same fuzziness. All engage the truth-building capacity of the text; all address the problematic relationship between the speaking subject and the world.

The problem raised by these fuzzy subjects is that they testify both to a lack and to profusion, to the absence and ambiguity of "specific" physical and biological trends, of definite sociocultural markers. In short, they point to the absence of referentiality in character development, while at the same time they underscore the inescapable need for heroes in literature. If, in Balzac's short story *Le chef d'oeuvre inconnu* (*The Unknown Masterpiece*) the old painter Frenhofer warns that "the human body isn't bounded by lines,"[39] then these fuzzy beings also stand as humanity's last unknown masterpiece, for they are drawn with a complete absence of lines, yet manage to occupy the full volume of our attention. The return to the subject pursued by fuzzy fiction then becomes the construction of an *epiphenomenous* self, of what Edgar Morin and Anne Brigitte Kern christen "unitas multiplex," whereby singularity can only be experienced as multiplicity.[40] The absent subject of the New Novel then turns into a fractal subject, a schizophrenic being—Robbe-Grillet talks of a "schizophrenic I" (je schizophrène) in his autofictional trilogy. Michel Butor further argues that plurality must precede singularity: "It is not the singular that comes first for me, not the individual, it is the plural, and it is inside the plural that the singular will come to be in a way."[41] Put differently, like the fuzzy subsets of sorite sequences, fuzzy protagonists end up being more than the aggregates of their parts, as with Redonnet's recurrent pairings, where the speaking "I" is bound to evolve into his or her double, only to find a new match, yet another double, and repeat the same movement, perpetuating the schizophrenic motion of the dyadic chain ad infinitum.

Further fragmenting the classic notion of "individual" (that which is indivisible), Volodine describes in his texts a dialogized being whose narrative authority finds itself dispersed among a multiplicity of voices. The narrative constraint at work in Volodine's fictions patterns itself after discrete systems, deliberately eliciting the notion of dissemination and blurring the lines of individuality. Voices intersect, overlap, commingle, completely or not, but none stands alone. Each endures as a minor interlocutor in a choir, as one narrative strand among many, in an archive where all strands potentially intercross. Yet no specific intersection can be pinpointed by the reader, as narrative overlaps are left deliberately vague, and intratextual seams are only evoked but never ascertained. Narrative space remains dialogic and agonistic, as different voices vie for narrative control but fail to rule out the innate heterodoxy of discourse. In Volodine's texts one is never more than "a minor angel" (ange mineur); one always speaks as oneself, but to a certain degree, between 0 and 100 percent. What matters then is not affirming the existence, the identity, of one speaking voice over another; what matters is the polyphony at play, the dynamics at work, the structuring nature of this perpetual *décalage*. Collective play is the aim of the game. No individual winners here, just mutual celebration.

If speaking, like writing, must become a testimonial relay between one poet and another, one voice and the next, it is because, for François Bon, we are "témoins" (witnesses, but also relays) between one another. Denouncing an openly monological imperative for the novel, Bon tracks the wavering, the hesitation that characterizes the human relationship to the world, "this splitting of the present, this sense of déjà vu even when it's not reasonably possible, this influence of the skies and the feeling you have that you're not walking but floating." Surveying the urban environment, Bon charts its antiutopian sensibilities, sketching "the disjointed cubes, the chimneys, all plowed down by highways," of the postindustrial heterotopia of our late twentieth-century urbanity.[42] Though the urban milieu may stand out as the worst part of the universe, it also remains the locus generis of postmodernity, and Bon warns against the threat of its invisibility, if not the danger of its disappearance. Exploring our inability to decode urban space, to make it signify within aesthetic and political registers, Bon depicts an "an interchangeable man," an everyman living in the urban everywhere. For him "the city displaces and modifies our categories of representation, our sense of simultaneity, our circular perceptions, our rituals and their symbols, affecting us as well as the locus of production of this representation. We are part of an immense collective subject that no longer exists as the thaumaturge of its own universe of representations."[43] Beyond social disaffection such symbolic and material displacement aims to outplay the very barrenness of the urban milieu by deporting physical space into textual space, grounding the elaboration of the self and its environment in language itself. For in order to resist (symbolic and physical) destituteness the writer must chart the deterritorialization of the self in language.

As different as Eric Chevillard's novels are from François Bon's, the two writers outline a similar vision of the (speaking) self as a random and heterogeneous being, not the absent or unreliable narrator of the New Novel but "the assembly of diverse cells," in the words of Eric Laurrent, or "the accidental convergence of thousands of foreign, even contradictory forces."[44] "All persons, living and dead, are purely coincidental," quips Kurt Vonnegut in *Timequake*,[45] and yet in these texts narrators affirm their pivotal position as the observers of the world in general and the human condition in particular. Not surprisingly, travelers, explorers, and land surveyors crop up time and again in the texts of Chevillard, Redonnet, Bon, Volodine, and Toussaint. I believe these figures to be eminently symbolic in the postmodern context, as they provide readers with strange attractors, anchor points around which the energies of the text coalesce, points from which readers can gaze into the swirling chaos of the text and the world. But the vantage point they provide is by no means a fixed one. On the contrary, it cuts across categories of self, gender, and identity, creating systems that invite interpretation and frustrate it concurrently. In this new dialogue with complexity the metamorphic heroes of Eric Chevillard stand once again as exemplars of the new epiphenomenous self, like Crab, a "skinchanging . . . Proteus," a postmodern "changeling."[46]

"Crab," notes Chevillard, "is ungraspable, not evasive or deceptive but blurry, as if his congenital myopia had little by little clouded his contours."[47] In the words of James Joyce, Crab is "almosting it"; he is nebulous, both profusion and lack, multifarious and unfathomable.[48] Crab permanently shifts between presence and absence, being and nonbeing, always hopping between states and identities. The problem then is not so much whether or not Crab will or can assume such or such an identity, endorse such or such an appearance, but that Crab comes to crystallize indeterminacy (not absence), yet not only "is" a character but spotlights the need for uniqueness and the investigation of its limits. Readers have known, from Ovid to Kafka, that in literature the metamorphic principle plays a liberating role, signaling the stochastic and liberating nature of change. Without a doubt, men-turned-beetles tend to be shunned by good society; they imply the abject, they suggest marginality, they might not even go to church. Yet they also climb to walls and ceilings; they turn our world upside down. They are slivers in the mind's eye, clefts across the picture. To the metamorphic principle Chevillard appends the notion of free play, the chaotic and permanent inception of the self, where identity reconstitutes itself, constantly, in palingenesic fashion, evolving and devolving in unpredictable ways.

Overall the paradoxical process of weaving and unweaving extends to the text itself. In Redonnet's minimalist pieces, for instance, the sentence weaves in and out of subjects, stringing out impressive numbers of constantly changing ideas that bump into each other like plastic ducks in a duck race. But rather than free-falling into chaos, Redonnet's sentence bubbles itself out and articulates itself around a triadic unit (subject-verb-object) that gives it a rhythmic constant. Readers may lose track of things, but the music of the text remains. The text then comes to function as a matrix, spelling out iterative patterns, as formal consistency ends up subtending topical randomness. Eventually the text opposes its own senescence, extolling both the loss of contiguity or sequentiality and the cathartic playfulness of its iterative processes. The universe, fuzzy fictions tell us, is not random, but gray. Chaos may be told, identities may be elaborated, but only within a textual framework that involves fuzziness and advances an "undifferentiated subjectivity."[49]

If the randomness of today's fictions seems to account for a world that is terminally chaotic, it is the very blurring of onto-logical boundaries and the persistent presence of formal determin-isms that give the text its sense of purpose. In this unpredictable environment it is narrators who function first and foremost as the text's chaotic attractors. In this sense fuzzy fictions are strangely close to older narrative genres in which archetypal characters car-ried the symbolic weight of the story. Even though today's nar-rators trudge on, beset with neuroses and schizophrenias, caught in uncertainties about themselves, their identities, memories, and contingent futures, they still carry on the traditions of old. In so doing they map out a road through chaos and display a persistent tendency toward pattern and order. Even death does not silence these fractal voices, for death, says Baudrillard, only suggests the most extreme marginality.[50] In light of this, speaking from an af-terlife only becomes the zero point of narrative consciousness, the end of one narrative cycle and its overlap with another, already begun, as both cycles have fused and merged at some point in the narrative. Thus in Volodine's postmortem polyphonias dead perso-nas come back to life and speak from the dead through the voice of the living, the game of possession referring here not so much to the classic topos of the out-of-body experience—as in Maupassant's fantastic tales, for instance—but to the very postmodern notion of the end of isolated subjectivity.

In the end fuzzy narrators are safely unreliable. They spell out an uncertainty principle for fiction. Though one never knows "who" is talking, as always, the show and the text do go on.

2. Jean-Philippe Toussaint
Reticent Narratives

> No salvation, save in the *imitation* of silence. But our
> loquacity is prenatal. A race of rhetoricians, of verbose
> spermatozoons, we are *chemically* linked to the Word.
>
> Cioran, *All Gall Is Divided*

Jean-Philippe Toussaint has achieved a celebrity that few will contest. Along with Jean Echenoz, he has established himself as one
of the leading modern French novelists, a fact that is confirmed
by the number of epigones that his work and Echenoz's seem to
have spawned, both at Minuit and elsewhere.[1] He is also an accomplished filmmaker and has adapted several of his works, including *La salle de bain* (screenplay); *Monsieur* (cinematography);
L'appareil-photo, retitled *La sévillane* (cinematography); and finally *La patinoire* (an original script). Toussaint's first novel, *La
salle de bain*, which sold more than seventy-five thousand copies,
was Editions de Minuit's second-biggest seller since the 1940s in
1997.[2] After *La salle de bain* (*The Bathroom*), published in 1985,
Toussaint wrote six other novels: *Monsieur* (1986); *L'appareil-
photo* (1988); *La réticence* (1991); *La télévision* (1997); *Autopor-*

trait (à l'étranger) (2000), more a series of vignettes than a full-blown novel; and finally *Faire l'amour* (*Making Love*) (2002). All in all, seven texts in nineteen years, all published by Editions de Minuit, for a total of 1,101 pages, at a spare average of 157 pages per novel. Of all these texts *La télévision* is the longest and, arguably, the least rigorous of Toussaint's works, clocking in at a hefty 270 pages.

Like many other writers today Toussaint questions literature's position with relation to the New Novel, more especially the relevance of the concepts of "experimental literature" and the "avant-garde." The issue remains a vexing one, for today's artists both embrace and oppose the notions at play here. For François Bon today's struggle lies elsewhere: "The avant-garde is old news. . . . To invent the unknown one must claim new forms, to quote from Rimbaud."[3] If, for Stéphane Mallarmé and until Philippe Sollers, experimental literature was considered an experience of the limits, formal and aesthetic experiments reached the limits of readability and intelligibility in the 1970s. Therefore since the 1980s literature has not so much challenged its limits as it has questioned the limits it sought for itself.

Impassivity: Between Action and Inaction

Toussaint situates himself at the crossroads of cultural and literary traditions, heir to the semioclastic and deconstructive tradition of Beckett and Robbe-Grillet but also to the more modernist influences of Nabokov, Kafka, Musil, and Flaubert. In a word, he proposes a rereading of cultural and aesthetic codes, particularly through the media of postmodern collages and cinematographic montage and the merging of semantic codes. Further, and most importantly, he shares certain tendencies with writers like Echenoz: impassivity, humor, an inordinate taste for the banal, and a certain sense of disengagement. The world of Toussaint is deceptively simple, unpredictable, and ludic. It is a world concerned with finitude and unpredictability, as seen through the eyes of a Pascalian observer, wedged between action and inaction.

Indeed, for Toussaint questioning literature's limits plays out first and foremost through a problematic of impassivity. As a literary trope impassivity has a long and venerable tradition, and Toussaint's characters most immediately recall Beckett's and Blanchot's lymphatic creations Molloy and Thomas l'Obscur. But before—and after—these two phlegmatic fellows there have been other examples of fundamentally reclusive and antisocial characters. The list one could construct contains an impressive array of names: Argon in Molière's *Le malade imaginaire*, Saint Anthony in Flaubert's *La temptation de saint Antoine*, the narrator of Proust's *A la recherche du temps perdu*, Des Esseintes in Huysmans's *A rebours*, the narrator of Nina Bouraoui's *Poing mort*, the sacrificial father in Barthelme's *The Dead Father*, Antonapoulos in Carson McCullers's *The Heart Is a Lonely Hunter*, the Boss in Haruki Murakami's *A Wild Sheep Chase*, Barabbas in Pär Lagerkvist's *Barrabas*, Robert Musil's protagonist in *The Man without Qualities*, Vladimir Ipatievich Persikov in Bulgakov's "The Fatal Eggs," the narrator of Dostoyevsky's *Notes from the Underground*, Goncharov's *Oblomov*, Melville's *Bartleby*, and on.

In Toussaint's novels, however, the offbeat impassivity of the protagonists does not merely seek to expose the arbitrariness of sociocultural conventions, nor does it have clear allegorical implications. One might of course read these texts as fictions that go no further than pastiches of the impassive literature mentioned above, but I believe that other elements belie that interpretation. More exactly, the absurd (yet normalized) behavior of Toussaint's protagonists articulates the need for an inventory of normality. In Toussaint's narratives what is *normal* (heimlich) functions paraxially with the *abnormal* (unheimlich), leaving the reader with a vague feeling of estrangement, but one that does not hinge on anything specific in the narrator's odd behavior.[4] In a nutshell the behavior of Toussaint's protagonists is neither normal nor abnormal; it does not in fact belong to either category but blurs them.

In this light the dogged impassivity of Toussaint's narrators should be key to understanding the fuzziness at work in these texts:

Toussaint's characters constantly hesitate between action and inaction and spend most of their time assessing the world around them
before they can make their move, for any action, even the most
trivial, may have tragic and unforeseen consequences. For each
narrator impassivity only serves to mask the chaos that threatens
our lives, as violence may, at any time, throw life out of balance.
Not surprisingly, the lackadaisical narrator of *Making Love* carries around his neck "a bottle filled with hydrochloric acid, . . .
with the idea of one day throwing it right in someone's face," as if
to remind the reader (and himself) that even the most unassuming
and serene individual may commit a violent act.[5]
  Let us understand that physical violence stands as the polar
opposite of inaction (or impassivity), since violence results in
the eradication of its object while inaction (toward something or
someone) consists in leaving its object undisturbed and untouched.
Not surprisingly, many of Toussaint's efforts go toward elaborat-
ing narratives that find protagonists poised in the fuzzy interval
between action and inaction. However, such dillydallying is not
the mark of plain indecision or ignorance on the part of the narrator, but an astute strategy of delay and temporization that allows
him to wait until the most auspicious moment before acting.
  One of the ancillary aspects of impassivity in Toussaint is the
banal and its psychological correlative, boredom. Patricia Meyer
Spacks observes that boredom appeared as a concept in eighteenth-century England, a cultural by-product of the growth of
leisure society. In the modern world, she contends, boredom appears as a construct more than as a natural state, conveying a sense
of anxiety, of cultural decline and lack of authenticity. For Spacks
boredom has come to permeate all of contemporary culture, and
not surprisingly, today's fiction has taken to using boredom as a
key paradigm to express feelings of estrangement and alienation.[6]
For writers like Donald Barthelme, Julian Barnes, Will Self, Jean-
Philippe Toussaint, and Hervé Guibert boredom serves largely to
frustrate the expectations of readers. A key aspect of Toussaint's
texts is that they proffer no teleological drive and refuse narrative

closure. But strangely enough, none of the protagonists of Toussaint's novels seems to experience boredom as we usually define
it—that is, as a state in which we are "weary by dullness, tedious
repetition" (*Webster*). They seem on the contrary to embrace boredom and to seek refuge in the endless repetition of banal gestures,
from Monsieur, who sits on a chair and stares at the heavens, trying to map the galaxy and scale down the chaos of the celestial
immensity into the smaller grid of the Paris metro, to the protagonist of *L'appareil-photo*, who finds peace sitting in bathrooms and
picture booths, letting his mind go blank and his thoughts run
freely, to the narrator of *La télévision*, who, reluctant to begin
working, argues that doing nothing paradoxically allows for "a
slow, progressive opening of the mind and complete accessibility
of the senses" (89).

Indeed, what Toussaint's protagonists really seek is leisure, not
boredom. Spacks quotes Josef Pieper, for whom leisure implies
"an attitude of non-activity, of inward calm, of silence; it means
not being 'busy,' but letting things happen."[7] Indeed, the narrator
of *The Bathroom* muses that "there's something suspicious about
the need to be diverted" (5); indeed, for Toussaint's protagonists
entertainment does translate a refusal of movement, a drastic re-
duction of physical activity. As the narrator of *The Bathroom* omi-
nously warns, "there was nothing I feared less than diversions"
(5), an opinion echoed by the narrator of *La télévision*, who rails
(gently) against the vacuity of a television that keeps viewers ar-
tificially awake and demobilizes them, leading them to a passive
and useless mental vagabondage (13, 26). One may fear, however,
that such self-imposed physical limitations may have serious consequences on the social and professional lives of these indolent
characters; not surprisingly, with the exception of Monsieur, Toussaint conspicuously avoids describing work environments. Exer-
tion, in other words, is left out of the frame. While one of the odd
working protagonists present in Toussaint's work would seem to
be Pascale in *L'appareil-photo*, her task seems precisely to devise
ways to avoid working: she goes and picks up croissants for the

narrator, closes the shop without much thought given to potential customers, and goes on shopping trips. As for the narrator of *La télévision*, he labors over two conflicting needs: writing a monograph on Titian and finding excuses to delay the project. Most of this novel in fact deals with the notion that a phase of reflection and contemplation must precede the beginning of work, the actual writing merely the end product of a long and convoluted developmental phase.

If in every novel vague allusions are made to the characters' professions, the stories largely take place during vacations, weekends, evenings, outings, museum visits, shopping expeditions, travel abroad, and finally at home. Even at work protagonists live at a sabbatical pace. The seriousness and urgency of such a festive and unhurried existence must not be underestimated, though. Protagonists enter this existence of reflective leisure with the dedication and solemnity of one entering monastic life:

> *Back at the hotel, I spent hours lying on the rung bed that stood in the center of the room. I did nothing, and expected nothing in particular.* (La réticence *14–15*)

> *Imperceptibly, Monsieur let himself sink into the hammock, lulled by the soft breeze, legs crossed, eyes open, his thoughts following the rhythm of the hammock's swinging movements, not anticipating nor provoking them. Occasionally, putting one hand behind him on the smooth trunk of the plane tree, he pushed for an instant to stop the movement; then, giving a shove, he started the hammock swinging again, from left to right,* for hours at a time. (Monsieur *27–28; emphasis mine*)

Such an earnest rendition of impassivity forces us to examine not only the need to "act" with regard to the danger of physical and mental exhaustion, and the ensuing need to think options through before acting. Faced with such choices, Toussaint's faceless characters elect to the last person to temporarily withdraw from the world until the most propitious moment when they may, at last, intervene: "There was no reason to hurry the end of that entelechy. Thought, it seemed to me, was a flux that should best be left alone so it may blossom in the ignorance of its own stream and continue to naturally produce innumerable, wonderful rami-fications that all end up mysteriously converging toward a fleeting stationary point" (*L'appareil-photo* 31–32). Of course this kind of project rarely lends itself to closure and manipulation, and ent-elechy cannot be regulated on a conscious level. Furthermore this wild romp through the woods of the psyche calls our attention to one drastic limitation of fiction: entelechy necessarily defeats any attempt at conceiving the world as a definable and finite object.

For Toussaint narrators are intellectual creatures that stand in as the chosen observers of the human condition. As such they look upon the world like dystopians, without hope or trust in either the *vita contemplativa* or the *vita activa* that provided Hermann Hesse's *Glass Bead Game* with its binary structure. In other words, our reluctant heroes are monastic figures of a sort, but unlike their Hessian brethren, they are not searching for metaphysical enlight-enment, nor are they active participants in social and political cru-sades. Standing in the fuzzy interval between action and inaction, they have evacuated what Gilles Lipovetsky calls "revolutionary eschatology" and bespeak an ethos of indifference and narcissistic isolation. Lipovetsky argues that "the modern ideal of subordina-tion of the individual to rational collective rules has been pulver-ized; the process of personalization has massively promoted and incarnated a fundamental value, that of personal accomplishment, and respect of subjective singularity."[8] Such rejection of engage-ment (in the sense of "being-in-the-world," not simply political engagement) is perhaps best epitomized by the quartet of writers whom Jérôme Lindon first associated with impassive literature: Jean-Philippe Toussaint, Jean Echenoz, Christian Oster, and Pat-rick Deville. For these writers political engagement and being-in-the-world engagement remain ideologically dubious, and politics and other orthogenic discourses (history, science) only serve to provide protagonists with interesting tidbits to share at cocktail parties, bits of information that carry no more ethical or cognitive weight than anecdotes on pop culture. This does not mean, however, that politics and ideology play absolutely no role in impassive literature. Rather, totalizing discourses are only another discursive strand of the chaotic mesh that the text encompasses.

It is a new era of suspicion that Toussaint and fellow impassive authors have chosen to usher in. Nonetheless, in Toussaint's work, although the aleatory may have subordinated the praxis of engagement, it does not operate as a principle of production. Instead in Toussaint's stories chance finds itself curtailed within the boundaries of the text and within a simpler, more accessible set of narrative rules determined by the *magister ludi*. The aleatory exists as a topos that generates a level of uncertainty and fuzziness only "within" the textual environment. Chaos is controlled, fuzziness reigns within.

Random Fictions

Ever since Einstein's theory of relativity, the concept of randomness has been a privileged staple of scientific discourse. For some the simple modernization of the atavistic desire to know the outcome of a game of chance, for others the realization that the universe is not deterministic, randomness has given birth to a new paradigm for scientific knowledge. It informs much of chaos theory, fuzzy logic, and the theory of complexity. In mathematics randomness serves to rationalize in statistical terms the degree of uncertainty that exists in an event based on chance. As such it constitutes the basis of probability theory. But beyond science the aleatory has helped problematize the related—and battered—notions of free will and determinism.[9]

In Toussaint's work the concept of the aleatory seems to inform much of the narrative peripeteia. Characters' decisions seem marked by indecision, as they do and say things apparently at random; go to foreign cities for no specific reason; stare at blank

TV screens; sit in bathrooms, on beds, in picture booths, and on toilets for hours on end, just for the sake of being there instead of elsewhere. They make love not so much on account of passion and desire—even though passion may play a major role in their lives—but chiefly to avoid disappointing expectant partners (and putting an end to a relationship) or, conversely, to avoid giving in too quickly to desire (and burning too quickly through the different steps of intimacy). Neither passion nor logic provides a rationale here. Only fuzziness proves to be constant, as reluctance to act dominates characters' lives, and none of the traditional trappings of the psychological novel seems to operate.

In effect the world of Toussaint appears to have expunged all traces of determinism. Yet such chaos is only relative; the aleatory remains carefully plotted, bringing some determinism back into the fictional universe, only at the level of narrative organization rather than plot. Toussaint's world, far from gradually sinking into utter disorder and finally exhausting itself, is nonentropic, given that in Toussaint's fiction randomness serves to organize the chaos of everyday existence and twirl the many narrative strands and discourses into a coherent whole that revolves around certain loci of the text, certain textual attractors. Each of Toussaint's novels articulates the problem of entropy in literary production and the exhaustion of the narrative.

Reading these texts simply for their deadpan humor and seeming nonchalance would lead us to misinterpret their urgency, as the omnipresence of death and disease from *The Bathroom* to *Making Love* casts a more ominous cloud over the triviality of things. It is telling that both *Monsieur* and *L'appareil-photo* conclude on a deceivingly simple lyrical note, in this case the image of "life," reminding us that these stories put the fragility of existence at the very heart of their problematics. If *Monsieur* ends with the apparently offhand remark, "Life, mere child's play for Monsieur" (107), *L'appareil-photo* concludes on a more caustic note: "I was watching the day break and thought simply about the present, the current moment, trying to pin down its fleeting grace—like you would immobilize the end of a pin in the body of a butterfly that would still be alive. Alive" (127). Like the butterfly the protagonist of *L'appareil-photo* finds himself transfixed in an ultimate moment of ataraxia (127). Finally, after turning off the TV set, the wearied protagonist of *La télévision* can only sink into an eternity of silence and darkness (270).

If Thanatos remains an emblematic figure, this is because Toussaint's novels proffer what Jean Baudrillard has called "the satellization of the real." For Baudrillard the much-contested and problematic concept of the real can be described in postmodern literature as the "putting into orbit of an indefinable reality without a common resort to the fantasies that once used to ornament it."[10] Accordingly Toussaint interrogates not only the possibility and necessity of describing the real but also the possibility of sustaining it in narrative form. For as soon as reality coalesces and loses its vagueness, its undecidability, once the narrator reaches his destination and completes his task, the story must come to a close, and the book to an end. For this reason Monsieur prefers to sit on a chair in his room, keeping his hands in his pockets because each expense of energy brings him one step closer to closure and death: "Monsieur, now more than ever, always sat on a chair. He asked for no more from life, Monsieur, than a chair. There, hovering between two compromises, he sought refuge in the calming performance of simple gestures" (85). An analogous problem dogs the protagonist of *Making Love*, who won't kiss his girlfriend, Marie, aware that a kiss, that wispiest of collisions between bodies, would mark the end of their relationship, just as another kiss kicked it off years ago. Challenged by Marie to explain his reticence, the narrator can only argue that he never said that he didn't want to kiss her nor that he did (10). But no matter how casuistically savvy the narrator may be, his diffident attitude is of little consolation to Marie, who concludes that he doesn't love her anymore and that their relationship must end.

To be sure, such tentative behavior forces readers to interrogate the provisional status of normality in the novel, even though

Toussaint's texts appear eminently realistic and do not present themselves as fantasies. Yet the quiddity of events is constantly questioned, and meaning cannot be extrapolated from the socio-cultural norms that inform the text. When hesitation becomes an overriding modus vivendi, all a man can do is spend his life in his bathroom (*The Bathroom*); or board with the parents of his estranged underage girlfriend even after their relationship has ended (*Monsieur*); or steal a camera from a stranger, terrified that the pictures the camera takes are visual markers of the passing of time (*L'appareil-photo*). In the same manner a man may become terrified at the thought of going to see a friend although this was the original purpose of his trip (*La réticence*), as if bringing this act to a close could have dire and unforeseen consequences. No less ominous is the situation of the TV junkie of *La télévision*, who foregoes watching TV at home but gives in to his audio-visual obsession elsewhere, like a smoker who only smokes in public. Lastly that same man may suffer from selective amnesia and still not have the foggiest notion whether he has declared his love to his girlfriend or not, even after years of life in common, since, if this liaison has truly begun, one may infer with good reason that it could (and will) ultimately come to an end (*Making Love*).

Consequently, far from constituting the white noise against which the story takes place, the randomness of events falls within a rationale of mental shilly-shallying and physical dawdling, as fuzziness works to hinder resolution. Instead of being fueled by the protagonist's desires, textual activity is activated by his protraction of desire. As with Lacan's signifying chain, the lack triggers production of meaning. However, instead of trying to remedy that lack in the most timely manner, here the protagonist tries to delay the outcome, for any movement, no matter how minute, may provoke uncontrollable emotions and result in "infinitely small disaster[s]" (*Making Love* 114). But even if Toussaint's narrators do not pursue relationships, or only pursue them in the most tenuous manner possible, relationships pursue them. And even if protagonists do not have a social life, or the faintest possible hint of one, they still receive invitations to cocktail parties and aerial jaunts and unenthusiastically accompany loved ones abroad for fashion shows. In short, no matter how much Toussaint's reluctant heroes resist the world's siren calls, society keeps on barging in, just like the text, which feeds off them to procure narrative material.

Exhaustion as Narrative Telos

Accordingly for Toussaint degenerescence occupies a privileged position in the economy of the novel, and it is in *La réticence* and *Making Love* that its importance is most notable. *La réticence* opens with the image of a dead cat floating in the port of a small town where the narrator is vacationing. From that inauspicious incipit the narrative weaves its way across virtual murders and disappearances, broken-down items and obsolescent places. Through the addition of small details the novel builds a picture of a depleted universe, where objects have reached the end of their functionality. In like manner *Making Love* opens, as noted earlier, with the alarming image of the protagonist carrying a bottle of acid with him at all times, with the idea of throwing it in his girlfriend's face: "I'd simply open the bottle (a small bottle of colored glass that once held oxygen peroxide), aim for the eyes, and run away. I'd felt strangely calm since procuring this corrosive amber liquid, which gave spice to my life and a keen edge to my thoughts" (5). All of Toussaint's fictions endeavor to build the same dystopic universe, where reality, at its most trivial, becomes worn down by the passage of time. Cars and baby carriages break down, furniture bursts at the seams, walls slowly crumble, love fades, like acid eating away the face (or flower) on which it was thrown. In short, the world of Toussaint, like contemporary fiction, ends up expended.

The walk on the beach that the narrator and his baby son take in *La réticence* is telling: it captures perhaps most acutely the sense of weariness that pervades all of Toussaint's work, from the characters' unremitting indolence through the sense of exhaustion that colors the world around them. In this scene a father and his toddler son take a walk on the beach and come across debris pushed ashore by the tide: "Sometimes, the baby would lean forward and try to grab some object that had drifted on the beach, and I kept on passing to him anything he wanted, pieces of dead wood brought ashore by the tide that now looked like strange talismans, stones, twigs (an old plastic sandal too, whose sole he kissed with woops of joy)" (14). If Toussaint announces "an onset of attrition" (un commencement d'usure [83]), he does so euphemistically. In fact, the narrative act itself is a terminal one, death looming large on the symbolic and structural horizon of Toussaint's novels.

For this reason exhaustion stands as the mal-du-siècle of Toussaint's narratives. While in realist novels like Zola's *Nana* and Dumas's *La dame aux camélias* the typology of diseases fell within a logic of moral retribution for past sins, in the twentieth century disease came to be viewed as radical consumption. Schizophrenia (characterized by splitting and a lack of personality integration) came to replace hysteria (a diminishing of willpower, chiefly in women) as the foremost psychological affliction of the era, just as AIDS (a serious and often deadly disease of the immune system) came to replace syphilis (a common venereal disease). But if the testimonial literature of AIDS victims has evolved into a sui generis category, and a medical and textual experience of the limits, and if schizophrenia has given birth to an entire subgenre of medical thrillers, for Toussaint the grim process of biological, mental, and fictional degeneration fails to crystallize the horror evoked by Guibert's *Cytomégalovirus*, Collard's *Les nuits fauves*, or Maurice Dantec's serial-killer stories. Instead in Toussaint's subdued fictions the abjection of disease finds itself diffused and downplayed, in no small part because of the deadpan humor that accompanies most medical problems.

Still, it is not insignificant that each of Toussaint's protagonists should suffer from at least one relatively minor illness and that being (as in "existing") and being sick (as in "beginning to die") should always coexist here. The first incarnation of Toussaint's valetudinarians, the protagonist of *The Bathroom*, must endure sinus problems, while Monsieur has a sprained wrist and bunions in *Monsieur*, and rheumatism and back problems ail the narrator of *L'appareil-photo*. As for the wandering writer of *La télévision*, he gets sunburn, whereas *La réticence*'s reluctant tourist endures small bouts of tachycardia. The traveling author of *Autoportrait* must put up with episodes of melancholia, and finally the morose lover of *Making Love* ends up catching a cold after walking semi-barefoot in the snow with his distraught girlfriend. One may deem these ailments unimportant and even insignificant in the general economy of the text, but like the wear and tear of objects, the deterioration of bodies is critical. The decaying body of the narrator iconizes the decay of the text itself, while the need for preserving the body dramatizes metanarratively the problematic survival of the text and the need to defer its closure through strategies of fuzzification.

However, delaying the onslaught of disease or the resolution of the text presents considerable risks. The body of the protagonist, like the body of the text, can be a ticking bomb, ready to go off should the accumulated pressure run too high. As Monsieur coldly assesses: "Monsieur became suddenly aware that he was too calm. He should, he knew well enough, try to get a little more pissed off in life, little by little, in steps, to avoid the tensions he was storing up exploding all of a sudden with one big bang" (81). The narrator's throwing a dart into his girlfriend's forehead in *The Bathroom* represents one such breaking point, when the accumulated energies of the narrator are no longer containable and break loose, with sudden and unforeseen results. In the same manner, in *Making Love* the narrator's decision to carry a vial of acid demonstrates that the smallest of decisions (carrying a small vial) may have larger, dramatic consequences.

Even a reader untrained in scientific matters and terminology will realize at this point that Toussaint's work emulates a known pattern of unpredictability, otherwise known as the "butterfly effect," whereby small initial conditions may have significantly larger consequences. In *The Bathroom* the protagonist settles in

his bathroom and in so doing provides an odd and somewhat banal starting point for what is to become an epic of banality; in *La
réticence* the initial reluctance of the narrator to meet his friend
Biaggi has a ripple effect that not only changes the life of the narrator but transforms the text into a neo-Kafkaesque thriller. Finally,
in *Making Love* the protagonist's initial reluctance to kiss Marie
eventually affects the rest of the narrator's life. Each time, from an
initial condition that is all insignificance and tedium, the narrative
matrix inexorably proceeds—albeit slowly and with many twists
and turns—toward its own end, its own heat-death.

As *Making Love* opens up, the narrator's relationship with his
girlfriend seems to be coming to an end, leaving him to wonder:
"Given that we were breaking up, was traveling together the best
solution? To a certain extent, yes, because separation would have
drawn us together just as much as proximity was tearing us apart.
We were in fact so fragile and emotionally disoriented that the
other's absence was probably the only thing that could still bring
us together, whereas being with each other would only accelerate
the breakup in progress and make our parting official" (14). Even
if the solution that the protagonist embraces in this case seems to
be the most radical, since it will precipitate the end of the relationship, there is among Toussaint's protagonists a deep-seated fear of
the future, of the deterioration of things and bodies. Besides, after
leaving Marie, the narrator finds himself temporarily at peace with
the world, and somewhat more sheltered from it, when he seeks
refuge at an old buddy's house in order to nurse a cold and his broken heart. There he seeks the numbing comfort of simple gestures,
as his predecessor had in *The Bathroom*:

> *Sitting on my bed with my head in my hands (always
> these extreme postures), I told myself that people were
> not afraid of the rain; some, coming out of the hair-
> dresser's, might want to avoid it, but no one was actu-
> ally afraid it would never stop, would become a contin-
> uous downpour obliterating everything. It was I who,*

> *standing in front of my window and misled by the dread*
> *inspired in me by the movements taking place before*
> *my eyes—rain, moving humans and automobiles—had*
> *suddenly felt afraid of the bad weather, when what had*
> *really terrified me, once again, was the passing of time*
> *itself.* (The Bathroom 20–21)

The emblematic use of Mondrian's paintings in Toussaint's first novel further serves to underline the protagonist's phobia about evolution: "What I like about Mondrian's painting is its immobility. No other painter has come so close to immobility. Immobility is not absence of movement, but absence of any prospect of movement, it is dead. Painting, as a rule, is never immobile. As with chess, its immobility is dynamic. Maybe that's why Edmonsson thinks Mondrian is such a crushing bore. I find him reassuring" (67–68). However reassuring they may be, the Mondrian paintings also remind us of one essential "truth" of textuality: a narrative is always poised between the unstoppable and chaotic rush of things—death by exhaustion—and the equally present danger of stalling life and the narrative matrix.

Both the narrator and the text thus find themselves between the Charybdis of exhaustion and the Scylla of immobility, and it is precisely death as narrative closure that the text seeks to avoid. Paradoxically what threatens the text is the text itself, or rather the inevitability of narrative progress. But rather than following the plethoric extravagance of Flaubert and Céline, Toussaint chooses to represent death through absence, rather than excess, and in that regard the endemic apprehension of his narrators is of particular significance. The etymology of *apprehension* points to the paradoxical relation between the self and the world: *to apprehend* comes from *apprehendere* (to grasp). Its first meaning alludes therefore to the physical relation between the self and the outside world. The word also takes on a more figural meaning, pointing to the fact of understanding, of "grasping" the meaning of something. Finally, the last meaning of *to apprehend* is "to be afraid of," as

if, after having completed contact (through body and mind) with
the outside, the survival of the individual and the self depended on
thwarting that very contact. If epistemology is traditionally built
on the relation between the subject and the world, the fact that the
relationship between the problematic subject of Toussaint's novels
and the even more problematic world is one of distrust and fear
must severely undermine the truth-building capacity of the text.

Pascalian Figures

On that account all of Toussaint's protagonists seek to minimize
physical and intellectual contacts with the outside, while most of
their active life is turned inward. Although they all seem to be
"active" members of society, they are first and foremost Pascalian
figures who observe and meditate upon the fate of things from the
margins while the world is held at bay, as if to prevent its final collapse: "Monsieur, now more than ever, always sat on a chair. He
asked for no more from life, Monsieur, than a chair. There, hovering between two compromises, he sought refuge in the calming
performance of simple gestures" (*Monsieur* 85). Likewise the text
feeds on its own temporizations and hesitations. It geminates upon
itself, as in *The Bathroom*, where with the excipit the reader goes
back to the incipit of the text: "the next day I left the bathroom"
(8) ("je sortis de La salle de bain" [16]) comes four pages into
the text, and "the next day I left the bathroom" (102) ("Le lend-
emain je sortais de La salle de bain" [123]) concludes the text.[11]
The text of *La réticence* loops within itself: it is divided into three
parts, and at the end of part 2, we return to the beginning of part
1. Then the beginning of part 3 takes up a new narrative strand,
but one that does not necessarily carry more authority or finality
than the embryonic and virtual storylines of the first two parts. In
La télévision, after having decided to stop watching TV, and after
having fought the effects of this severing during the whole course
of the novel, the narrator begins watching again, only to savor the
intoxicating pleasure of turning the TV set off.

Such effects testify to the uncanniness of banality and everyday life in Toussaint's textuality, because it is not the monsters and chimeras of folklore and fantasy that challenge narrative authority here, but the most ordinary, banal, boring elements of everyday life. These narratives know no exotic threat, no intrusion from the outside. It is within the ruins of the self and of the unitary subject that the uncanny resides. Fear then is no longer fear of the other, but fear of the self. It becomes decentered, pervasive, and again, chaotic. Finally, it no longer articulates a struggle for personal and textual authority between an identifiable self and an "other" but problematizes the possibility of establishing narrative competence.

Fear manifests itself through refusal: refusal to act, speak, and even think and believe. The reticence that inscribes itself at the threshold of Toussaint's fourth novel seems to occupy a liminary position in every one of his novels. The etymology of reticence—"to be very silent"—underlines the importance of the empty spaces of the text, of moments of stillness. Reticence alludes to the unsaid, whereas impassivity signals unwillingness to show feeling and to act. Not surprisingly, Toussaint's impassive protagonists recoil from doing, feeling, and saying anything. They attempt to remain frozen in place, like the ideal "dame blanche" (a dish consisting of vanilla ice cream with whipped cream and warm chocolate sauce) in *The Bathroom*, only to find out that beings and bodies (just like the dame blanche) must eventually melt down and burn away. As the apprehensive protagonist of *La réticence* states at the very beginning of the novel, "I did nothing, and expected nothing in particular" (14–15), as absence of engagement entails absence of expectation.

The emblematic presence of Pascal in *The Bathroom* grounds the malaise of its protagonist in the reflections of the French philosopher: "But when I thought more deeply, and after I had found the cause for all our distress, I wanted to discover its reason, I found out there was a valid one, which consists in the natural distress of our weak and mortal condition, and so miserable, that

nothing can *console* us, when we think it over (Pascal, *Pensées*)"
(87).[12] This passage from Pascal addresses of course the topic of
human foibles and mortality, but beyond the obvious realization
that man and the universe are finite, the presence of Pascal allows
Toussaint to playfully underscore the obsolescence of rationality.
The ludic angst of his claustrophilic protagonist in *The Bathroom*
defeats any attempt at rational exegesis on the reader's part, as the
small Pascalian vignette provides the reader with a metaphysical
blueprint for the impassivity of all of Toussaint's protagonists.

In *The Bathroom* the narrator's fantasy of a frozen and eternal
"dame blanche" melts in the burning furnace of reality, which demands that thing after thing, seme after seme, be fed to it. The show
must go on regardless, through the sheer impulse of the sentences
adding to each other. Nothing must derail the text, in spite of the
narrator's attempts to slow it down. In *Monsieur* the story and its
protagonist strive to attain equilibrium, as the pun on *centralien* in
the following passage indicates: "Madame Dubois-Lacour found
him a remarkable young man, this Monsieur, knowledgeable, calm,
serious, punctual" (85) ("Mme Dubois-Lacour trouvait que c'était
un jeune remarquable, ce Monsieur, *centralien*, calme, sérieux,
ponctuel" [89]).[13] Monsieur tries to attain a Montaignian "juste
milieu," so as to avoid being caught in the maelstrom that threatens to engulf him. Yet in spite of the almost painful platitude of
the sentences, their even and almost repeatedly stalled rhythm, the
number of pauses (note the abundance of punctuation marks—especially commas and semicolons—in Toussaint's work), the inescapable reality of narrative progression brings the text and its protagonist constantly closer to narrative exhaustion and announces
its closure. The reluctance to act confronts the actors of the tale
with the specter of absence and lack. In the game between presence
and absence the unsaid correlates with the tendency toward non-
presence, toward a reality beset by vagueness, as Toussaint's texts
unfalteringly thwart the reader's expectations for narrative closure
and semantic totality.

Consequently each text only reluctantly identifies the fuzzy

speaking voice that tries to remain hidden behind a screen of anonymity. The pantomime of Monsieur, who tries to hide behind his
superior during administrative meetings, testifies to the need for
protagonists to be out of the narrative loop:

> *Monsieur sat at the seventeenth seat on the left where, he*
> *knew from experience, his presence went the most un-*
> *noticed, beside Madame Dubois-Lacour who, as super-*
> *visor to a large part of his activities, responded to most*
> *of the questions asked of him and, throughout the meet-*
> *ing, calmly smoked his cigarette. Monsieur was scrupu-*
> *lously attentive to remain in line with her body, drawing*
> *back when she moved backward, so as to be never too*
> *directly exposed. Whenever the Chief Executive said his*
> *name out loud, Monsieur leaned forward, as if surprised*
> *and, inclining his head respectfully, responded straight*
> *away in dry, precise, technical, professional terms. Hip,*
> *hop. After which, fingers trembling slightly, he retreated*
> *into his neighbor's shadow.* (11–12)

From *The Bathroom* to *Making Love* reality remains a stifling
force, and the protagonists show a single-minded reluctance to
confront it. As a result they are disinclined to reveal themselves
and speak themselves into existence. If Toussaint's first three novels use reticence as their leading trope, the fourth evolves into a
performance of reticence, as do *La télévision* and *Making Love*,
but in a minor key. It is obvious, however, that *La réticence* marks
an apex in the problematic balance Toussaint negotiates between
movement and immobility, between the fear of entropy and the
dread of absence or lack. In *La réticence* life is all but vicarious and, as Baudrillard would have it, must then be apprehended
through the virtual.

Intersecting the various discourses on chaos (Prigogine, Schrödinger), Toussaint's novels engage in a radical reexamination of
the nature of the narrative act. As a result the narrative gaze is
constantly reassessed. Yet Toussaint makes no attempt to refute

its subjectivity. The use in Toussaint's fiction of vagueness and uncertainty does not serve to establish the authority and truth of
the latter. Instead the epistemic status of truth-building discourses
finds itself in the spotlight. At the end of *Monsieur* the eponymous
protagonist informs his date:

> *According to Prigogine, in fact, quantum theory de-*
> *stroys the notion that physical description can be ac-*
> *curate and that its language can represent the properties*
> *of a system independently of observational conditions.*
> *Well, well. Beside him on the bench, in perfect evidence,*
> *was Anna Bruckhardt's hand. Discreetly watching Anna*
> *Bruckhardt's hand, Monsieur, his eyes lowered, eventu-*
> *ally lifted one of her fingers, prudently, then a second,*
> *and finally, he took her hand in his. He stayed like that*
> *for a few moments, Monsieur, holding Anna Bruck-*
> *hardt's hand, then, not knowing what to do with it, he*
> *delicately put it back down on the bench. Well, shall we*
> *go, he said. (105–6)*

If Prigogine provides us with an a posteriori topical figure for
the random nature of the narrative peripateia, the episode that
immediately follows the description of the Prigoginian theory illustrates how fiction and science interface, dismantling categories
of monosemic versus polysemic discourses. When faced with the
realization that life is not always what it seems (a potential relationship between Monsieur and his date), the protagonist becomes
reluctant to engage in what might be an illusion and falls back on
reticence as a way to defuse the situation. The narrator of *Monsieur* willingly admits that the gaze is only theoretical: "Sight, said
Monsieur. The mind's eye, yes. In the opinion of science at least,
he added for the sake of honesty, and included with a vague hand
motion the Copenhagen interpretation, the Tutti Quanta theory
and all that" (105). In this sense attempting to ferret out the truth
is like going on a wild goose chase, as truth observably resides in
the eye of the beholder, and reality becomes a cultural artifact. As

a result the framing and centering of the narrative gaze occupies a privileged position in Toussaint's narratives.[14]

The object of the narrator's gaze becomes a vague presence, undefined and sometimes inexpressible. The problem seems to lie in the fact that the gaze does not allow the onlooker to seize the "totality" of the real. Toussaint reminds us of one fundamental truth of literature: that we only see part of the puzzle, and even that "remains to be seen." Quantum and atomic theories state that neither light nor matter is continuous, and this concept resonates strongly within the field of literature, raising the question of narrative continuity. We can say that if continuity is visible, the visible providing for the continuity of the narrative fabric, then it is discontinuity that is invisible, fragmenting the text within its deep structures. At the level of the infinitely small, things break down, revealing the holes in the overall cosmic tapestry.

The presence of a quirky and irksome crystallographer in Toussaint's second novel might appear, to the unsuspecting eye, to be just another of the writer's oddities. However, this oddball character adds to the overall sense of dislocation and fragmentation, since his crystals, like any crystal, seem perfect at first sight yet, at the submolecular level, are inherently "flawed." In fact, crystals, unlike other amorphous materials, have properties at the submolecular level that vary depending on the direction in which they are measured. Indeed, Schrödinger's experiment concluded that, depending on the position of the observer, significantly different results are obtained, underscoring the painful fact that truth, because it is narrative and narrated, is no longer crystal-clear.

Vague Borders

Because narrating is beset by vagueness and subjectivity, the world of Toussaint is one of loose moorings and imprecise borders. In an episode of *L'appareil-photo* the protagonist, his girlfriend, and her father get lost in a newly constructed area of the city, whose postmodern architectural features provide the narrator with a locus to

expose the artificiality of his surroundings and, by extension, of
existence:

> *As we walked out of the mall, hesitating as to what our*
> *path should be, we started down a little thoroughfare*
> *of the new city, lined up with ranks of street lamps, at*
> *regular intervals, like so many pathetic and apocryphal*
> *props. The whole block, incidentally, with its cold and*
> *impersonal architecture, gave the impression of being a*
> *disproportionate scale model where we could move, at*
> *our own scale, between two rows of buildings. . . . Fur-*
> *ther on, while we had apparently gotten lost, we ended*
> *up at an immense artificial lake, whose horizon was*
> *filled by the grayness of an industrial zone. (65)*

In the rest of this passage, as in each of his novels, Toussaint multiplies the use of the modifiers "like" (comme un), "in a manner
of" (façon de), and "as to" (manière de), as each object that falls
within the narrative gaze becomes blurred, vague. And while the
gaze of the narrator can't establish the permanent status of truth,
the world inside and outside the narrator remains provisional, the
city an apocryphal *non-lieu*.

Here Toussaint takes the reader beyond the *chosisme* of the New
Novel, questioning the neutrality of the narrative gaze by focusing
on the very need for subjective narrativization, since for Toussaint
the narrative gaze should remain more inquisitive than ever. It is
important to notice that if Toussaint's texts willingly accommodate
a polyglossia that undermines the normality of certain scholarly or
intellectual discourses, by combining them with slang or snappy
patter, they leave little room for polyphony. There is one single
narrative voice in Toussaint's novels, and this voice is resolutely
anchored in the first-person singular. Unlike François Bon and Antoine Volodine, who articulate polyvocal and polymorphous uni-
verses where multiplicity and diversity submerge identity,[15] Toussaint crafts a chaotic world that we see through one single lens.

Such a lens, however, does not only have one setting. In *Monsieur* it is at least bifocal, as the narrative gaze constantly shifts between two narrators (one homodiegetic, the other heterodiegetic) who in reality are two shades of the same narrating persona. For his part the narrator of *La télévision* admits that he is at a loss to distinguish between newscasters on television: "[While] I was still gazing at this grave and affected face made of three million light dots, which, at a rate of six hundred and twenty-six lines per image, and fifty frames per second, was still reporting the news on the screen, I told myself that this bespectacled newscaster was not Jürgen Klaus, but Claus Seibel, I do mix them up, these news anchors, despite the three million small dots that characterize them" (124–25). Gazing with accuracy, or truthfully, is a tall order in Toussaint's novels, for the gaze obviously affects the object it is gazing at, as the object affects the gaze. And yet, armed with awareness of its limitations, the narrator decides he must look on.

The inquisitiveness of the narrative gaze is most obvious in Toussaint's novels and, as paradoxical as it may seem, is inversely proportional to its fuzziness. Not surprisingly, *La réticence*, Toussaint's most symptomatic study of the effects of the gaze, reads like a parodic whodunit, that is, an attempt to find the hidden narrating voice of the story, spiked with the awareness that discovery must necessarily close the text. Caught in a problematics of presence and potentiality, *La réticence* opts for using the prolonged search of an apprehensive would-be narrator, an epistemological detective who conducts an inquiry into "his" own death to delay the finality of narrative teleology.

Symbolically, throughout the story the narrator comes across objects that might put him on the track of the ever-elusive Biaggi: a typewriter, a camera, and an answering machine. All three objects are important clues in the textual puzzle, all pointing not so much to the potential body of Biaggi and the text but to the object of the crime: narration and its discontents. The typewriter remains unused; it is a dead presence and does not serve so much to produce a text as to signal impediments to the narrative project. As for the camera, even though it might have been used to capture the narrator on film, or so he surmises, it fails to produce one single picture. Finally, all that the answering machine captures is the silence of the narrator, who had previously called Biaggi's villa without leaving a message. Ultimately these objects remind us that it is precisely in the unsaid that meaning resides. Only in the shadowy corners of *La réticence* do we ever see the light.

Not surprisingly, Toussaint's apathetic protagonists are often at pains to make the world signify, despite their cultural and scientific competence. Indeed, all the protagonists have the same sociocultural status in common: they are intellectuals, scholars, businesspeople, and writers; in other words, they think for a living. But their privileged position in society in general, and in the intellectual community in particular, seems inversely proportional to their ability to map out and understand their respective environments. Most characteristically here, academic style finds itself subverted by ludism, and style, rather than content, becomes the object of the reader's focalization. A constant interplay of levels of language blurs the distinction between "serious" and "playful," and the isotopic combination of jokes and scientific or intellectual truisms points toward the constructed status of truths and truth-claims. Rather than ferreting out the truth, or a truth, the protagonists fulfill a subversive role, one that frustrates the reader's expectations and foils the process of identification with the characters, who at best remain vague and always (partially) out of sight.

Likewise the cold, detached, and quasi-scientific observations that each of Toussaint's narrators shares with the reader are meant to stand in contrast to the human drama that fills each page of his novels, as if fiction must take the form of confessional literature to hide the fragility of the narrator behind a facade of impassivity. But these narrators are alienated figures, hovering between presence and absence, unwilling or unable to physically affect the course of the narrative. Mieke Bal reminds us that "characters resemble people. Literature is written by, for, and about people. That remains a truism, so banal that we often tend to forget it. . . . The character is not a human being, but it resembles one. It has no real psyche, personality, ideology, or competence to act, but it does possess characteristics which make psychological and ideological description possible."[16] One would think that Toussaint's refusal to psychologize in his fictions defeats the process of identification, but that is not really the case. Because Toussaint's protagonists enjoy a wide range of emotions and feelings, they still allow readers the luxury of partial identification. In fact, these protagonists may seem quite "realistic" to a contemporary readership, as their feeling of estrangement from the world and from themselves comes across as an earnest rendition of postmodern anxiety, while their overriding sense of dismay and distress brings to mind a number of contemporary worries. Among these, "man" only exists as a verbal construct, lost in a sea of ambiguous random information, locked in fearful hesitancy, reluctant to fulfill his obligations as a social being. What's more, knowledge proves to be at best limited, at worst ineffectual, and most if not all instances of cross-cultural and multilingual encounters lead to frustrating and disappointing results, which Toussaint alleviates with a light comic tone:

> *At the airport—Marco Polo—I made the acquaintance of a Soviet. . . . Since he was as multilingual as me, but along different lines (Russian, Romanian), and was explaining in Italian, I didn't quite catch what he'd come to do in Venice. . . . Standing behind our glasses, between silences in which he would doubtfully heft his attaché case, we talked about contemporary history and politics. After a brief overview of the history of Italy in the twentieth century (Gramsci, Mussolini), we ordered more beers. Then, moving on to the history of his country, a touchier subject because of the yoke, we said Krushchev, Brezhnev. I mentioned Stalin. Musing, he swallowed some beer and, with a fatalistic expression, presumably hoping to change the subject, pointed through the glass windows to the landing strip outside.*
> (The Bathroom 97–98)

Even names (signs whose authenticity seems unquestionable) appear largely ineffective with regard to the creation of meaning; rather, they can only point to the fallacy of metanarratives (history in this case). More exactly, the names that serve to fill in the blanks of the conversation underline by and large the impossibility of one individual reaching beyond him- or herself. Each individual is hopelessly alone in Toussaint, a solitary figure lost among peers, for whom knowing the other proves to be as frustrating as knowing the self.

Clearly Toussaint's fictions prolong the New Novel's attack on the psychological novel. They demonstrate that the novelist can never gaze with absolute certainty into the protagonist's mind. And yet the novels of Toussaint fundamentally differ from the New Novel, since they also articulate a resurgence of the subject, but a polymorphous one. If, in Toussaint's semioclastic universe, toponymy plays a singular role, this is because it undermines the normalizing and categorizing role usually played by names in the economy of the novel. Unlike a Balzac novel, in which characters' monikers typically situate them within a sociocultural grid (Eugène de Rastignac versus Vautrin, for instance),[17] the New Novel and most of today's formal fiction use a fuzzy toponymy to increase the level of polysemy, as characters' names no longer signify in terms of a cultural economy, but rather as signs of the dislocation of the process of characterization.

Toponymy then alerts the reader to a reading strategy of naming-qua-difference, as names come to signify linguistic and cultural divergence. For all intents and purposes, in Toussaint's novels characters' names "sound" out of the ordinary. A sampling of names taken from Toussaint's first two novels would net: Edmonsson (a woman), Kabrowinski Witold, Kovalskazinski Jean-Marie, Polougaïevsky, Il signore Gambini, Biaggi, Rafa, Fulmar and Puffin (two driving instructors), Parrain, Kaltz, Dubois-Lacour, Pons-Romanov, Anna Bruckhardt, and Eigenschaften (the Austrian ambassador). Regarding the latter, Sophie Bertho notes: "Toussaint's wink to Musil's *Man without Qualities*, through the name of Ei-

genschaften, which he gives to the Austrian ambassador, a character who represents outside space in the narrative, social space,
leads the reader to believe that Toussaint's heroes are essentially
'men without qualities.'"[18] Names become signs of alterity because
they disrupt patterns of linguistic and semantic traditionalism: few
of them are French, or if they are, last names precede first names
or seem unreasonably short or long. They thus fail to signify referentially; instead they create noise, though that noise is by no
means meaningless or absurd. Thus even though the eclecticism of
toponymy ranges far and wide across the *hors-texte*, these names
suggest, first and foremost, the anonymity of the characters, that
is to say, not their lack or absence of identity, but the vagueness
that comes to characterize them. In other words, we know these
people, their names ring a bell, but which bell do they ring? The
question remains open.

If Toussaint's novels lead us to interrogate the notion of identity
and its epistemological foundations, it is highly significant that a
number of scenes in Toussaint's stories should tackle the topos
of representation through some of its most traditional tropes: reflections in mirrors, puddles, and TV screens; pictures and photo
IDs. For each of Toussaint's texts is a search for the self and a
flight from it. For that reason, because he is caught in the tension
between absence and presence, the narrator of *L'appareil-photo*
appears oddly reluctant to have his picture taken, and yet the
moment he steals a small instamatic camera marks a fragile and
ephemeral moment of epiphany for him. However, this moment
does not last; it can't last. The narrator can't find the figure in the
narrative carpet because he can't visualize it all, since coming to
terms with his own self means ending the search and closing the
text, and since the dying body of the narrator only points to the
discontents of narration itself.

A narrative can operate in three different modes: description,
monologue, and dialogue. We have seen that in Toussaint's texts
descriptions are eminently subjective and hazardous and that
monologues often sink, progressively and unremarkably, in the

murky waters of ataraxia. As one would guess, the dialogical imperative of Toussaint's fiction remains problematic. At the level of the story the reader elicits little if any information from discussions. For instance, throughout *La réticence* the narrator refuses to ask the questions that would bring the story to a close. After having played a game of cat and mouse with the innkeeper of Biaggi's villa, the narrator fails to elicit from him the information that would solve the puzzle of Biaggi's absence. As in the rest of Toussaint's work, dialogues here function as noisemakers, and vagueness rules, along with uncertainty and incompleteness. Dialogues' referential function is conspicuously inoperative; it is first and foremost on the phatic level that they operate.

Small Talk

Not surprisingly then, all that Toussaint's characters end up exchanging with each other is small talk, literally and metaphorically. Their verbal exchanges are short and scarce in information, minimal. In addition, the free, indirect discourse that Toussaint often uses displaces dialogues one notch further from any potential discursive veracity and relevance. And if most discussions remain anecdotic, this is precisely because it is on the terrain of the anecdote that Toussaint's characters feel most comfortable. Like the entelechy into which they sink occasionally, anecdotes are virtual dialogic strands, fragments of narratives, embryonic, fuzzy, and incomplete insofar as they do not lead anywhere. They might be complete stories in themselves, with a beginning, middle, and end, but as they appear in the text, they make for a fragmented, entropic whole. Like many other aspects of these stories, they point toward the danger of exhaustion and investigate the notion that any exchange of information between individuals, any "contact," may have unfortunate results, no manner how minute. The first meeting of Monsieur with Anna Bruckhardt is particularly edifying in this regard:

> *Monsieur knew almost nothing of Anna Bruckhardt. . . .*
> *They'd spoken together for two hours, hardly more, sit-*

*ting opposite each other in the kitchen among the empty
glasses. . . . Anna Bruckhardt and Monsieur . . . hadn't
exchanged the slightest bit of information concerning
each other. No, they told each other anecdotes instead,
taking turns, which, as they went on, became more and
more insignificant, about people that the other didn't
know and that they themselves hardly knew anyway.
. . . They lingered a moment in the hall, exchanged one
final story in the dark, and then fell silent, immobile,
looking at each other with melancholy eyes, Monsieur
with his back to the wall, she facing him, a hand on his
shoulder. (90–92)*

Like descriptions and monologues in Toussaint's work, dialogues eschew the reader's attempt to elicit information. Here
there appears to be no motivation, desire, or envy—at least on the
surface—and conversation adds up to a simple exchange of information, but information that does not signify referentially. Instead
the dialogical universe of Toussaint is a world of fuzzy, free-float-
ing associations and meaningless anecdotes, dialectical pirouettes,
all of which aim to prevent the distress of emotional and physical
contact and fulfillment. If centuries of fictional exploration of the
love story, from the *roman courtois* to the pornographic novel,
have taught us that the aim of the game is ultimately to "get the
girl," Toussaint counters that the aim of the game is precisely the
opposite: to not get the girl, or at least to delay the getting of the
girl if one doesn't have her (*Monsieur*), or to delay the losing of the
girl if one has her already (*Making Love*). In short, for Toussaint
the game (which he compares to chess on more than one occasion)
consists of striking an awkward balance between getting and not
getting (to kiss a girl, to see a friend, to obtain a driver's license),
being and not being (in love, separated from, with, committed to
a project)—that is, occupying a fuzzy place within the scheme of
things, which explains why the Pascalian observer should be such

a significant figure in Toussaint's fiction: both inside and outside the world, both acting and observing, without ever settling for one or the other entirely.

For that matter, Monsieur and Anna Bruckhardt's conversation follows the same pattern as Monsieur's entelechy; both are chaotic systems, unpredictable, with results that might or might not go beyond the scope of the original conditions (a potential love story, for instance). Threatened by entropy, these discussions may falter at any moment and reach a point of exhaustion, which is what occurs, inevitably, at the end of the novel. So between Monsieur and his date there can be no follow-up discussion; indeed, Monsieur drops Anna's hand once it becomes clear that they have told each other everything. The narrator of *The Bathroom* has a similar experience with Edmonsson, his fiancée, and declares peremptorily: "[We were] not speaking. We had said everything, we didn't agree. . . . In the face of such a deliberate refusal to cooperate, I had nothing to say: no, not another word" (61). At this point their relationship has run its course, and Edmonsson wisely elects to return to Paris.

Yet as inchoate as they seem, these narrative strands underscore the (seeming) return of the plot that takes place in today's fiction. In the 1970s the texts of Philippe Sollers and Jean Ricardou, among many, attempted to rid the narrative of plot and characters, placing the emphasis on the process of writing itself. Nonetheless, Peter Brooks argues, plot has been a constant fixture of narratives since Aristotle, "the very organizing line, the thread of designs that makes narratives possible." What Toussaint and Robbe-Grillet may have in common then is that both refute the "final plenitude of meaning" that characterized most prewar literature. Rather, today's fiction encourages readers to engage in the reconstruction of narratives, and "plot," as Brooks puts it.[19]

Toussaint builds narratives that demand several readings, for at first sight these fictions may seem deceptively simple, minimalist in style, short in peripateia, and almost bereft of ideology. But the lackadaisical attitude of his protagonists does have ideological implications in terms of reader response, as it frames each narrative in a rhetoric of reticence. The reticent protagonist then becomes important beyond the confines of the text, serving as a mouth-piece for the author, not a mere character with whom the author might identify, but the exemplum of what the ideal reader might or should become: a Pascalian reader. Several critics have recognized the figurative presence of *Les pensées* in *The Bathroom*. Yet the presence of Pascal extends beyond Toussaint's liminal work: "The sole cause of man's unhappiness is that he does not know how to stay quietly in his room," says Pascal.[20] Like Toussaint's ideal reader, the homo toussainis is a recluse by choice, an intellectual skeptic who attempts to soften reality before reality (in all its min-ute manifestations) bangs him up too badly, forcing him to spend himself out until depletion.

In Toussaint's stories readers are called upon to construct fic-tions that, for lack of an unambiguous plot, become metafictions. Undeniably, in order to make Toussaint's fuzzy pieces cohere and signify, readers must first accept that the story may not signify in a referential way, but rather metanarratively. For that reason the various extratextual signs—locations (Venice, Paris, Milan, Lon-don, Berlin, Orléans, Brussels, Prague, Nara, Tokyo, Kyoto, Tu-nis, Elsinore, Ropongi, Hanoï), artists, writers, historical figures (Mondrian, Zappa, Trénet, Pascal, Jean Moulin, Prigogine, Breyer, Schrödinger, Titian, Charles V, Plato, Leonardo da Vinci), commer-cial brands (Stanley Blacker, Fiat, Mars, Nuts, Milky Way, Crunch, Tuborg, Thermogaz, Butagaz, Naphtagaz, Mammouth)—that are dropped isotopically in the text don't illuminate the demeanor of the characters, but rather displace meaning. What matters, how-ever, is that each sign becomes the agent of its own semioclasis; from the pieces they pick up readers attempt to build a narrative within the bounds defined by the author.

Narrative Meanderings

Let's observe that in Toussaint's novels the return of the plot (and its "fuzzification") has a distinctly baroque edge. Events and episodes seem to be loosely connected, while the story ostensibly lacks any real narrative drive to take it forward and bring it to a close, reminding us of the structural vagary of picaresque fiction, such as Cervantes's *Don Quixote*, Tasso's *Jerusalem liberata*, and Ariosto's *Orlando furioso*, all loosely structured as a sequence of episodes united by the presence of one or several characters. Significantly, discrete systems, of which picaresque fiction offers a literary illustration, articulate the paradox between internal dislocation and external coherence that is at the heart of Toussaint's literary project. However, unlike the maximalist experiments of Tasso and Cervantes, the minimalist works of Toussaint implement a much tighter control of the general direction of the narrative. And even though the randomness with which passages follow each other is not always determined at the level of the fabula, or story, there is in Toussaint's texts a follow-through via synecdochic and metaphoric links.[21]

Further, whereas in *Quixote* the knight and his page wander the roads of Spain in a seemingly random manner, each episode coming higgledy-piggledy on the heels of another, in the works of Toussaint protagonists' movements are often restricted and carefully choreographed within a specific space. The protagonist of *L'appareil-photo* goes over the same circuit over and over again with his driving instructor. The narrator of *The Bathroom* lives in and around the bathroom. Monsieur mediates between his room, his roof, and his office. The narrator of *La réticence*, when he ventures out of his room, always follows the same route between his hotel, the villa of Biaggi, and the port. As for the meandering narrator of *La télévision*, he curtails his movements to a specific routine between his apartment, the park, and the swimming pool, with few excursions outside. Finally, the forlorn lover of *Making Love* wanders between the hotel in Tokyo (where he is staying with his girlfriend), his friend's house in Kyoto (where he is trying to leave her), and the art museum (where her works are exposed). The iterative nature of these movements is of particular significance since iteration allows a sense of cohesion and order to appear in the confusion and incoherence of the text. Peter Brooks comments: "Repetition is one of the few factors of the text that allows a reader to see patterns of coherence, and thus at least the incipience of meaning, and to perceive how modification works, how the idea of repetition is linked to the idea of variation, indeed how an entire narrative might be constructed on the minute variations within repetitions."[22] Iteration is a crucial issue in Toussaint not only from the point of view of literary technique but also from a philosophical standpoint. N. Katherine Hayles underlines the notion that "in deconstruction, as in the science of chaos, iteration and recursion are seen as ways to destabilize systems and make them yield unsuspected conclusions."[23] This might be partly the case in Toussaint, where repetition only allows for variations, narrative swerves, but these always happen around the same loci of stochastic self-organization. Around these specific loci—"stable chaos," as James Gleick says—the fictional universe is often meaningless and chaotic, noisy in fact because it is not divulging clear information.[24]

Paradoxically the most significant iteration in Toussaint's fiction is the repetition of "non-acts," as it is mainly through the absence of movement that Toussaint's characters create a sense of regularity and normality, while the ataraxia (or perfect peace of mind) they try to achieve allows for tighter control of the environment by the narrator. In fact, in his most formally rigorous fictions (especially *L'appareil-photo* and *La réticence*) Toussaint plots events as he would chess moves. Indeed, one particular chess move piques the interest of the protagonist of *L'appareil-photo*: the Breyer variation. And because this variation depends upon delaying tactics and maneuvers to achieve victory, it becomes apparent how such a tactic plays a much larger role in the general economy of Toussaint's novels: "The driving lessons were going fine. . . . We always drove the same way, with few changes, following a course that was not unlike that of the knight in the Spanish Breyer variation; that is, we went around the area, slowly, and seemingly without a sense of purpose, with indifference for all the other chess pieces (that Breyer variation was quite interesting: though full of deceptive procrastination and suspicious equivocation, it casually laid out the foundations of a killer position)" (41). Attempting to lessen the drama of his impending breakup with his girlfriend, the narrator of *Making Love*, though sick with a cold, manages to re-establish a sense of balance in his life by limiting his moves to the most familiar and trivial of places, that is, the bed, the bathroom, and the kitchen:

> *I was enjoying this state of weakness and fever. . . .*
> *The hours were empty, slow, and heavy; time seemed*
> *to be standing still: nothing was happening in my life*
> *anymore. No longer being with Marie was like having*
> *a nine-day blow of stormy winds die away completely.*
> *Every instant, with her, was intensified, dramatized,*
> *strained, crazed. I would constantly feel her magnetic*
> *power, her aura, the electricity of her presence in the air,*
> *the saturation of space in the rooms she entered. And*
> *now, nothing anymore, afternoon calms, boredom and*
> *fatigue, one hour after another going by. (96–97)*

If for the narrator indolence seems to trump volatility, it is because saving time, playing with time, and ultimately denying time are prime concerns throughout Toussaint's oeuvre. For his part Monsieur attempts to teach his twin nieces that by going east, one goes in the direction of the earth's rotation, subtracting from the time that goes by (69). Likewise through mental and physical immobility he attempts to slow down the passing of time within. But like all of Toussaint's protagonists, he finds this process to be impossible; like all the other harried protagonists of Toussaint's unhurried fictions, he can't subdue the anguish of being part of time's flow.

Likewise, after a particularly trying quarrel with his girlfriend, the protagonist of *Making Love* hopes against hope that the sun will not rise over Tokyo, because he knows that "daylight would bring proof that time passed, relentless and destructive" (43). The only way for Toussaint to reverse this effect (or negate its effects, temporarily at least) is to stack the deck against the wearing effect of time by constructing a world whose probability tends toward zero. We know that probability only allows us to look forward, in an attempt to guess at the future. Commenting on Lucretian physics and in particular on the concept of the stochastic clinamen, Eric White affirms: "The future does not derive from the past in strict linear fashion. The deterministic unfolding of the universe has repeatedly been punctuated by catastrophic bifurcations, by chance swervings in unforeseeable directions. Nature, in more venerable parlance, is ruled by Fortune."[25] In his account of Lucretius's *De rerum natura* Michel Serres singles out the concept of the clinamen as emblematic of the intrusion of the aleatory into determinist symmetry.[26] Warren Motte characterizes the concept of clinamen in the following terms: "Democritus argued that atoms, the prime and irreducible components of all matter, fall with unvarying linearity: this motion sets up causal patterns that determine everything from physical phenomena to human thought and action. Epicurus chose to refute this notion of an endless chain of causality in its most crucial point: linearity. He argued that the atoms do not always fall straight down, but rather swerve from time to time; it is precisely this swerve that becomes the locus and the guarantor of free will."[27] Toussaint's twist on the aleatory nature of the real is that, if seen in reverse, history falls into an unquestionably deterministic pattern, each event logically leading to the event that caused it. So in his first and fourth novels Toussaint opts to cheat chronological time: in both cases the narrative geminates upon itself, forcing events and characters to veer back to the past and repeat themselves in palimpsestic fashion.[28] By doing so Toussaint reduces randomness to a minimum, but not to zero, and freezes down the universe in a repeating time-loop.

Besides, the epigrammatic presence of Pythagoras's theorem in *The Bathroom* reminds us that the progression of the narrative can be rational and predetermined.[29] Indeed, the Pythagorean theorem lies at the heart of the modern notion of optimality; that is to say, it allows us, through mathematical means, to find the best solutions to a problem based on chance and therefore to minimize randomness. If one decides to read *The Bathroom* in a loop, without stopping at the end of the book—and this is clearly one of the reading strategies suggested by Toussaint—one's knowledge of the unfolding events of the story defeats randomness. The universe is once again deterministic, provided that one replaces the novel's eschatology within the framework of a self-perpetuating system.

Few critics have caught on to the performative nature of Toussaint's textuality or to its profound subversive intent. Toussaint suggests to us a readerly praxis of tranquility, of distanciation and doubt. His design proves to be revolutionary, all the more so because subversion comes here under the accouterments of the already seen, of the already read, while the very "listless drive" (*Monsieur* 57) of the text softens up the reader's resistance to its subversive intent. And the first trap laid by the text comes with its effortless skepticism, as if this were all that the text had to offer (see Yvan Leclerc).[30] But Toussaint's skepticism dissimulates a more somber urgency: the anguish that these texts are suffused with, the fear of finitude, the stifling feeling that time is running short.

Besides this skepticism, the texts' accessibility is also one of their most prominent features, but their "readability" successfully dissimulates their semioclastic intent. One has to look for clues in the text, beyond its prosaic immediacy, that reveal the political and philosophical causticism of Toussaint's work: "In my opinion, Pascale [but also the reader] misunderstood my method, and did not understand that my entire plan of attack, though seemingly rather obscure, effectively intended to weaken the reality against which I was colliding, in the same manner one would soften up an olive, for instance, before successfully picking it up with a fork. My tendency to never rush anything, far from being prejudicial, would lay the groundwork for me; when things were ripe, I would go for it" (*L'appareil-photo* 14). Learning to read Toussaint implies learning how to go beyond expectations of textual totality à la Ricardou, as well as mimetic fiction à la Stendhal. Such an enterprise is bound to be frustrating, but its very inconclusiveness, the fact that the text is left in suspense, points to the fact that the letter of the text is pending (*en souffrance*), that is to say, never completely realized, part of a praxis of suffering, suffering as reading, reading as suffering: "I spent several days in the hotel. I didn't go out, didn't move from the room. I was feeling feverish. During the night sharp pains dug into my forehead, my eyes burned, were boiled. It was black, I hurt. Suffering was the ultimate, the only confirmation of my existence" (*The Bathroom* 78). The stoicism of Pascal echoes in the pages of Toussaint—the stoicism of protagonists faced with a real they can never vanquish, the stoicism of readers faced with a text they can never fully absorb and that continuously escapes them. Such inconclusiveness is necessarily painful, not only for the reader who expects narrative closure but also and primarily for the reader trained and transformed by the New Novel, who expects the kind of spectacular and self-important stylistic experiments that seem utterly absent from Toussaint's patently banal textuality.

Toussaint has chosen to engage the conventions of the realist novel and the New Novel through an aesthetics of banality and a return to Barthes's concept of the readerly. He lays bare the narrative structure, stripping narrative conventions down to their simplest and most basic possibilities: verbal exchanges are minimal, and often inconsequential and meaningless, characterization is sketchy at best, and the plot seems to revolve around unachieved and embryonic narrative strands. His novels offer a world that is resolutely alien, aleatory, and yet strangely fuzzy. Outside the text there is no absolute truth, inside the text only the glimmer of one. In an age of suspicion Toussaint calls attention to himself by resolutely standing at the heart of chaos like a skeptical passionaria at the foot of the cross.

3. Eric Chevillard
Building Babel

> We will preach against insensate laws until they are re-
> formed. And meanwhile we will submit to them.
>
> Diderot, *Supplément au*
> *voyage de Bougainville*

Comedy: Mapping Fuzziness

Ever since Plato and Aristotle comedy has suffered from compari-
son with its nobler counterpart, tragedy. In Umberto Eco's *The
Name of the Rose* Guillaume de Baskerville laments the loss of
the mythical treatise Aristotle supposedly wrote on comedy.[1] Such
a treasure, had it existed, would undoubtedly have filled a void
and given comedy (and humor) a place in the canon it doesn't
have today. In the same vein Bakhtin deplores the fact that the
grotesque—which E. K. Fisher calls "mythological comic"—has
been rejected by Western aesthetics.[2] For many critics, humor, in
its various forms, seems trite or inconsequential, as if meaning and
humor were at odds with each other. But the comic novel, like dramatic comedy, has been one of the literary forms most susceptible
to change and development, and its history is a long and fruit-

ful one, extending from Cervantes to Queneau and Calvino. This creative versatility is due both to the intrinsic nature of laughter and to what Bakhtin would call the protean nature of the novel. Yet critics study the absurd in Ionesco and Camus, the nihilism of Beckett, the anti-Semitism of Céline, autobiographical trends in Genet, the *chosisme* of Perec, but only rarely the humor that predicates their aesthetic and ideological choices.

Humor implies ambiguity, fuzziness, and a deconstruction of the real. In *Le rire* (*Laughter*) Bergson suggests that overly mechanistic behavior, or, to put it differently, an excess of normality or an aberrant use of the natural, is the source of laughter. He concludes his argument by stating that laughter serves as a regulating device against the degeneration of the social body: "Society will therefore be suspicious of all *inelasticity* of character, of mind and even of body, because it is the possible sign of a slumbering activity as well as an activity with separatist tendencies, that inclines to swerve from the common centre round which society gravitates: in short, because it is the sign of an eccentricity."[3] Although Bergson's position clearly inscribes itself within a modernist perspective, that embodied best by Foucault's panopticon, it accurately pinpoints the mechanisms of laughter. If humor can serve to underline the asocial nature of eccentric behavior, conversely it can function as a subversive force by focusing on the mechanistic or formulaic behavior of normative ideals. Thus humor fulfills both centripetal and centrifugal functions; it binds together and takes apart. The humorist, by deconstructing human endeavors and straining their normality, deals anew the ontological deck. This reshuffling then opens the way to representations of ambiguity, abnormality, and marginality.

If the New Novel was characterized by intense self-criticism and metanarrative work, and not a little self-consciousness, some of today's novelists, although very critical of the subjective nature of language, have decided, through humor and ludism, to question the truth-building capacities of language and its ideological and structural precepts.[4] Yet by contriving to avoid the seriousness and

affectation that sometimes characterized their predecessors, new
humorists like Chevillard are faced with a new challenge.[5] They
must convince readers and critics that comic fiction, although
funny and seemingly without depth, tackles in earnest and quite
thoroughly very critical issues and has as much "weight" as existentialism or the New Novel.[6] For Chevillard in particular the
meaning and purpose of art in an age of ideological rupture has
increasingly emerged as a crucial matter, one that is tied to the
nature and function of humor.

Chevillard has chosen to explore all the facets of the comic,
from parody to the grotesque and the nonsensical. His eclectic
and highly original oeuvre includes *Mourir m'enrhume* (1987);
Le démarcheur (1988); *Palafox* (1990); *Le caoutchouc décidément* (1992); *La nébuleuse du crabe* (*The Crab Nebula*) (1993);
Préhistoire (1994); *Un fantôme* (1995); *Au plafond* (*On the Ceiling*) (1997); *L'oeuvre posthume de Thomas Pilaster* (1999); *Les
absences du Capitaine Cook* (2001); *Du hérisson* (2002); and *Le
vaillant petit tailleur* (2003), a retelling of the Grimm fairy tale.
His texts introduce us to one of the most complete and challeng-
ing practices of fuzziness to appear in recent French literature. His
humor is as ferocious as it is seditious, yet it marks a passion for
language and its discontents. Like Barthes, Chevillard listens to
and explores the rustle of language, its labyrinthine intricacies, its
yawning gaps and insurmountable barriers. He is one of today's
most brilliant exemplars of a noble tradition of carnivalization
that began with Rabelais and continued with the philosophers of
the Enlightenment. But Chevillard's humor evacuates Rabelais's
joyous and rejuvenating comicalness, instead harking back to the
darker side of eighteenth-century comical fiction, to a *fin de siècle*
ethos that permeates the bleaker writings of Diderot and Sade,
as well as the burlesque writings of Scarron, Charles Sorel, and
Cyrano de Bergerac, and the baroque in general.[7]

"Dying is giving me a cold, that's funny" (Mourir m'enrhume,
c'est amusant), Mr. Théo prattles in the incipit of Chevillard's first
novel.[8] On the eve of his encounter with the Grim Reaper Mr.

Théo has found solace in Montaignian stoicism. For him, as for Montaigne, the world is nothing but a theater of cruelty, a bedlam scarred by violence and death. Everything is fragmented, unstable, fuzzy, and Mr. Théo's erratic reflections follow the same pattern of confusion and chance. The zany old man is a relativist and, much like the other protagonists of Chevillard's extravagant narratives, has a taste for cryptic metaphors and a tendency to diverge and digress almost continually, like a modern-day Lazarillo de Tormes.

As Jean Rousset noted, the baroque is "change, inconstancy, trompe-l'oeil and ornamentation, funereal spectacle, fleeting life and an instable world . . . , metaphor and ostentation, movement and scenery."[9] Born in an era marked by brutal change, confusion, and political and religious conflicts, in a society on the verge of collapse, the baroque expressed a growing defiance of immutable truths and systems. Four centuries before the New Novel it was the harbinger of an *ère du soupçon*. Stendhal, who cannot be charged with being baroque, let alone a humorist, conclusively stated in *Vie de Henry Brulard* that he harbored a passion for the rigor of mathematics and could not tolerate "hypocrisy and vagueness, the two things I loathe."[10] Yet we would be ill-advised to draw conclusions regarding the rigor of classicism and the ambiguity of the baroque. In point of fact Chevillard's texts wonderfully manage to bring one along with the other, framing baroque ambiguity (or fuzziness) within unusually rigorous narrative structures. His humor is deceivingly gentle and adheres to an astute form of subversion. Most importantly, it alerts the reader to the emergence of a new paradigm in contemporary French fiction, one that has become the hallmark of several Minuit writers: impassivity.[11] Contrary to popular wisdom, humor and impassivity naturally match. Indeed, Bergson defines humor thus: "Here I would point out . . . the *absence of feeling*, which usually accompanies laughter. It seems as though the comic could not produce its disturbing effect unless it fell, so to say, on the surface of a soul that is thoroughly calm and unruffled. Indifference is its natural environment, for laughter has no greater foe than emotion."[12] Impassivity does not

imply detachment, and humor, unlike pathos in tragedy, does not
work on an emotional level. Humor addresses the intellect in an
effort to challenge our belief in finality, totalization, logic, nature,
representation and truth, causality and temporal continuity. The
impassive humor of Chevillard actually develops into a formidable
semioclastic force, one that resonates within the Nietzschean—or
post-Cartesian—paradigm, after the demise of some of modernity's most unquestionable certitudes.[13]

In a time of ideological doubt and moral frigidity Chevillard's
comical novels raise a crucial and timely question: are there any
moral or deontological boundaries the novelist is not supposed to
cross? Putting this in a nutshell, Mr. Théo, the main protagonist
of *Mourir m'enrhume*, asks his child accomplice if one may laugh
at everything (109). Only a few lines into the novel the question
already demands an affirmative answer. For Chevillard one of the
functions of art is precisely to push against the boundaries of good
taste, of *idées reçues*—in a word, against the tyranny of cultural
conformism. To use Michel Leiris's metaphor, Chevillard's textuality stands as a *tauromachie*, a cannibalistic revisiting not only of
the canon but also of what constitutes normality.

Encyclopedic Folly

Chevillard's purpose is simple, yet one of the most radically ambi-
tious in contemporary fiction: to deconstruct and carnivalize the
Encyclopedia, or the "Dictionnaire raisonné des Sciences, des Arts
et Métiers" (rational dictionary of sciences, arts, and trades), and
with it the *homme rationnel* described by the philosophers of Ancient Greece and the Enlightenment. Only after the completion of
this grand project will the artist, and the individual, be free to start
from zero:

> *Soon, Monge will be alone in the world. First measures:
> lay waste to libraries, set them on fire since books can
> swim, butterfly-stroke, then, sitting on the lukewarm
> ashes, like a kind forebear without offspring, tell the*

passing wind marvelous and barely believable stories.
. . . Touch up masterpieces with acid, a cavalier and
amusing perspective, frame his own drawings, big round
yellow suns, humble cots. . . . Music will shut itself up,
on her own authority, an incompetent body. By precau-
tion, slam the cover on her fingers. Then sing . . . , and
*the whole world will laugh out loud. (*Le démarcheur
55–56, 70)[14]

From Rabelais to Flaubert's *Bouvard et Pécuchet*, through Diderot
and d'Alembert's *Encyclopedia*, Buffon's *Histoire naturelle*, Balzac's *Comédie humaine*, and Zola's *Rougon-Macquart*, writers
have tried to embrace the totality of the world in an all-encom-
passing vision, or to show the fallacy of such a scheme. Whether
the grid is predominantly sociological, psychological, scientific or
political, poetic or metaphysical, the desire to totalize has been a
recurring trope of literary history. For his part, ever since his first
novel, in which a dying narrator attempts to exhaust the doxa
before passing away, Chevillard has focused upon the narrating of
totality. For him it is the very desire to set pan-normative ideals,
to limit intellectual freedom, to construct an ontology based on a
rigorously rational approach to reality, to sacrifice fantasy on the
altar of reason for reason's sake, that goes most against the grain
of poetry and art. His writing, therefore, posits itself as resolutely
antisystemic and marginal:

> *For instance, Furne is opposed to April showers. If it was*
> *only that, he would face it, or shoulder it, but there is*
> *nothing about which he doesn't have something to say.*
> *Without looking for something he finds it, a legal flaw or*
> *construction defect in everything, grave imperfections,*
> *excesses, pettiness—those are his own words—and con-*
> *cludes that a reshuffle is called for, a total methodical re-*
> *organization of the system at work: since it doesn't meet*
> *our most basic needs and thwarts our most legitimate*
> *dreams, let's revise it. (*Le caoutchouc décidément *7)*

Such a complete reorganization of the system in place (*le système en vigueur*) suggests that in order to escape a lifeless world, where "there is nothing to be learned, to be discovered, to be invented," where there is "nothing new under the sun of identity," one needs to question every single facet of human knowledge.[15] One must, in Furne's words, force reality to step back (*Le caoutchouc décidément* 98) and mollify the discourses of knowledge through a poetics of fuzziness. Thus by opposing the Aristotelian paradigm Chevillard takes to task some of the fundamental constructs of human existence (time and space, history, literature and the arts, sexuality, nature versus culture) that underpin modernity. As for his characters, they leave no doubt about the need for unconditional relativism, which prompts the protagonist of *Préhistoire* to assert: "We would rather believe in our visions of the world, which are pure hallucinations, or delirious mental conceptions, that had to be said, but which end up constituting a universe after all, our universe, whose plausibility depends only on the precision of our encyclopedias and atlases, our liturgies, our classifications, our plans" (*Préhistoire* 104). In an attempt to debunk the encyclopedic ethos further, Crab, Chevillard's most archetypal polymath, (playfully) argues that any *grand oeuvre* should begin with a good dictionary. The writer, he argues, should first combine all the words of the dictionary in every possible way, add each sheet of paper to the growing pile, take out the ceiling, and make an aperture in the roof before he can, at last, climb the mountain-high manuscript to the top. But instead of gloriously contemplating the fate of the world from this new Olympus, he should proceed to reduce the summa to a more publishable size and start burning out all the mediocre passages, taking the work down to the *substantifique moëlle*, a one-hundred-page masterpiece, a unique, unrivaled, "unreadable intermingling of banalities and incoherencies" (*Crab Nebula* 91). The logic of this sweeping enterprise, absurd as it may be, knows no rebuttal. And yet the doxa, though exhausted, can only be born from its ashes: "To the devil with all these books, I've read enough, and I want to live! Crab exclaims, and rips handfuls of volumes from his library before throwing them on the ground, and stomping on them furiously. Then, without waiting any further, fortified by his resolution and anxious to follow through, Crab sets himself at the table and begins writing" (*Un fantôme* 111).

For Chevillard's narrators the totalization scheme, though conveyed in ruefully academic tones, is antipoetic by nature, refuting any allusion to fuzziness or uncertainty. For these freewheeling narrators it is in history that encyclopedic mania ultimately finds its most deleterious expression. To be sure, the Old Testament philosophy of history, which assimilates Greek and Roman philosophies, assumes that the human being grows and unfolds in history and eventually becomes what he or she potentially is. It is precisely the fact that, for many, history has become synonymous with eschatology that prompts Chevillard to tackle modernity's most radical dogma of totality and closure. For Furne, the insane theoretician of *Le caoutchouc décidément*, it is one's duty to expose the dogmatism of historians, as well as their prosaism:

> To him, historians are the foulest henchmen of the system at work, immortal doting Visigoths; they never tire of reminding you of its erstwhile triumphs over innocence and fantasy. By complacently showing it at work since the world was born, they give it all the characteristics of fate—with apocalypse on the heels of the sound of boot steps. . . . Nonetheless, most of History's lessons deal firstly with tactics and strategy: which hat you should choose to conquer the world, how you can institute Terror, how you can proclaim yourself king without wetting your sheets, how you may become a prosperous grocer during food shortages, which steps to follow, which traps, which mistakes to avoid. (116–17)[16]

Echoing Chevillard, Jacques Lesourne argues that classical historical narratives always tend toward orthogenesis, and thus narrative closure. For the historian who gives the unfolding of events all the characteristics of fate, matters could not have happened any other way.[17] Indeed, orthogenesis would seem the natural counterpart of eschatology, and the combination of both accounts for the rational and centripetal tendency at work in traditional history. Speaking of the "nineteenth century's obsession with questions of origin, evolution, progress, genealogy," Peter Brooks explains that the rising tide of secularization rendered the existence of a "sacred master plot that explains the world" obsolete, but that in turn it foregrounded "historical narrative as par excellence the necessary mode of explanation and understanding."[18]

Wary of all centripetal discourses, Furne launches a revolutionary project, a "grand design" (7), from the most irrational of places, the yard of the asylum where he has been committed. For Furne, heir to Jarry's Docteur Faustroll, logic must be subordinated to fantasy, orthodoxy to heterodoxy, faith to fuzziness, and normality must stoop before monstrosity and madness. Steadfast in his diatribe against the system, Furne seeks the help and expertise of a number of inmates for his project. From the shell-shocked veteran to the suicide survivor, through the paranoiac and the bulimic, all suffer from a number of psychological and psychosomatic afflictions, and all are perfect for the task at hand. For Furne, in this gallery of freaks, the real freaks are not the ones you think; reforming the system commences with averting the critical gaze from the scientific object—the inmates—to the scientific subject—Zeller, enthusiastic psychiatrist and medical zealot, "taxidermist and prison guard" (30):

> *Furne ignores why [Zeller] is called a professor, maybe it is the white lab coat, floating around him, unless it's him who's floating within the coat, or it may be his big domed forehead (even though phrenology is, nowadays, scientifically refuted, it is still recruiting followers among storytellers whose characters now sport as many bumps as they have ideas or vices, and that man with a pear-shaped head who walks briskly—don't turn the page, oh well-informed reader—he's going to his orchard).*

> But Zeller's big forehead may not accommodate a great
> idea; a minuscule ostrich brain exclusively fantasizing
> about a large feathered posterior would be just as much
> at home there. (32)

For what phrenology and literary realism share is a way of constructing a discourse based on particularization and coherence.
Thus Furne's argument conflates phrenological categories with literary types in realism. By refusing the imperative of verisimilitude,
and going past "written reality" (le réel écrit), as Flaubert puts it,
Furne affirms the subjective nature of language and the privileged
place poetry—and madness, the most vivid expression of uncertainty—must be given among discourses.[19]

Under constant surveillance from the personnel and psychia-
trists of the institution, studied and analyzed at length, in what
amounts for him to "sterile work" (31), Furne can only feel em-
pathy for nature's fuzziest creation, the anomalous cells that zo-
ologists strive (unsuccessfully) to track down and pigeonhole in
ready-made categories. What could be more nebulous than "these
unique, unclassifiable, uncategorized individuals, these monsters,
these hybrids, these errors of nature that win him glory and that he
dedicates to his spouse—who's too busy to give him a love child—
and that he baptizes with his own Latinized name even though he
would be incapable of creating the motif for a new butterfly wing"
(30–31)? Furne, on the other hand, "has his head full of new, un-
seen models, with an original form and brand-new colors" (31).
If there never was a case for creative madness and the debunking
of scientific sterility, Furne is determined to create one, making the
narrative a locus of subversion and a fuzzy space.

Accordingly Chevillard's fictions leave a significant place for
madness, which saves one from "mediocrity and boredom" (*Crab
Nebula* 12) and redeems the writer from blind subservience to
the system in place. With Furne and his heteronyms Chevillard
endeavors to thwart any finality of meaning by constructing the
dynamics of a debate between the centripetal impetus of reason

and the centrifugal forces of irrationality. Thus, very methodically, each novel touches upon different kinds of insanity, from the senility of the protagonists of *Mourir m'enrhume* and *Le démarcheur*, to the schizophrenia of *The Crab Nebula*, through the paranoia of *Préhistoire* and the delirious hubris of *Le vaillant petit tailleur*. However, if there is madness in Chevillard's texts, it is not associated with the supernatural, the fanciful, or even the extraordinary. Rather, madness finds itself wedged in the very heart of banality and becomes a praxis of liberation, as Chevillard decides to deconstruct normality from the inside, carnivalizing the real and the text. For the madness that truly threatens Chevillard's protagonists is not unfettered imagination, senseless folly, frenzy, or even rage. On the contrary, it is steeped in the coldest logic: "What stalks him now is a maniacal madness, devoid of comfort: niggling, cautious, meticulous, a frenzy for order and symmetry—not an immense park in which to wander, unkempt, eyes rolling, hands hanging limp, but a geometric hell as clean and cold as the depths of winter, run by a school of allergists, and Crab in the middle of it all, impeccably dressed, and the door noiselessly closing" (*Crab Nebula* 7–8). Against the cold meticulous madness of rational discourses, the poet (as madman and teller of fuzzy tales) must therefore mount a counteroffensive based on the same narrative principles. However, "how does one become mad?" Crab wonders. "For it's not that simple." Indeed, there must be method to the madness of Chevillard's protagonists, and to their absence of method:

> *Crab has chosen madness. Rest assured that this is no sudden brainstorm. Brainstorms are just so much wind. . . . The mind that ponders this problem will never come up with anything but methods, and any method is in the end an attempt to order the motion of the heavens. Will Crab have to invest in a trepan? Other tools? Tongs? A rasp? Or is it enough simply to concentrate, until he becomes so wired that he blows his intellectual fuses? So that this tough, all-too-lucid consciousness, this bril-*

liant star—sharp, trenchant, incisive, penetrating, able to graft night onto day—might suddenly disintegrate, dispersed, diffuse, defused: the birth of a nebula. (Crab Nebula 6)

In the end emancipation from the cold hell of rhetoric must pass through a deconstruction of the Aristotelian paradigm's exact symmetries and tidy predictions. And to carry through his parodic unraveling of the encyclopedic project, Chevillard opts to follow d'Alembert's own triadic method, spelled out in the preface of the *Encyclopedia*, which the mathematician sums up in three words: memory, reason, and imagination.[20]

Tackling the first of d'Alembert's precepts (memory), Chevillard suggests that access to memory, be it personal or collective, is a linguistic act. And for Furne language repeatedly betrays its limitations: "This failure of language is not without consequences . . . ; the lack of verbs restricts our freedom of movement. . . . Our desires, our vague impulses, our intentions even, fall into that lexical abyss" (*Le caoutchouc décidément* 111–12).

Trapped in the prison house of language, the postlapsarian man can no longer take the female chimpanzee to ecstasy—a sure sign of his downfall, according to Furne—and struggles to hide the shame of his fallen state by building an immutable paper fortress of self-perpetuating texts around him. Such a fortress, should it come to exist, would be the sum of human discourses, a monolithic neo-Borgesian library of Babel:

History is well known. We have the texts. Texts support one another. Often, texts repeat one another. So we are sure. Reading the texts is a bit boring, for sure, but it is precisely because they repeat one another, because there is only one truth. . . . The reader's expectation is rewarded, for the reader of texts would not appreciate a version of history that would differ too much from the ones he has already read, which all agree, to the point where they become one, the same good old story each

time, the same magnificent adventure, so now we know
for sure. (Préhistoire 88–89)

And if history fares poorly, autobiography fares even worse, bow-
ing as it does to the deadening predictability of chronology and
the hegemony of first-person narration. For the narrator and
would-be autobiographer of *Du hérisson*, who plans to write the
ultimate autobiography, aptly entitled *Vacuum extractor* (an exhaustive chronicle that would include every single moment, every single event, small or great, of the writer's existence), only the
most absurd of events (the untimely arrival of a hedgehog on his
desk) can put a stop to his enterprise. "All memories will be organized French-style in *Vacuum extractor*" (238), he promises, but
the dreaded autobiography never sees the light of day, thanks to
the hedgehog's untiring destruction of the writer's magnum opus.
Beaten by the hedgehog's resilience, and owning up to the fact that
"autobiography sucks" ([l'autobiographie], c'est de la merde [74]),
the unfortunate author is forced to feed the rest of his oeuvre to
the flames, succumbing to the sensuous delights of schizophrenia
as he gives up on himself and instead embraces the other: "I dream
about taking the place of the naïve and globulous hedgehog, so I
may reconquer my territory and live there as a sybarite" (211). In
like manner the heteronymous Thomas Pilaster suggests that, in
place of a classic biography, one should write a "biobibliography"
starting with "raie, mont, rousse, aile" (*L'oeuvre posthume* 35),
and, through the emblematic presence of Raymond Roussel, abdi-
cate the diktat of verisimilitude for the delight of fantasy. For biography, far from being an exercise in fact finding, should inscribe
itself under two principles: the need to invent and the need for
narrative constraints—that is, in both cases, the need for fallacy,
or literary madness.

Buoyed by this need Chevillard's protagonists (here ostensibly
inspired by George Sorel and Bakunin) lash out at the unpoetic
discourses that constitute memory. In relentless attacks on the system in place they condemn, in turn, literature, painting, sculpture,

criticism, linguistics, semantics, philosophy, sociology, history, geography, paleontology, anthropology, zoology and its various branches, medicine, psychiatry, psychology, mathematics, cosmology, physics, and chemistry (and this list is far from exhaustive). Calling upon the authority of the discourses he parodies, Chevillard creates his own discourse that is "fully documented and refereed," draping itself in scientificity.

Among Chevillard's novels *Le caoutchouc décidément* pushes this process the furthest. History provides the first list of canonical figures, from Pépin le Bref, Pépin de Hastal, Pépin l'Ancien, Clotaire II, Dagobert Ier, Sigebert II (16), Antinoüs (28), Vespasian (57), Saint Louis (61), Christopher Columbus, Magellan, Tasman, and Cook (100), to Dutch admirals Marteen and Cornelis Tromp (117). From art history come Botticelli, El Greco (35), Michelangelo (42), Rembrandt (79), Manet, and Monet (101); from music Stradivarius (93) and Nicolo Paganini (121); from religious studies and mythology Buddha (9), Minos, Dedalus, Icarus (27), Anadyomene (Venus) (50), the Danaides (70), and Jesus (93); from philosophy Pascal (68), Saint Thomas Aquinas, and the Abbé Drioux, his translator (82); from literary studies Rimbaud, Shakespeare (38), and Hans Christian Andersen (67); from psychoanalysis Freud (58); from psychology Rorschach (105); and from zoology Cuvier (26). The following inventors close the list: Alexander Bell, Thomas Edison, Karl Benz, Auguste and Louis Lumière, and Limonaire (112). But this historical and cultural "who's who" goes no further than deconstructing the "encyclopedic epistemophilia" denounced by Chevillard."[21]

At first sight the lexicophagy of Chevillard's protagonists would seem symptomatic of the epistemophilia he denounces, but lexical excess only serves to deconstruct the fallacy of encyclopedic accumulation and totality. One key figure among his literary anarchists is the "naive, fuzzy" hedgehog of *Du hérisson*, who begins by breaking up the author's autobiographical logorrhea into segments of nine to eleven lines. Eating away at the text, figuratively and literally (the hedgehog actually eats the pages that the author

attempts, with little luck, to write or preserve), the beast knows
that the act of listing and cataloging in no way connotes scientific
competence or realism but, at best, amounts to scholarly mimicry.
Fortunately, as the author attempts (unsuccessfully) to write his
memoirs, the fuzzy, naïve hedgehog forces him to diverge from
the straight recounting of chronologically ordered memories (each
drearier and duller than the last) and jump randomly from one
subject to another, on and on, constituting in the process a narrative whose thematic exuberance is proportional to its poetic in-
ventiveness.

If the hedgehog throws himself into the midst of things, attempting to impede the writer's work and prevent him from finishing his
autobiography, this is because autobiography and encyclopedia are
analogous insofar as they endeavor to map out, exhaustively, all
of life's events and experiences. But for the hedgehog, and Chevillard, such attempts only beget "a cacophonic torrent carrying all
the figures of rhetoric like so many bloated cadavers, flooding our
prairies in bloom, our long avenues, drowning our poets" (55).
Against the cold hell of epistemophilia, "the main preoccupation
of the hedgehog seems to be to sow confusion in my work and disorder in my pages," protests the disgruntled autobiographer (186).
But this romp through the field of knowledge and across categories
prompts a thorough investigation of the political implications of
normative thinking and especially of the encyclopedic project.

For reclaiming language—and the freedom of language—must
be the first step in the carnivalization of the system in place. Furne
says it best: "He deserves all the words" (*Le caoutchouc décidément* 71). Against the system's rigid organization of knowledge by
discourse and lexis, Chevillard's protagonists transgress boundaries and pass indifferently from geology to numismatics to zoology
to necromancy to genetics to phrenology to archeology to sexology
to religion to medicine and so forth. Not surprisingly, as an author
Chevillard feels compelled, in his frontal attack on the system, to
take on some of the more vicarious manifestations of "literary"
epistemophilia, from realism, through naturalism, surrealism,

modernism, the *nouveau théâtre*, romanticism, the Enlightenment, the avant-garde, autobiography, and minimalism, to maximalism. More surprisingly, however, we find items in the catalog consti- tuted by the system in place that we do not usually associate with the encyclopedic project or with modernist ideologies of totality. Such is the case with automatism in the visual arts (*Le caoutchouc décidément* 104); sleep (*Mourir m'enrhume* 49); poultry—"too much screeching, too many legs, too many droppings" (*Le caou- tchouc décidément* 77); bones—"the last annoying stiffness, in a time of ideological decline" (*Les absences* 30), gravity (*On the Ceiling*), and twenty-two-year-old women (*Un fantôme* 129).

No matter how much one looks at it, it would be difficult to find common ground among these random items, other than their appearance on the same list (things that should be reformed). Like Borges's laundry list, Chevillard's fuzzy set is equal to an ensemble where elements find themselves collocated in a particular category because of the (arbitrary) necessity for the category itself. And like Borges's list, Chevillard's fuzzy set emphasizes two things: the cat- egorization of semes by semantic field partakes of encyclopedic epistemophilia, and the subjectivity of the list underlines the sub- jectivity of epistemophilic ratiocination. Tellingly, it is the temp- tation to constitute things into a list, no matter how haphazard, the impulse to catalog, the need to order in encyclopedic form, that Chevillard satirizes. More than the encyclopedic project itself, it is the encyclopedic principle, its pretense to rationality, bound in a totalitarian narrative logic, that finds itself deconstructed in his texts. Thus, following a clear parodic intent, Chevillard's style rigorously structures itself along the same rational imperative as the *Encyclopedia*, complying in the process with the second of d'Alembert's precepts: reason.

Accordingly Chevillard's own texts are rigorously constructed from a formal standpoint, the ontological systems and paradigms built by his protagonists quite methodical in their own right. But like the Ouroboros, Chevillard's dialectic bites its own tail, as it relishes making use of the various faulty reasonings, malaprop-

isms, and paradoxes that are an appendage to conventional rhetoric and tend to sidetrack resolution or forego closure. "How may
one not regret the importance given to proof?" muses the narrator
of *Les absences du Capitaine Cook* (13), casting doubt upon the
ideological and formal veracity of progress, or logic. For his part
Crab, the elusive protagonist of *The Crab Nebula*, is a rhetorician
who, at first sight, follows in the footsteps of Aristotle, subscribing
to the old Roman maxim "Sapiens nihil affirmat quod non pro-
bet" (The wise only assert what they can prove). Yet he is as far
removed from Aristotelian teleology as one could be:

> *Crab never bases his decision on a given object's purely
> utilitarian superiority over another. He cares nothing
> for such petty concerns. If he has concluded that on the
> whole the dog outstrips the needle, that the dog is glob-
> ally superior to the needle, and he must then sew on a
> missing button, Crab uses the dog. A passerby, watching
> him struggle at his task, will inevitably point out to him
> that he would have long since finished the job if he had
> used the needle. And Crab will have to loose his dog on
> him, to prove to this genius that he had reasoned rightly,
> and even forcefully. (2)*

The example of the dog and the needle is a textbook case of Aristotelian principles, providing a perfect illustration of both *dem-
onstratio ad absurdum* (proof obtained through absurd reasoning)
and *argumentum ad baculum* (appeal to force to win an argument).[22] In the same mystifying manner Palafox uses a double
analogy to demonstrate that by throwing a fisherman in the water, and counting the ripples, one will know the age of the river
(*Palafox* 85).[23] Finally, Crab might argue for one thing and for its
opposite in the same breath. Georges Braque, whom Crab ostensibly emulates in his deconstruction of realism and reason, alleged
that we always need two ideas: one to kill the other.[24] Furthering
Chevillard's parodic intention, the metanarrator of *Un fantôme*
informs us that the operating principle of a narrative resides in a

paradox: "to write things and the opposite of these things" (7).

If anything, the paradox becomes the emblematic figure of Chevillard's fuzzy logic. From a rational standpoint the paradox always seems "aberrant," since it binds together ideas that are at odds with each other, concepts that are irreconcilable and violate the laws of reason. Always the master of paradoxes, Crab maintains that if you look hard enough for an object that is not in a room, you must and will find it there (*Crab Nebula* 17). There is no light at the end of the tunnel in such incongruous logic, only the marmoreal quality of the *quod erat demonstrandum*. The narrator of *Préhistoire* even argues that "reason, unleashed, is a type of lyricism . . . , a wild deductive folly that orders all as it goes, and only quiets down at the end of its implacable demonstration" (41). Following a modus operandi of associative links, the logic of the narrated finds itself subverted by the logic of the story and ends up "giving birth to [rhetorical and poetic] monsters," to a polyphonic and polychromatic reality (*Les absences* 161, 177), that is, to figures of vagueness and excess. Describing the dictionary, the narrator of *Les absences* marvels at "the infernal game of cylindrical, conical, double-helical, chevron-patterned, helicoidal, and globoid gearings" (68), as if the dictionary itself had turned into some Eischeirian transformative structure and could provide a paradigm for a systematic investigation of randomness and chaos, or, in other words, a fuzzy set.

Finally, following the third of d'Alembert's precepts (imagination), Chevillard's rhetoricians elect to act like compulsive dreamers, "aggressive dreamers who don't seek refuge in their dreams, but violently oppose them to reality."[25] William Paulson notes that if, for d'Alembert, "in light of the seemingly definitive triumph of Newtonian science . . . , the place of imaginative creation had been inevitably reduced," Chevillard's perspective is decidedly post-Newtonian, for his characters live within what Baudelaire would call the reign of imagination.[26] Emblematic of this cataclysmic encounter between reason and fantasy, between the world and its oneiric double, Furne, Albert Moindre, Crab, Mr. Théo, Palafox,

Monge, Thomas Pilaster, the naïve fuzzy hedgehog, and the other anonymous narrators of Chevillard's texts have elevated nonsense to an art form; like Lewis Carroll's Mad Hatter, they weave sense out of nonsense.[27] Representative of this narrating of fantasy, Albert Moindre, the eco-warrior anthropologist of "Trois tentatives pour réintroduire le tigre mangeur d'homme en Lot-et-Garonne," concludes, after judging the noxious dreariness of human behaviors within the ecosystem, that only the tiger can bring meaning and poetry back to our lives: "Living far away from tigers means settling for a false immortality, among the stones; it's being dead instead, since only the dead do not fear tigers. The tiger is indispensable to Man, just like the sun and the shadow, whose colors he defends. The tiger is the real diviner of sap and blood—with him, chlorotics and anemics find good reasons to be at ease about their health: dark red is the blood that flows profusely from their open throat" (22).[28] If Albert Moindre and his heteronyms deploy logic as a subversive strategy against the deadly humdrum of *les idées reçues*, it is in order to develop a new relation to an environment that can best be described as chaotic. Two centuries earlier Diderot commented with some irony on *le bon goût*, castigating our unwillingness to depart from commonly held views, from the safety of discursive closure.[29] Today Albert Moindre and his doubles expose the same flaw in our character. But if Diderot based his argument on scientific materialism, heralding the emergence of modernity and its implicit notion of human happiness through material progress, Chevillard's perspective is resolutely postmodern. The political and industrial revolutions of the eighteenth and nineteenth centuries marked the displacement of the concept of providence from the spiritual province to the world of science and politics (*l'état providence*). But postmodernity in general, and Chevillard's fiction in particular, place the individual in a state of epistemological uncertainty.

Already in 1908 Poincaré had foreseen the importance uncertainty would assume in certain systems that demonstrated the shortcomings of transcendental determinism and exorcised Laplace's Demon from the field of epistemology. Subsequently the twentieth century saw the generalization of Poincaré's views to all fields of human expression, from the sciences to the humanities. Today N. Katherine Hayles suggests that the new science of chaos develops and synthesizes the discourses on the aleatory and has deep affinities with other cultural and linguistic factors that all emerged from the postmodern context.[30] For chaos theory, as well as other postmodern discourses, not only is the post-Newtonian paradigm a new set of concepts and ideas, but practices themselves should only be read as culturally situated. Language, rather than being the means to an end Sartre thought it was, shapes as it articulates thought.

Chevillard harps on this illusion that language could be purely instrumental, taking apart the ideological project of the system in place. Language, like culture, falls short of reality here. For Furne and his heteronyms the exuberance of the world and its growing complexity defeat our attempts at representation and objective organization: "Furne is not naive enough to still believe in the power of the word . . . , in sentences, empty discourses, vain poetry; the more the parrot speaks, the less he flaps his wings, getting fatter as his vocabulary expands; he loses his colors, puts his feathers away in a quill box, puts on a lorgnette, and steps on the platform. Today, we are going to talk about the great scientific discoveries: open your books" (*Le caoutchouc décidément* 62). The parrot functions as a source of humor because of its mechanistic imitation of human speech. Its counterfeit command of language and its false erudition point to the fallacy of traditional science and the meaninglessness of its pedagogical and ideological aims. If Chevillard's parody targets all forms of education, this is because in his carnivalesque narratives the system in place recycles itself through the sclerosis of academicism and the ratiocination of knowledge. Like Rabelais's Gargantua, Chevillard's characters remind us of the vacuity of our intellectual efforts within the stifling environment of the system. Via education Chevillard ferociously lambastes the totalitarian arbitrariness of the social and cultural codes that compound the system, from our dressing standards ("a thousand-year-old system that bullies us" [*Le caoutchouc décidément* 47]) to our mating rituals and, of course, our pedagogical principles:

> *We surrender to laws that we didn't vote for, that constrain us, and weigh on us since childhood—do not trust the newborn's apparent carelessness or his mental backwardness, anxiety grows with him. . . . Painful apprenticeship of life at the end of which the little imp will be appointed rural policeman and receive a nice uniform. . . . The apprentice ignores what rights he has. Spitting his compote in grandfather's face may seem quite innocent, but no, for the latter tries to strangle him with a napkin; now he knows: one does not spit his compote in grandfather's face—where to then, and what should he spit in grandfather's face? He finishes his meal crying, salty and sweet in the same plate. The first lessons are quickly learned. . . . The arms change, the slaps keep on coming. Professors with diplomas, whose undeniable erudition scarcely justifies the exploitation of limestone deposits since half a chalk is enough to exhaust it. . . . These sad civil servants, guards of the state of things, take the child's education in hand, and grab him by the ear, which they pull if need be, if he won't lend an ear, torturers then, but badly equipped, no blades, no pincers, a strong grip, however, and goodwill, they don't ask for another penny for all the extra work, forty ears to pull in a day.* (Le caoutchouc décidément 11–12)

Avoiding the dreariness of such a predetermined fate, not to mention the odd slap in the face, seems to keep most of Chevillard's protagonists busy. They are like Plato's gadfly, invariably disputing the inexorable order of things, drawing into question the claims of scientific discourses to achieve unambiguous meaning. If chaos theory dispelled the illusion of a universe ruled by simple mechanisms, and fuzzy theory endeavored to verbalize imprecision, Chevillard's fiction then has a double task, that of deconstructing the system in place and searching for alternatives in the investigation of knowledge, in a new dialogue with complexity.

Once again Chevillard's argument hints at the *Encyclopedia*. Indeed, both the organization of themes and the humanist views that inform the *Encyclopedia* point to its anthropocentric ideology ("the general picture of the efforts of the human mind across genres and centuries"); the encyclopedic project betrays a transcendental ego bound up in a logic of dominance and control, one that ignores the unpredictability of the ecosystem in which we evolve. *Fin de siècle* observers, Chevillard's protagonists flaunt a misanthropy that is symptomatic of their dystopic sensibility. They question the pertinence and relevance of such "efforts," of testimonies to our cultural achievements that disclose first and foremost an ethos of anthropocentrism. In so doing they challenge two key idiolects of humanism that still inform contemporary conceptions of self: humanity and its opposite, animality.

Fuzzy Figures: Between Man and Beast

The philosophical discourse on animality has always been fertile ground for discussing the quiddity of man. From Descartes's theory of animal-machines that demonstrated the transcendence of the ego ("mind over matter" [mens agitat molem]) and comforted the supremacy betokened by Judeo-Christianity, to the more equalitarian views of the romantics that transposed to the animal sphere the debate on human rights, the discourse on animality has always served a different purpose; specifically, it functioned as an all too obvious apologue on the human condition.[31] Aesop and La Fontaine made it an explicit prerequisite to their fables, and it stands as one of the fundamentals of the bestiary. More recently texts like Lautréamont's *Chants of Maldoror* and Michaux's *Space Within* revisited the bestiary form for more openly parodic purposes. Instead of being a collection of moralistic fables, the bestiary becomes in these texts a fantastic universe where the chaotic recombination of animal categories—including human—leads to indictment of the immanence of epistemological and ontological certitudes.

In the seemingly inexhaustible range of semantic fields explored by Chevillard, animals rank first in number of incidences. They appear 175 times in the 114 pages of *Mourir m'enrhume*, 154 times in *Le démarcheur*, 81 times in *The Crab Nebula*, 73 times in *Le caoutchouc décidément*, 70 times in *Préhistoire*, and 79 times in *On the Ceiling*. Mentions of animals or animal parts number in the hundreds in *Palafox*, as the exhaustive cataloging of zoological categories and subcategories, groups and subgroups, allows for a topsy-turvy rendition of scholarly discourses that implodes under the pressure of such inflationary practices. At the other end of the spectrum few animals are referred to in *Du hérisson*, but its small eponymous hero is mentioned hundreds of times over the 252 pages of the novel.

Taken as a whole, Chevillard's zoophagous obsessions foreground a parodic exploration of our world-view. Extrapolating from Darwin's theory of the species, Chevillard pictures man as a mere incident in the evolution of the earth's ecosystem. For him the rise of man is not the product of one mishap, but of a series of mishaps, chance swervings in the unfolding of the universe. Yves Copens argues that the multiplicity of prehuman species renders our genealogical provenance even more mystifying and aleatory than is usually thought. For Copens (and for Chevillard) we do not know (exactly) who we are or where we come from. Rather, man's occasional certitudes fail to hide the hypostatic presence of chance in his genetic development. Copens states that, in the course of evolution, among all prehuman species only one family survived—Homo sapiens—and this is largely because of events whose occurrence we could neither predict nor control. Copens shows further that when gigantic earthquakes created the valley of the Rift, cutting East Africa in half, the species that were on the western side of the rift evolved into the higher simian species we know today (chimpanzees, gorillas). Those on the eastern side developed into the human race.[32]

If humanity depends on nothing more than being on one side of a rift, for Chevillard man's behavior proves that humans may have been on the wrong side. Illustrating this point, in *Préhistoire* he pushes antiessentialist logic as far as arguing that humans are indeed the usurpers of their own existence: "Today, we are the descendant of a species, both close and rival to the lost human race, whose prestige and privileges we usurp, and whose civilized manners we ape. The lice are not fooled, and neither am I; everywhere, all I see are chimpanzees applying themselves . . . , but clumsily, brutally, and insistently, carried away by their monkey logic, going beyond all measure, their smiles eaten away by their grimaces, their excessively brusque gestures, and all the words, laboriously learned, thrown away when they're angry" (90–91). Clumsily aping other species better equipped than they are to endure, humans try to emulate them in order to conform to the new world order, but to no avail. The human being, this genetic freak of nature, does not eat Colorado beetles (*Le démarcheur* 95), lacks instinct, has a weak constitution (*Préhistoire* 169). Human intelligence only amounts to "the plain distinctiveness of easy preys" (*Préhistoire* 69); unlike the hedgehog, the human cannot roll up before danger, failing to form the "more or less perfect globe" that makes the hedgehog the paragon of the animal kingdom (*Du hérisson* 50, 143). In an attempt to evolve past his all-too-mortal condition, the narrator of *On the Ceiling* opts to leave the world behind and goes to live on the ceiling instead, in a radical reversal of space and being.

As for Furne, undaunted by the task, he proposes to reform human anatomy and analyzes the causes of our inferiority in the following terms: "Our bad hair does not protect us from the cold or from blows, let's say nothing of our feathers; our nails hardly compare with the scales of reptiles or the cuticle of shellfish, they are crumbly and scattered, useless, they can only feed anxiety" (*Le caoutchouc décidément* 52). But besides physical ineptitude, humans' primary handicap in the race for evolution might be their propensity for violence. In fact, even the elaboration of art and music here is but the offshoot of humans' atavistic brutality: "Man, that bloody degenerate . . . discovered music by chance, while eating his brother with his hands. . . . All was going as well as possible . . . , until that thousand-time damned day when the creature improvised a martial rhythm while chewing on his bone, and, bashing to death a passing turtle to amuse himself, he sounded out the rhythms of war (*Le démarcheur* 47). Yet, unbeknownst to him, the warmongering human sometimes serves the higher purpose of other animal species when going into battle: "Heartening news from the front. The enemy is in retreat. Our brave boys are gaining ground for our cows" (*Palafox* 54).[33] Yet in the end humans testify to their poor adaptation to the world and their deplorable lack of survival skills: "It isn't unusual for animals caught in a trap to mutilate themselves to gain their freedom. Badgers and flying squirrels gnaw on their trapped paw, chew until it gives, it gives, three bites by a fox are enough; does, hares, and birds of prey make the same sacrifice—all of them do it with the exception, however regularly chained to an unfriendly policeman, of man, who never has the courage or even the imagination to do this" (*Palafox* 53). A fervent admirer of Nietzsche's perspectivism, Crab alleges that the human being is the sole creature who has forgotten that belief systems were tailored to serve the impulse to survive and succeed: "Evolution continued, natural selection; in a world where life is experienced by the senses and maintained by force, each of these animals saw its intelligence shrink little by little, saw its mind grow dim, its memory and reason decline even as its agility improved, along with its particular beauty, its instincts, its bounteous good health. Harmony was established at last, and only one straggler continues to disrupt it with his anxieties, his shames, and his endlessly reiterated adolescences. Only man was unable to do away with his consciousness" (*Crab Nebula* 101). This carnivalesque rereading of essentialist tropes goes beyond mere disparagement of our ecological pusillanimity and indictment of our appetite for bel-

ligerence. Rather, Chevillard contests the notion that our putative
cultural development has allowed us to outgrow plain biological
determinism and ignore the need for relativism. Soberly summing
up the issue, and putting a new twist on Truffaut's reflections in
L'enfant sauvage, the narrator of *Préhistoire* submits that a child
raised among wolves will conform to the standards of the lupine
race, but that a wolf growing up in a human environment will
finally eat his parents—and be shot by a gendarme (170)—defini-
tively proving that human survival is contingent on change and
testifying to the iconic presence of metamorphosis and ambiguity
throughout Chevillard's texts.

The fact that the ambivalent figure of metamorphosis—through
the twin figures of anthropomorphism and bestialization—occupies a privileged position in Chevillard's aesthetic confirms that
for Chevillard narrative order only arises from the consistent fragmentation and recombination of (zoological) categories. In this regard the emblematic figures of Palafox illustrate best the hazards
of the construction of identity. A being whose physical appearance
is in a state of constant flux, ceaselessly morphing, Palafox is also
affected by these metamorphic fluctuations, his behavior totally
unpredictable. Palafox, once a baby giraffe, grows into a shark,
a mosquito, a leopard, a snake, a leonine poodle—which wins a
beauty contest for representing, paradoxically, the "ideal of the
breed" (121)—a sheep, a crocodile, and hundreds of other animals, and all, and none. Palafox is, above all, "crude and chaotic
stuff" (130). In other words, he is a nonspecific (or fuzzy) being.

If Newtonian science taught us that form commanded matter
and energy, and that intelligibility resulted from this formal determinism, Palafox, like Crab, demonstrates that energy exceeds
form, that form is subordinated to the unstoppable process of
transformation. Metamorphosis, Bakhtin tells us, commonly partakes of an aesthetic of the grotesque. Bakhtin quotes L. E. Pinsky,
for whom the grotesque, like paradox, makes the most incoherent and disparate elements cohere: "In the grotesque, life passes
through all the degrees, from the lowest, inert and primitive, to

the highest, most mobile and spiritualized; this garland of various forms bears witness to their oneness, brings together that which is removed, combines elements which exclude each other, contradicts all current conceptions. Grotesque in art is related to the paradox in logic."[34] It should come as no surprise then that the grotesque of Chevillard's motifs, the proliferation and disintegration of identities, complements the madcap logic mentioned by the protagonist of *Préhistoire* (41), as the fuzzification of the ego manifests itself through the multiplication of paradoxes and the deconstruction of reason.

Bakhtin also notes that in baroque literature the motifs of transformation and identity, "which began as matters of concern for the individual, are transferred to the entire human world, and to nature, and to those things that man himself has created."[35] Chevillard's discourse on animality, which owes much to contemporary ethology and sociobiology, suggests that humans have inherited archaic behaviors from their ancestors and from other animal species. By undermining the antithesis between man and animal, and using transformism as a leading trope, Chevillard prolongs the denunciation of humanist orthodoxy that was set in motion in the works of Lévi-Strauss and Foucault. No longer a figure of perfection, or the measure of all things, humans must accept being an "imperfect pearl" whose future may not hold much to be desired or hoped for.

For this reason the dystopian protagonist of *Préhistoire* decides to look the other way, toward the past, and begins to live the life of a prehistoric cave dweller, in a tentative attempt to go back to the human golden age. So, neglecting his professional responsibilities as guide and guardian of the caves of Pale, the apprentice paleontologist decides to moonlight instead as a primitive artist, one who is fully aware of the variance between the exhilarating heterogeneity of the past and the stifling uniformity of the present. Rather than fulfilling his mission, and opening his grotto to the public, the narrator chooses to wander the underground maze, meditating on the aesthetics of troglodyte painting, where, tellingly, one image is the composite of several, a hotchpotch of human, animal, and vegetal forms, a fuzzy figure whose "truth" is at best partial and whose identity remains undefined. For the troglodyte image is by no means immobile; its boundaries are indistinct and unsteady, and the onlooker fails to seize their meaning:

> *Among these indefinable figures . . . , you may think you first recognize the head of an izard, and you wonder what the problem is, only the izard possesses that kind of curved horns, but then you make out two smaller lines that continue them and branch out to become the powerful antlers of an Irish elk. So that was the answer, the mystery was not very difficult. Then, in the entanglement of the antlers, your eye extricates the genuine silhouette of a roaring feline, and all organizes itself differently."* (115–16)

The game of shifting perspectives and recombination of forms does not stop there, and the fuzzy figure on the wall becomes in turn a bird of prey, a mammoth, a buffalo, a salmon, and a crab. Finally, the painting keeps its secret and its polysemanticity intact, for in the end only the paleo-artist's divergence from the dictum of realism can empower both painter and spectator:

> *To reproduce is to admit, so it is to submit, to accept following the herd of reindeer throughout their migration, like one of the coprophagous flies. But the bond between man and the world changes when his imagination comes in. . . . It no longer is a relation of constant humiliation, of subjectification. On the contrary, the opposite occurs, as the situation turns to man's advantage—from now on, four-legged beasts will have four left legs, and won't go far. And so it was.* (117)

No wonder then that it is in the field of zoology that Chevillard's lavish use of metaphor is at its most dazzling, serving here as a narrative bridge between disparate and contradictory elements. It is the energy of the transformation, the constant change of perspective, that drives the narrative forward in a carnivalization of traditional zoology and, synecdochically, of the system in place (be it the sciences of nature or the complete *Encyclopedia*).

However, like progress, evolution remains a dubious measure by which to gauge the future of man (or beast). As a result in Chevillard's narratives the evolutionary drive soon becomes a need for devolution, as if, in devolving, ontological closure (and failure) is deferred. More than Darwin's theory of evolution, then, it is Buffon's transformism that illuminates most of Chevillard's zoophatic poetics, and madness ("zoophatic delirium" [*Le caoutchouc décidément* 15]). In *Histoire naturelle générale et particulière* Buffon speculated on the degeneration of the species, and although he granted humans a privileged ontological status, his naive anthropocentrism did not prevent others from developing his theories and applying them to all life forms.[36] In Chevillard's texts transformism plays a doubly symbolic role: life evolves and metamorphizes; conversely life may have to devolve in order to endure, for it is in in-between forms, in-between identities, in the ever-happening game of transformation, that humans' inherent uncertainty may blossom.[37]

Thus Chevillard does not exploit devolution for nostalgic ends. Even the narrator of *Préhistoire* does everything but play out a modern rendition of the noble savage, and the caves of Pale do not partake of utopia or uchronia.[38] There is no hope for finality, as evolution no longer inscribes itself within an eschatological vision of the world. As the failed autobiographer of *Du hérisson* dejectedly confesses, "My own past seems suspicious to me now; the few memories I can find and sort out may be just as illusory as the so-called bones from which paleontologists remake the world" (184). Yet the role ascribed to the metamorphic principle remains an emancipatory one, and the multiplication of identities only increases indeterminacy and free play, as Chevillard invites us to participate in this debunking of determinism and explore the stochastic and liberating nature of change. "Only metamorphosis truly exists," Eric White argues, commenting on Michel Serres's description of stochastic self-organization in complex systems.[39] In the chaotic chronotope of Chevillard's narratives identity must re-create itself constantly, in palingenesic fashion, evolving and de-volving in unpredictable ways.

A Crab Nebula

But if Chevillard's oeuvre can effectively be described as a fuzzy bestiary, it is in Crab's stories that the usage of transformism as investigation of singularity is at its most effective. Indeed, the poly-morphous Crab is as "unstraightforward" as his animal namesake and resists all attempts at characterization. He can be, in turn, beautiful, ugly, small, gigantic, fat or thin, suicidal or not, rich or disenfranchised, grotesque or divine, and on. He possesses a penis that can stretch to the moon, and tree branches grow from his body, which he must defend against foraging squirrels and treat against worms. Crab has the advantages of a god—he can fertilize all that he touches—and the drawbacks of a loser held in universal contempt. In short, he integrates all known physical and psycho-logical traits. He is an Ur-being, the ultimate global hero, the en-cyclopedic confluence of all and everything. Finally, as the title of *Un fantôme* underscores, he is a ghost, not the kind that usually comes with gothic castles and screaming maidens—although he is some of that as well—but a simulacrum (or "phantasma") and as such the vaguest of individuals.

Crab serves as the text's sole pole of reference, nebulous and indeterminate, surdetermined because all and everything at the same time, coming to represent both pure meaning and absence of meaning in one fell swoop. Crab may seem an abomination be-cause "[he] exceeds the very basis of classification, language itself: [he is] an excess of signification, a strange byproduct or leftover of the process of making meaning."[40] He is monstrous because he de-fies reason and devilish because, as William Blake observes, "Good is the passive that obeys Reason. Evil is the active springing from

Energy."[41] Julia Kristeva remarks that *evil* comes from "ubils" and "über," that is to say, "excessive."[42] Accordingly, if evil is the deliberate transgression of meaning and truth, or the manifestation of unfettered and excessive desire, Crab is a devilish and entropic force, and everyone suffers from the anxiety of his influence:

> *Crab's influence on his entourage is such that we can't ignore it; it affects us sometimes, without our noticing it, directly or not, more deceitfully when chance brings you in its range, an immediate influence, irrepressible, like the contagion of a laughing fit or yawning, and it propagates just as quickly: on all the faces, then, Crab's tics, on all the lips, his grimaces. And his speech impediments, his defects, affect each one of us now; the confusion of his thought troubles all minds, and all bodies become stooped like his. Our step falters, our mimetic gestures are his. This is the state of things. If we don't vigorously fight his growing influence, right now, with no hesitation, or regard for spilled blood, it will soon be impossible to know which one of us is Crab. (Un fantôme 10)*

In like manner the hapless writer of *Du hérisson* observes that the hedgehog that has settled in his house and on his desk "influences his every thought" (27), to the point at which he wishes he could become the hedgehog himself, not in the hope of trading one body for another but in order to become one with uncertainty and, like an Army recruit, be all that he can be.

   In Chevillard's hazy world-view being becomes a performance, and existence excludes essence. "All the world's a stage," Shakespeare wrote, paving the way for the ubiquitous Crab and his doubles.[43] Caught in the satellization of the real, in the specular relation to the self, Chevillard's hypothetical man only exists as a simulacrum of himself, his own fictional counterpart: "From now on, Crab's shadow will walk up on its feet, and Crab will crawl after her, which will be more true to the importance of their respective situations in the world" (*Un fantôme* 25).[44] Crab is Palafox is Furne is Monge is Mr. Théo is the anonymous narrator of *Préhistoire*, is the hack biographers of *L'oeuvre posthume de Thomas Pilaster* and *Du hérisson*, is Albert Moindre, is the valiant little tailor, is an undefined figure, fragmented, that has lost all notion of individuality, and his name is legion, for he is many. And for Crab truth, like identity, remains *en souffrance*: "It is too much dispersion, too much scatter for Crab to follow his nature without knowing, anywhere, and, at the same time, give in to irreconcilable desires, temptations, fears, and the slightest velleities of commitment or flight. He risks dislocating, dissolving, volatilizing, a disintegrated body, being no one anymore; he's already losing his hair" (*Un fantôme* 81). In an attempt to map out this latent multiplicity Edgar Morin argues that each human being potentially contains a stream of personalities, that each psyche is a smorgasbord of feelings, ideas, fantasies, and pulsions. For him singularity may now only be experienced as multiplicity, or what he calls "unitas multiplex."[45] But the substantive "nebula" carries more than one meaning, which is as it should be. A nebula is both an interstellar cloud and a hazy smudge of light in a telescope. As the title *Crab Nebula* announces, Chevillard's Ur-protagonist is nebulous; that is, he is both profusion and lack, multiple and unknowable: "Crab is ungraspable, not evasive or deceptive but blurry, as if his congenital myopia had little by little clouded his contours" (*Crab Nebula* 1).[46] In the world of fuzzy logic Crab stands as the epitome of "fuzzy" characterization.[47] Bart Kosko explains that the space between being and nonbeing is inherently fuzzy, indefinite. In other words, a thing may not be simply A or non-A, but may fall in an intermediary state, an in-between, fuzzy state, somewhere between presence and absence.

Glossing Descartes's experience with the beeswax plug and his fruitless search for a continuity between being and nonbeing, Kosko shows that the problem lies in the way we appropriate the grayness of the world, with black and white discourses (A or non-A).[48] For his part Chevillard sets out to both invalidate and flush out the notion of literary character by composing an Ur-character that, beyond his multifacetedness, also exists in between states and across identities, in perpetual motion. "There is in fact no difference between a young lass nimbly chopping a cucumber into thin slices and a big brown bear barreling in the snow," asserts the narrator of *Les absences du Capitaine Cook* (12). For man is "an incoherent being" with "an inscrutable nature," "an ectoplasmic character," and ultimately "a ghost" (*Les absences* 33, 61, 73). If Palafox, who jumps from one incarnation to the next without ever stopping, already offers a probant picture of nebulousness within the confines of the animal world, it is Crab, the hero of two novels (*Crab Nebula* and *Un fantôme*), who pushes ontological indeterminacy to its farthest limits and paints an almost perfect picture of life as "a fleeting reality," a condition that the narrator of *Les absences* describes with a patent sense of glee (142).[49]

The question then is not so much whether or not Crab will or can assume one identity over another, pick out one specific appearance, but how Crab comes to crystallize ontological indeterminacy (not absence) and yet "is" a character. *The Crab Nebula* and *Un fantôme* explore Crab's existence, his age, sexual habits, physical characteristics, philosophical views, and social standing, but the picture the reader gets of Crab does not resolve itself as either narrative progresses. As information on Crab increases, so does his fuzziness. Not only does Chevillard draw our attention to the "subjectivity" of characterization, but he also questions the nature of identity. There is a very meaningful correlation between Chevillard's stylistic choice—the comic novel—and his approach to characterization, in view of the fact that the fuzziness of the character ties in with the structural and epistemological ambiguity inherent in humor.

And yet, despite his fuzziness, Crab's chaotic search emblematizes the crucial pursuit of identity, for Crab's life is a perpetual quest for selfhood and an exploration of its confines. At the end of *Un fantôme* Crab dies and is buried at the cemetery:

*We are leaving the cemetery. Let's go home. We slow
down. Tears cloud our eyes, still wet; a tiny smile plays
about our lips; slowly, we start to daydream, and relish
that precious tenderness that unites us to Crab, beyond
death, which explains our irritation when, upon arriv-
ing home, we notice that the morticians have done a
bad job and that Crab still lies on his back, his hands
joined, his eyes closed, and has become again that both-
ersome, cumbersome cadaver who monopolizes a bed
and causes so much trouble. Will we ever get rid of him,
and if so, how?* (158–59)

In the end Crab tells us that the universe is not random, that it is
deterministic but vague. Crab is its constant, its permanent feature, inescapable, and yet we do not know what Crab is. Crab is
always—to some degree—all and everything. The part always partially contains the whole, Kosko states.[50] In mathematical terms
Crab is the potential subset of all known physical and psychological characteristics, somewhere between absolute space and nothingness.

Ultimately Crab proves not only that readers need characters
they can identify with but that there can be no death of the character, since the character is always there, to some degree, even if
that degree is o: "In any other book, Crab would be a secondary character, the cold corpse around which the riveting detective
story would be built, one of the troops, a shape far away, Sancho
Panza's mule, footsteps in the night. One would pay him little attention, the author would despise him, like the other characters;
the reader might even use him to turn the pages. Crab is the only
hero of this book. He will behave like one until the end, to everybody's surprise" (*Un fantôme* back page).

Like Crab, the eponymous hero of *Le vaillant petit tailleur* is initially a man destined for mediocrity. He is, after all, only a tailor,
and a small one at that. But through sheer chance and not a little
confusion he manages to bamboozle a king and his court, marry a

princess, and receive half a kingdom as dowry. The tailor's liminal exploit (killing seven flies), honorable as it may be (the author of these lines has never killed more than one fly at a time, for instance), soon snowballs into a succession of high tales of heroism and bravery, all based on the vagueness of the initial claim: he (the tailor) killed seven (seven what?) in one blow. From that initial misunderstanding (the tailor kills seven flies, who become seven knights, seven giants, etc.) a hero is born, a kingdom is conquered, a princess is wed, and order emerges from uncertainty.

In this fairy tale, as in the rest of Chevillard's texts, the elusive hero cannot be ruled out, or his importance downplayed. This is a matter of great importance in the field of fiction, because if the New Novel was animated by the desire to rid the narrative of character—if it was, in Bernard Fauconnier's words, "dominated by the desire to found a rhetoric of nothingness that accounted for the dissolution of the self"—Chevillard's narratives demonstrate that such rhetoric can only be erroneous.[51] To come back to Foucault's reading of Borges's "Chinese" laundry list, Chevillard's fuzzy protagonist constitutes more than the accumulation of items contained in the list, more than the simple assembly of semes, and, because of his "vagueness," thwarts the purpose of encyclopedic epistemophilia. In this sense Chevillard's nebulous hero escapes the ethos of realism, as there are no visible borders around him, no physical, psychological, or metaphysical certitude. As the object of the readerly gaze he remains blurred, out of focus. Only the two extremes of the hero's limits are known: totality and nothingness. The in-between is more problematic, but at any rate, there is always something on which the curtain never falls:

> *At the end of the performance, the curtain did not fall— stuck in the flies no doubt—and since the audience expected the show to go on, Crab had no choice but to keep it up. He hesitated a moment; they thought he'd forgotten his lines, and the indulgent crowd gave him an ovation. Crab bowed and resolved to perform the whole*

play again from the beginning. There were a few catcalls at first, of course, but the more enlightened members of the crowd understood that this was a daring metaphor for the eternal return, or even a fierce satire of our serial existences, and urged silence upon the carping dullards. The second performance was applauded far more warmly than the first, but still the curtain did not fall. (Crab Nebula *125*)

A third representation follows the first two, and then Crab starts improvising, randomly mixing in famous monologues and frequently pulling Yorick's skull out of his bag of tricks. Then he begins singing, dancing, telling stories, reciting prayers, listing capital cities and rivers, counting as far as humanly possible, exhausting moral and philosophical questions, inventing stories, telling his life story, and finally dissecting his own organs. But the curtain stays up:

And then Crab sank into silence, slowly, inexorably, vertically; he sank in and eventually disappeared from the gaze of the audience. There was some confusion among the spectators, a moment of uncertainty, of incomprehension, but they quickly settled on the only credible hypothesis: a trapdoor had opened beneath Crab's feet—of course, there was a trapdoor concealed in the stage—and, by common agreement, this symbolic burial of the character, replacing the fall of the curtain or the sudden blackout that traditionally signifies the end of a show, was in itself worth the price of admission; with one blow it erased the long days of boredom that had preceded it. (Applause*) (126)*

Reticent Endings

"Ends," says Peter Brooks, "have become difficult to achieve." Indeed, for lack of a coda, "one is condemned to playing: to concocting endgames, playing in anticipation of a terminal structuring moment of revelation that never comes, creating the space of an as-if, a fiction of finality."[52] Brooks asserts that in this fashion postmodern fictions reject final plenitude of meaning by frustrating the reader's desire for narrative closure, and this is clearly the case in Chevillard's novels. For Chevillard it is narrative teleology itself that has become problematic. And when the narrator of *Préhistoire* admits his reluctance to begin working, it is the writer's unwillingness to start his story that transpires:

> *Don't I risk being crushed by trying to go against the grain of things, carried away by my tale, all of a sudden, following the rules of the genre and inexorably running till the book's end, and mine, once all the pages have been turned? Is there in fact any difference between the page that you promptly turn after reading it and the one that you tear out bluntly, roll up, and throw on the embers to kick up the fire? The reader's left hand only contains ashes: I have no interest in hurrying the pace of this story and even less in throwing myself wholly into it; that will happen soon enough. (47–48)[53]*

Without fail Chevillard's protagonists deploy an intense activity, mental, physical, and above all verbal, which fuels the narrative drive until its end, after all energy and narrative possibilities have been exhausted. The final scene of *Le caoutchouc décidément* sums up this chaotic telos. On their way back from a farm they have just visited, where they identified the aspects of the system in place that need to be reformed, Furne and his investigative team (of mental patients) board the bus that will take them back to the institution, but the bus does not start. Instead it coughs a couple of times and, in metatextual fashion, stalls; the novel ends on the word "smoke" (fume [126]), as the smoke coming out of the exhaust signals the end (and exhaustion) of the story. For the reader, as well as the protagonist, this is where the trip ends. Fighting against the same exhaustion Crab goes on speaking, partly to keep his wax tongue warm and mobile and prevent it from hardening. "He is fighting for his life," the narrator cautions readers (*Crab Nebula* 9). For his part the protagonist of *Préhistoire* shows similar concerns for his impending demise, as well as the text's, a fear that explains his reticence to engage in any course of action. His obdurate silence may strike one as odd when compared with the loquacity of Furne, or of most of Chevillard's prattlers, but it testifies to the same fear of death.

In order to avoid or delay the entropic termination of the text, and explore a dizzying amount of narrative possibilities in the meantime, Chevillard deploys two narrative strategies. The first one, used from *Mourir m'enrhume* through *The Crab Nebula*, consists of slowing down the progression of the narrative with a set of delaying tactics.[54] I will call this "delayed plotting." *Préhistoire* marks a significant shift in perspective and narrative strategy and the emergence of "regressive plotting." I do not mean that there is no plotting taking place in this novel, as that would indicate the absence of narrative per se, but that Chevillard playfully deconstructs the designs and intentions of traditional narratives. Regressive plotting in fact appears as far back as *Palafox*, but on a minor scale. Delayed plotting also plays an important role in *Préhistoire*, but as an adjunct to regressive plotting.

In his most recent efforts (*L'oeuvre posthume de Thomas Pilaster*, *Du hérisson*, and *Le vaillant petit tailleur*) Chevillard has combined both strategies effectively. If these novels evoke picaresque fiction, this is because they are divided into small segments (consider the nine- to eleven-line-long segments of *Du hérisson* or the seven different parts of *Thomas Pilaster*), each dedicated to a specific topic, or a specific incident, or, in the case of *Thomas Pilaster*, a specific genre: the journal, the detective story, the collection of aphorisms, the short story, the monologue. These telegraphic narratives privilege episodicity and aleatoriness, rather than the tight chronology of traditional texts, and promote an aesthetic of fragmentation and incompletion. Unlike Cervantes and Diderot, however, Chevillard uses these combinations of sequences not so much to provide the fabula with peripetaeia, nor to create a fini-

tude of meaning, but to forego, once again, narrative closure.[55]
"Will I have time to finish my sentence?" Mr. Théo asks, wonder-
ing whether death will cut him cold in the middle of one of his
meandering digressions before he has a chance to tell the whole
story, or in this case all the stories (*Mourir m'enrhume* 23). But the
storyteller keeps on rambling, trusting that the end will come only
when everything has been exhausted.

Despite the centrifugal impact of delayed plotting on the course
of the narrative, it still functions as a structuring force. The narrator of *Préhistoire* couches the purpose of digression in the following terms: "I may have progressed more than it seems—maybe
digression is the shortest route from one point to the next, to think
of it, since there is so much traffic on the straight lane" (66). This
contradiction is echoed by the narrator of *Les absences du Capitaine Cook*, for whom every turn taken away from the straight and
narrow is really a shortcut (227). In fact, the function of the digression is double and paradoxical. It takes the narrative forward,
from point A to point B, through some "roundabout ways," as the
narrator of *Préhistoire* puts it (48), but it doubles backward upon
itself when it ends. The narrative then progresses, ever so slowly, in
weaving/unweaving fashion, but always reaches its point—even if
this is its point of departure, as in *Préhistoire*. Accordingly Palafox
speaks of "the tangents that punctuate this story, or make it unravel, since we always manage to make our way back to the point"
(*Palafox* 98).

Narrative continuity in Chevillard's texts is virtually nonex-
istent, as digressions constantly interrupt the primary plotline.[56]
These digressions constitute a series of logical spin-offs that seem
at first to derail the plot; patterns of communication are constantly
interrupted by noise, by unprocessable information. However, it
soon becomes clear that they function instead as seemingly random swerves of the narrative, as stochastic moments of semantic and rhetorical self-organization. Each swerve of the narrative,
each moment of clinamen, marks another development in the chaotic "madcap logic" and adds to textual complexity (and uncer-

tainty).[57] By using the very fragmented and aleatory form of the narrative—jumping from topic A to topic B to topic C in seemingly random manner—Chevillard frustrates our desire for narrative resolution and syntagmatic cohesion.

Within each segment he makes an extensive use of *enchaînements* (1–2), *enchâssements* (1–2–1), and *entrelacements* (1–2–1–2), emphasizing relations based on causality. Between segments relations are based on contiguity, but all develop into a splatter structure. In *The Crab Nebula*, for instance, the center of the splatter structure is the ubiquitous Crab, although that center clearly is embattled. Characters provide for narrative cohesion, yet Chevillard's infinitely unknowable subject triggers a narrative flow that organizes itself around him and defeats the reader's interpretive maneuvers. The center of the structure is a nebula, opaque and fragmented, and this structure geminates at the deeper levels of the narrative.

Further, like discrete systems in mathematics, each segment is a splatter structure in itself, a subset and an open set, an attractor in the chaos of the text. From this nodular point the reader interfaces with other texts, as in hypertext, in what Umberto Eco calls "inferential walks"—that is to say, juncture points in the text where the reader branches out to other related narratives.[58] As for discursive articulations, within and between segments, they ensure narrative continuity and become, paradoxically, moments of liberation, loci of free will where the narrative cheats the system in place:

> *Ah, the hinge! Allows one to come and go at will, provides a link and some play between two distinct, maybe opposite, orders of reality. There is one between day and night, vice and virtue, salty and sweet; it connects them, articulates them. When logic abuses it, it grates, it jams. General harmony depends on it, and even delirium owes it its singular coherence, the evidence of its most audacious metaphors. It will serve our needs; if used well, it will give us access to everything everywhere. In it resides the only tangible truth. There is always one be-*

tween what precedes and what follows. (Le caoutchouc
décidément *125)*

For Peter Brooks plot is "the principal ordering force of [the]
meanings we try to wrest from human temporality," where the
narrative permits the articulation of "man's time-boundedness, his
consciousness of existence within the limits of mortality."[59] Here
Chevillard's narrators play with the encoding of history in narrative time, impeding the march of the narrative with digressions, introducing chance in narrative logic, but hazard and narrative time
remain carefully plotted: "There is no more hazard than source
for the winds. The plot is run a lot better than may seem; its rigor
drives me to despair. The obstacles I throw in make up its necessary peripateia; it assimilates and swallows everything that was
supposed to throw it off course—there's no way out" (*Préhistoire*
84). Cognizant of the inconclusiveness of delayed plotting, the apprentice narrator understands that the text itself is the problem.
Textuality is bound in time, and history is a textual construct. The
sequential ordering of events in a story invariably introduces the
notion of narrative logic, and with it the two related notions of
story time and discourse time. For the narrator of *Préhistoire* historical time has no transcendental value as "time of reference"
and is tied to story time. For him it would be perfectly possible to
"tell history backward" (129), and so to plot his story regressively:
"One would see then a logic of progress, the inversion of cause and
effect; the string of events would appear to be just as inexorable
as the one we depend on. . . . It's movement that counts, evolution
(whatever its flow), no design, no necessity. Nothing justifies History as we may reconstitute it. Life plows on, it digs in and wants
to endure, but we can't give it shape or purpose; it is a principle
without consequence, pure energy, useless" (130). The goal of regressive plotting therefore is to take the narrator before the event
of the text, to its prehistory. In fact, *Préhistoire* can be read as an
incipit to textuality, to another work yet *en souffrance*, to the sum
of all texts. It is, in short, the story of a story that never begins, just

as *Du hérisson* tells the story of a book that is being burned, page by page, until even the author has given up all pretense of existing. Playfully these texts pronounce that before history, there was life, but life unshackled, not yet the prisoner of linguistic determinisms, and harmony prevailed:

> *The end of prehistory was precipitated by the arrival of writing. More exactly, we consider that the arrival of writing marks the end of prehistory, that, in fact, prehistory ends when the story begins. Present on the Earth for three million years, and tired, as one would be with less than that, unchanged despite morphological transformations that, little by little, drove him away from the monkey without bringing him any closer to the tiger, man became that fictional character whose extraordinary adventures will continue from book to book until the end of writing, for these adventures, too, will tire readers out, since it is true that rapid and uninterrupted succession makes up the most perfect figure of immobility that has been known since the Quaternary ice age.* (Préhistoire 43)

To break this palimpsestic retelling of the same, the narrator invites us to read "backward" (in the same fashion one would read delayed plots "sideways") and thus unravel the proairetic code. Instead of precipitating the narrator toward his ends, acts and events now push him back to his—and humanity's—beginnings. "Only cave paintings seem good enough to last," reads the epigraph of *Préhistoire*. Heeding Gaston Chaissac's advice, *Préhistoire*'s protagonist slowly slips back into the body and mind of a paleo-artist. But rather than being a Bildungsroman, in which the reader would follow the protagonist's development, his or her troubled quest for identity, *Préhistoire* is Chevillard's most exemplary "Rück-Bil-dungsroman" (or reversed Bildungsroman), the narrator's quest for identity passing through a deexperiencing, an unlearning of humanity's cultural and historical atavisms.[60] Because of its pre-

textual status, prehistory—not capitalized in Chevillard—offers
the artist the only possible space of creative freedom: "As long as
we know nothing for sure about prehistory, we understand almost
nothing, we are forced to invent" (*Préhistoire* 89). Like the painting on the cave wall, prehistory allows for instability, hazard, and
mystery. And prehistoric humans personify incomprehensible otherness: "These [troglodytic] men have become foreign to us. The
generation gap—widened and flooded in zoos to keep monkeys or
lemurs from sneaking into the company of visitors—this famous
trench seems deeper still . . . , which keeps us from the carcasses
and other fine remains of our direct ancestors. All one need do is
show their gently prognathous skulls to a contemporary to judge,
and listen as their laughter overflows" (*Palafox* 62). But pretextual
Eden is by its very nature hazardous, and "sooner or later" the
story will begin, and with it all textual necessities. The need for
representative strategies—first pictural, then textual—will lead to
interpretation and closure. Even the prehistoric world, the narrator concedes, was "awfully organized" (*Préhistoire* 69). "We will
come out of fuzziness" (flou), he tells us (169), out of the cave, and
into the text. Thus *Préhistoire* goes on and takes to task Plato's
theory of ideas, his concept of man's gradual emancipation from
the cave, from mere imagination (*doxa*), and ascent toward the
world of ideas (*episteme*). But coming out of the cave—the prese-
mantic matrix—may not liberate or empower the individual, the
narrator of *Préhistoire* warns us. Only in the cave do we imagine
ourselves for what we are, in this ephemeral moment of freedom
before the first picture takes shape. But as the saying goes, the
writing is on the wall, and the show, as always, must go on.

Only a change of cast, humanity giving itself a secondary role
in the zoological order of things, might help humans swerve away
from thanatocratic textuality. Then they could live a vicarious life,
in awe of more developed animal species. Their burgeoning interpretive schemes would entail zoomorphic representations and
shun anthropomorphism: "Will man ever take himself for model
and subject of his painting? I doubt he will ever be so presumptu-

ous, nor that he will think so highly of himself to judge himself worthy. Besides, for whom would he make these pictures? For his peers, what for? A man's portrait could only interest a living being, someone intelligent and sensitive, and someone who would not be a man" (*Préhistoire* 170). Through these desperate attempts at survival, at finding a niche for man in the order of things, Chevillard's protagonists only tell the reader that life is but an interlude. And like most artists, they seek to evade this condition through immortality and achieve it through the immolation of the text. Monge, whose writing is cast in stone—he is a mortician who, in his own terms, "labors for eternity"—has chosen to eradicate all potential locutors and won't even stop at castrating the mute (*Le démarcheur* 35, 76). Furne's manifesto against the system in place is entirely devoted to textuality and literature (*Le caoutchouc décidément* 70), and the ceiling-dwelling narrator of *On the Ceiling* entertains nothing less than "a general reorganization of things" (20). More modest in his goals, the narrator of *Préhistoire* confesses that his hopes for fame and grandeur do not exceed a very reasonable period of forty or fifty thousand years (169). Mr. Théo, the geriatric killer of *Mourir m'enrhume*, simply wants to go out in style, and to do so he must have the last word, "musical and light, like a blade of grass between taxidermist's teeth" (9). And last but not least, the hedgehog of *Du hérisson*, after having laid waste to the biographer's work and expectations, makes himself a home in the ashes of the book, so that he may, like a fuzzy Phoenix, rise again one day.

4. Marie Redonnet
The Mourning After

> The Sirens: it seems they did indeed sing, but in an un-
> fulfilling way, one that only gave a sign of where the real
> sources and real happiness of song opened.
>
> Maurice Blanchot, *Le livre à venir*

Dead Man & Company

Since 1985 Marie Redonnet has been writing what can best be
described as an elegy to contemporary literature. She exposes an
aging culture that is ebbing, haunted by history, revealing a paradigm shift—Thomas Kuhn's term—that is troubling the old order.[1]
To be sure, the end of the millennium has prompted many *fin de
siècle* writers to search out the past, rekindling the fires of memory
in order to elucidate the aporias of the present.[2] In the winter of
France's discontent, however, few of them have elected to explore
so thoroughly the inertia that seems to hold the old world in its
grip in order to reinvent literature in the aftermath of what Michel Leiris called its *mise à mort* (murder).[3] As a result Redonnet's
heroines struggle between resistance and abandon and attempt to
live on, finding meaning in eroding worlds, haunted hamlets, val-

leys and islands abandoned by populations too old or too weak
to resist. Critics have noted Redonnet's propensity to use images
of death and desolation—Jordan Stump has spoken of her cult of
the dead—as well as her tendency to formalize the theme of mortality in a series of remarkably coercive narrative structures.[4] In a
very personal rendition of the apocalypse, where one should stop
thinking in order to forget everything,[5] where identities do not exist or only barely so, episodically emerging out of nothingness, art
leads to death ("art is a relation with death"), as Maurice Blanchot
says, testing our limits, "because death is the extreme" (l'extrême).
"He who includes death among all that is in his control," he adds,
"controls himself extremely. He is linked to the whole of his ca-
pability; he is power through and through. Art is mastery of the
supreme moment, supreme mastery."[6]

Redonnet began her fictional necrology in 1985, with the publication of a series of minimalist poems, reportedly inspired by
a personal death, in *Le mort & Cie* (*Dead Man & Company*).
One year later twelve short texts followed, which she auspiciously
introduced as "twelve little machines of failure and death" (*Doublures* jacket notes). Moving from short, fragmented pieces to full-
length literary works, in 1988 she wrote a play entitled *Tir & Lir*,
the grim tale of an old couple slowly dying in a room. *Mobie-Diq*
(1989) chronicles the last days of another couple of elderly folks
who spend their last days drifting away on a nameless ocean. *Seaside* (1989) tells the story of drifters hovering between worlds at
the end of time, closing the triptych initiated with *Tir & Lir*. Her
last two plays, *Le cirque Pandor* and *Fort Gambo*, written for children and published together in 1994, depict used-up worlds, worn
out by corruption and decay and inhabited by transient, ghostlike
figures.

Her biggest contribution, though, is in the field of the novel, with
eight texts that articulate one of the dreariest formation cycles of
contemporary literature, eight dystopias haunted by her personal
ghosts. Her first three novels (*Splendid Hôtel* [*Hôtel Splendid*] in
1986, *Forever Valley* and *Rose Mélie Rose* [*Rose Mellie* Rose]

in 1987) form the novelistic counterpart of her theatrical triptych and bespeak a Beckettian influence. Leaving Minuit—and Beckett's shadow—for Gallimard, in 1990 she published *Silsie*, the story of a young teacher embarking on a quest of self-discovery in a world still marked by the influence of the dead. *Candy Story*, published in 1992, upped the ante, through the gradual emancipation of the heroine from her past. In 1994, however, *Nevermore*—published by POL, like the preceding novel—reminded the reader that the nefarious influence of the past can in the best of cases only be held at bay and that the pathos of life is bound to repeat itself endlessly. Finally, Flohic's publication of *Villa Rosa* in 1996 and Grasset's of *L'accord de paix* in 2000 add two other (minor) chapters to Redonnet's obituary of fiction. Overall her oeuvre makes up an extremely coherent ensemble. Her most recent novels (*Nevermore*, *Villa Rosa*, and *L'accord de paix*) close, for the time being, what I will call her elegiac cycle.[7] In addition she wrote an essay on one of her main influences, Jean Genet, in 1999 (*Jean Genet: Le poète travesti*).

Like Beckett, Redonnet tells of desolate spaces inhabited by crippled beings. Yet unlike Beckett's, her world does not irremediably crawl toward extinction. Rather, it builds up the narrative from where Beckett left it. Beckett's Clov and Hamm fret over the fact that their acts and words might impress some meaning on the world: "Hamm: We're not beginning to mean something? Clov: Mean something! You and I, mean something! (*Brief laugh*). Ah that's a good one!"[8] Redonnet's characters seek an escape from the impoverished contingencies of Beckett's characters. Jordan Stump notes that, although *Tir & Lir* recalls Beckett's *Endgame*, it fails to empty itself of things; things accumulate instead—here in the form of letters that parents and children send each other and that provide the play's narrative tension.[9] Likewise, from her first works through *Candy Story* Redonnet's plotlines have tended to increase in complexity with each new text (*Hôtel Splendid* concerns the life of an old maid and her two sisters, while *Candy Story* describes the parallel lives of about forty characters), as if the accretion of characters mirrored and echoed the accumulation of objects.

Though novelists and playwrights in the 1970s still labored in the wake of Brecht and Beckett, the 1980s marked a return to storytelling, and notably the narration of the ordinary, the anecdotal, as the texts of François Bon, Pierre Michon, Xavier Bazot, Emmanuelle Berheim, Michel Vinaver, Yasmina Reza, and Marie Redonnet readily show. But for their part Redonnet's texts have retained an aesthetic of poverty and lack that is common of Beckett and untypical of much postmodernist prose, with few notable exceptions (such as Christine Angot and Annie Ernaux). In fact, ever since her beginnings Redonnet has led an uncompromising struggle against what she describes as "the shallow talent of postmodernism."[10] Instead like Yem, the sailor of *Rose Mellie Rose*, she has chosen to navigate a more austere route.

Her writing is unadorned and terse, rejecting both the flourishes of good style and the pyrotechnics of postmodernism. Articulating itself on a basic triadic pattern (subject-verb-object), her denuded language makes extensive use of what Claude Prévost and Jean-Claude Lebrun have called "verbs that were used up before being used (to do, to have, to say)," performative verbs that shun metaphors, yet, in the words of John Barth, suggest more by saying less.[11] Not surprisingly, her seeming discomfort with language—she speaks of her "initial disagreement with language"—her flat prose and minimalist ethos, in a word her unfashionable tendencies, have by and large kept Redonnet from the limelight.[12] Although three of her plays, *Tir & Lir*, *Mobie-Diq*, and *Seaside*, were produced at the Avignon Theater Festival by Alain Françon (the first two) and Gilles Gleize (the third), and although she has been published (and anointed) by Minuit, in addition to Gallimard and POL, her "relative" lack of visibility has kept her out of the media limelight and distanced from the literary awards that are such a key part of the French publishing world. Paradoxically, if Redonnet's *romanesque* owes much to theater—she even thought at one point of entitling one of her novels *Théâtre*—because of their resolutely nonludic and nonpostmodernist tessitura, her plays are rarely produced and performed.

Growing Indeterminacies

Warren Motte has justly underscored Redonnet's "simplicity of conceit and transparency of style,"[13] for her stylistic bareness is precisely one of the most bedazzling aspects of her prose, as the almost endless repetition of small sentences—each of them a matrix of textuality that seemingly displays the same void, the same absence of meaning—that is so characteristic of her writing endeavors to numb readers and lower their defenses. Not surprisingly, critics have pointed out the formal similarities between Redonnet's early texts and fairy tales. As in fairy tales, or songs, the constant recurrence of small verbal units in her fiction takes on a nearly hypnotic effect, very much like the serialist music of Schoenberg, Stravinsky, and Messiaen. Yet the faint rustle of Redonnet's language cannot entirely mask the buzzing chaos under the surface, the fuzziness at play, nor does it try to do so.

Hence the rhythm of her language (the repetition of triadic units) goes hand in hand with a continual swerve between lexias, for the subject of her story always seems to change, as if each of her narrators could never keep her mind on one single topic for more than a few sentences, and sometimes even less than that. Accordingly over the first twenty-three sentences—in twenty-three lines—of *Hôtel Splendid*, the narrator addresses a mounting array of topics, arranged isotopically, each event having the same importance and meaning as the next, each sentence following upon the one before without any transition other than a metonymic one, as if events were piled, rat-a-tat, on top of each other. Like the growing number of characters, the dizzying accumulation of events serves here to prevent any narrative resolution. Instead even the most banal events remain nonspecific, open, and only lead to other, equally ordinary occurrences, the whole tableau a masterpiece of vagueness, of perpetual transformation.

Over these first twenty-three lines the reader is confronted in turn with the deterioration of Hôtel Splendid, the clogging of the toilets, the effect of humidity on the wallpaper, the presence of a subterranean water source, the responsibility of the narrator's grandmother for having built the hotel in such an unreliable and unsanitary spot, the grandmother's long-lost hopes, the addition of modern toilets to all the rooms of the hotel, the uniqueness—and oddity—of the hotel's presence in the area it was built at the time it was built, the presence of the grandmother's portrait in the hotel's main hall, the grandmother's show of pride in the picture, the detail of the cane on which she leaned, the good impression produced by the picture, the loss of the hotel's former reputation, the vanity of the narrator's sisters, the manifest senility of the narrator and her claim to still being in her prime, the healthy looks of Ada, her sickliness, her fainting spells, and the displeasure Adel experiences when Ada faints; this litany goes on, unabated, for 126 pages.

Words for Redonnet have weight and a propensity to oppose the deliquescence of the universe, its senescence, through their re-iteration, creating order in the face of chaos. Each of Redonnet's fundamental tropes and figures—all of which return to the performing of identity and memory—functions like an attractor or magnet around which lexial dissemination is organized.[14] Thus topical clutter finds itself counterbalanced and regulated by the internal logic of language and the permanence of certain motives. It is not inconsequential either that Redonnet's economy of means should point to the spatial cohesiveness and constraints that are typical of the theater. Thus most of her characters' movements, no matter how repetitive and frequent, no matter how seemingly trivial and small, are rigorously organized along set topographical lines, like those of actors onstage, and between a limited number of points that mark the limits of the text, borders beyond which narrators may not venture without risks; indeed, several of her characters do die after attempting to cross into the offstage.

Bob, the apprentice border guard in *Forever Valley*, has a heart attack after trying to rally the border, and Mademoiselle Marthe, the mayor's substitute, passes away after the failure of her professional reconversion in the new world (*Rose Mellie Rose*). Yem, the young sailor of *Rose Mellie Rose*, vanishes with his boat, *The Fairy Queen*, after exploring a mysterious off-world (and off-text) sea passage. Like Mab, the fairy queen of Shakespeare's *Romeo and Juliet*, who is both mistress of magic and deceitful illusionist, Redonnet's fairy queen serves to underscore the double bind of hope and disillusionment, for Yem sails into the unknown but finds himself immersed in (and probably killed by) it.

Apart from inducing formal and aesthetic constraints, Redonnet's fight with language also reveals an emblematic figure of loss and absence, a void of great congruity on which her narrative chronotope is predicated: death. Death stands at the center of her web; it is an entropic force that pulls everything in its wake. It is the dominant ethos of her work and, not surprisingly, has haunted it since its beginning: "[The dead:] that was the inaugural word from which my writing was born," says Redonnet.[15] In this her texts intersect those of several of her acknowledged poetic predecessors, like Franz Kafka, Bruno Schultz, and Danilo Kis—all of whom took to task the absurdity and the cruelty of human fate—but also, and above all, those of Beckett and Genet, whose key contribution to Redonnet's mythopoetics is "the theme of death, and history."[16] *Silsie* begins with an epigraph from Kafka, an epigraph in the form of a farewell, as *Silsie* is the first text written after the Minuit triptych and, as such, marks the end of the unimpeded rule of the dead. *Nevermore* is dedicated to the memory of Danilo Kis, whose 1962 novel, *Psalam 44*, inaugurated the cycle dedicated to the question of the Final Solution, "the family circus," in Kis's words.

For Redonnet the figure of the dead is emblazoned in her personal history, written, as it were, on the body. "The personal project of the [female] narrators [in *Hôtel Splendid* and *Rose Mellie Rose*] has as an objective the inscription in the symbolic, the autograph," writes Anne-Marie Picard; "it's the body that signs."[17] Indeed, Redonnet has commented on numerous occasions on the death of her father, a traumatic event that compelled her to begin writing several years later.[18] After her father's demise, Redonnet admits, she undertook a psychoanalysis that lasted seven years

(1977–84), a period of bereavement and exploration that was followed by the cathartic writing of *Dead Man & Company*. From then on the figure of the (dead) father has not only remained a key figure but has functioned as a monadic presence, an ultimate signifier in her literary cosmogony: "God and the dead, whatever names you may want to give them, seem to me like the main two cards in the game of writing. Other cards are variable."[19] Around these two incontestable textual anchors there can be no absolute truth or falsehood, no certainty, except the drag that pulls each and every character, each and every thing, toward them.

"Redonnet's autobiography gives birth to fiction, and feeds it," states Yvette Went-Daoust,[20] and indeed, the apologetic and exhibitionist nature of such texts as "Redonne après maldonne" and "Redonnet, Marie" (an entry Redonnet wrote for Jérôme Garcin's dictionary of contemporary writers) seems to leave no ambiguity as to the autobiographical bent of her fiction. From the outset her characters and the situations in which they evolve have seemed to mirror episodes and actors from Redonnet's own life. Her father was the son of a miner and a baker (some of the characters in *Doublures* have the same occupations); he was a railroad man (see *Hôtel Splendid*, *Silsie*, and *Candy Story*); her mother worked as a seamstress (see *Doublures*, *Silsie*, *Nevermore*, and *Villa Rosa*). Redonnet's own professions (as teacher and writer) are evoked in *Dead Man & Company*, *Silsie*, *Candy Story*, and *Nevermore*. And what is true for the socio-professional environment of her novels is also true for psychological data. Speaking of her Minuit triptych, Redonnet says that "the three novels form a triptych that tells . . . how Martine L'hospitalier [her 'maiden name'] became Marie Redonnet."[21]

If the triptych narrates the fight against the symbolic presence of the father—the genitor or one of his symbolic doubles—and the difficulty of reestablishing a filiation with the mother, the post-triptych works describe the recurring struggle against the father's ghost and the resulting onslaught of neurosis. "After leaving Editions de Minuit . . . , I thought I had to grow on my own, without

the fatherly presence of Jérôme Lindon," says Redonnet, in an example of what Elizabeth Fallaize has called the passage from the
patrilineal to the matrilineal.[22] Yet *Silsie*, *Candy Story*, *Nevermore*,
and *Villa Rosa* still shape some of the same symbolic genealogies
and archaisms already exposed in the two triptychs. In *Hôtel Splendid* the anonymous narrator must endure the decomposition of her
hotel, a parable for the stifling presence of the father's memory,
the word *hotel* alluding metonymically to "(L')hospitalier."[23] In
fact, the words *hotel* and *hostile* share the same roots: "hospitalia"
(apartments for strangers or guests), but also "hostis" (a guest,
stranger, but also an enemy). And *hostel* also refers to the Biblical "host," another fatherly presence that hinders the narrator's
longing for liberation. As the action takes place, literally, in the
name of the father, matrilineal transmission is often jammed, haphazard at best. "Mother is always blurry in those photos, in the
background," laments the anonymous narrator of *Hôtel Splendid*
(95); and again, "in the background, you can see mother, blurry as
usual" (102). The image of the mother is veiled, fuzzy, and fails to
transpire through the paternal order. This symbolic obliteration of
the female figure recurs throughout Redonnet's texts, as in *Silsie*
(89) and *Villa Rosa* (26–27). And if the rose of *Villa Rosa* plays
out like a parable for the name of the mother—whose real name
is Marguerite, another flower—the name of the mother has only
been written, once again, over the name and space of the father.

Thus the novelistic cycle of Redonnet goes from the Hôtel
Splendid—*locus patris*—to the Villa Rosa—*locus matris*—where
it ends a cycle, that of Redonnet's personal mythology and fu-
neral song.[24] *Villa Rosa* is a Künstlerroman that tells the story of
Monsieur Jean, a painter. Some of his paintings represent head-
less "castrated" women, fuzzy and eternally reproducible figures
who find themselves literally and metaphorically framed as subjects of the paintings. Each painting that appears in *Villa Rosa* is
in fact double, thus superimposing one erasure upon another. For
instance, Matisse's 1914 painting is entitled "Woman on Chair at
the Window" (Femme sur chaise à la fenêtre [26]), and the paint-

ing that doubles it in the text becomes "Lola on the high stool, on the podium" (Lola sur le haut tabouret du podium [27]). All of Redonnet's themes hark back to the same scenario, Yvette Went-Daoust says, to the problematic relation of a girl with the law of the father: "a young girl . . . experiences great difficulties in freeing herself from the law of the father."[25] This atavistic attachment to the past has symbolic overtones throughout Redonnet's texts; the image of Hôtel Splendid leaning over like a boat run aground, decaying but unsinkable, is perpetuated in fact until *Villa Rosa*, except that the "home" has turned feminine.

Vague Mat(t)er

This unveiling of the semiotic—Redonnet speaks of "unveiling the imaginary"—remains embryonic in the first part of the triptych, while the language of the narrator oscillates between logorrhea and aphasia, colliding constantly with "the symbolic abutments" that paralyze it.[26] But liberation only fails partially, as some images begin to puncture holes in the Oedipal order. Such would be the case with the episode of the railroad line swallowed by the swamp on which it has been erected (*Hôtel Splendid* 73), which should be read as a parable for the poet's ability to unsettle the father's order (Redonnet's father worked for the Régie des Transports Parisiens, which includes all the train lines of the subway and the RER) by calling to the semiotic space on which the symbolic rests (the swamp representing female space in traditional mythologies and in psychoanalysis).[27] Still this incident does not conclude on an epiphany, only hinting at the possibility of liberation. Likewise *Forever Valley* closes on an acknowledgment of failure on the part of the anonymous narrator, physically and emotionally tied to the father, whom she buried herself, although this burial has not prompted her emancipation from him (110). Describing herself as anemic and "still not developed" (102) ("pas formée" [125]), and thus still a child from a physical standpoint, she is also illiterate, remaining an intrinsic part of the (father's) Imaginary.[28]

It is not until *Rose Mellie Rose* that the female narrator—named for the first time, thus severing herself from the name of the father—can swerve from the deleterious rule of the patrilineal. "The dwarf scratches his name until it bleeds," writes Redonnet in *Dead Man & Company* (32), for the homunculus, the writer-to-be, must erase the father's name before reinscribing another name over it, before dealing anew the ontological deck, as the title "Redonne après maldonne" suggests ("mal-donne" alludes, among other things, to a "bad hand" in a card game). The same parable of escape from the symbolic order is used in *Villa Rosa*, where Henri Matisse, a young man named after the fauvist painter, finds he must grapple with the difficulty of severing himself from the figure of his elder. Only when he succeeds in changing his name from Henri Matisse to Monsieur Jean (his grandfather's name) does the anguish disappear, and does he become able to fashion his own identity: "It's the name that came to him. His anguish died out" (31). But Jean is a painter himself, and his paintings are identical to, or rather supersede, Henri Matisse's real prints. In fact, young Matisse's pressure to emancipate himself from the presence of his artistic double plays like another variation of Redonnet's own account of her coming of age as a writer. In "Redonne après maldonne" she explains that she only became a writer when she was able to inscribe herself in the symbolic: "The dilemma only ended at the end of the analysis, when I settled the question of the Name, as, for me, this question has a lot to do with becoming a writer, it's even one of the key reasons for it happening. It's as if, having given birth, through writing, to the name that was not given to me (Redonnet, my mother's maiden name, instead of Hospitalier, for the father), I had to bring back a universe that was completely lost, a memory that was inaccessible, another tongue."[29] Though the image of the mother gains more resilience and appears more sharply, the father's ghost—or trace, as Derrida would put it—still makes an impression. In so doing it continues to haunt Redonnet's later texts, like the ghost of Hamlet's father haunts the battlements of Ellsinore.[30] As for the president, Patter, in *Nevermore*, Redonnet's next-to-last novel, he stands as one of her most salient images of the father as omnipresent being. Not only is he a testimony to the father's ubiquitous presence in Redonnet's elegiac cycle, like a remanent ghost showing through on every picture that Redonnet conjures up; he is also a "president," that is to say, the one who, literally and figuratively, "sits in front," preventing other images from coming into view.

That the father functions as the centripetal force of Redonnet's mythology is never in doubt, and in this Redonnet intersects Kafka by evoking the errant quest of disenchanted beings, trying to find a meaning in their lives beyond the burdensome influence of the father. However, at the same time Redonnet proposes to "mourn (and forget) the accursed, crucified writer," that is, to engage the Kafkaesque aporia.[31] "It's a past with no archive," says Silsie of the castle's history (125), for the castle was drowned under the waters of the lake, its memory erased. An identical scene takes place in *Forever Valley*, at nearly the same point in the plot. But as the title indicates, even when underwater, the valley of the dead remains the center of the narrator's attention, an inescapable force that feeds her nostalgia. If the quote from Kafka that serves as the epigraph to *Silsie*—"What will you say when you see this wardrobe full of dresses?"—comes from the last chapter of *The Castle*, this is precisely because Redonnet's novel proposes to go beyond the Kafkaesque dead end, beyond its symbolic fiasco.

Entropy

What Kafka's and Redonnet's characters do share is a social unease. But if Kafka's protagonist (K) eventually finds meaning in his Sisyphean attempts to become part of the social order, Redonnet's characters struggle with the rigidity of social ties and the hierarchy that they imply. In consequence the landlady of *Hôtel Splendid* finds that her customers have little patience or gratitude for her enormous—and desperate—efforts to improve the comfort of the hotel, while the customers of Monsieur Codi's "Hôtel de Texe" (in *Silsie*) and Marion's "Hôtel de la Mer" (in *Candy Story*) show even less appreciation. If hostelry does not seem to offer a very promising situation, other professions fare hardly better. Manual workers (blacksmiths and butchers in *Doublures*, sailors in *Rose Mellie Rose* and *Candy Story*), civil servants (customs agents in *Forever Valley* and *Fort Gambo*, police officers in *Candy Story* and *Nevermore*, administrative secretaries in *Rose Mellie Rose*), and members of the liberal professions (architects and photographers in *Rose Mellie Rose* and *Candy Story*) all fail to manage their affairs effectively.

Manual workers toil till they drop, sailors routinely drown, butchers let their stock of meat rot, customs agents go missing at their post, police officers don't complete their investigations, architects have no money to finish their projects, and photographers lock themselves up in the darkroom where their pictures should be. Even the world's oldest profession can't avoid this fate; the local dairy maids who moonlight at the dance hall (and brothel) of *Forever Valley* end up losing their jobs after the hall closes: "The girls from the dairy miss the dancehall already. To them, it's irreplaceable. They are not sure it will be so easy to work for themselves on Saturday nights. . . . Away from the dancehall the girls will lose their appeal, they know it and it torments them. . . . They are bitter" (75). Identity, social as well as psychological, becomes mediated through performance, for failure to perform has two corollaries, engendering not only pauperization but also loss of identity. Even artists and intellectuals experience the same bitterness as prostitutes. Aspiring writers willingly whore for success, like Kurtz, Rotz, and Witz in *Candy Story*, but may find the price too high to pay. Failed artists, such as dancers and circus performers, are no less common, as in *Seaside*, *Nevermore*, and *Le cirque Pandor*, and try to recover from past accidents that broke their careers and their lives. As for the librarian of *Rose Mellie Rose*—a man with a reputable position—he becomes disenchanted too, for, after having given up his translation project, "he is no one" (20).

Often *mal formés* (badly trained, but also physically handicapped), Redonnet's characters must labor under the debts that they incurred or inherited from ancestors, as in *Doublures, Hôtel Splendid*, and *Forever Valley*. The most remarkable of these poverty-stricken creatures is undoubtedly the proprietor of the less than grand hotel of *Hôtel Splendid*, condemned to unblock its everlastingly clogged-up pipes, riddled with debts to the plumber and the electrician. As for Yem, the young sailor of *Rose Mellie Rose*, he owes money for his boat and the house he has built for Mélie and himself: "Yem comes back more exhausted every night. He works harder and harder at fishing. He needs a great deal of money to pay for the boat and the house. It is beyond his strength to go on fishing this way" (83). For her part the eponymous heroine of *Silsie* runs up debts with the local Madame (Madame Gilda) to buy herself clothes and food (73), but in doing so she comes to owe Madame Gilda more than money. Identity too is reified, and Silsie, like Mélie with Mademoiselle Marthe in *Rose Mellie Rose*, finds she must first define herself through the gaze and economic strategy of another. As seems logical in a world where identities are bought and traded, the changing of clothes comes to play a significant part in this constant trading of identity. "In her new clothes, she already feels she is another," confirms Sister Marthes, a young woman who abandons her convent for a new life outside of its walls (*L'accord de paix* 15).

As well as an economic construct, identity is a legal one, as being and being owned become increasingly hard to distinguish from one another, a fact that becomes critically clear to Mélie when she needs to declare her identity at the *état civil* (*Rose Mellie Rose* 34)—the registry office, but also, literally, "being or existing within a given state or society." Only once she has filled out the necessary paperwork does the registry office grant her access to the social— and symbolic—order, inscribing her in the registers and giving her a temporary ID. (Her number is 3175, which adds up to Mélie's age: sixteen.) She then receives her final ID, after her picture is taken and captured, photographically as well as symbolically (36). "Without my papers, there wouldn't be any proof that I am the

schoolteacher who was appointed to Dolms," states Silsie (*Silsie*
15)—no proof of her professional existence ("schoolteacher") and
no proof of her social and symbolic legitimation ("appointed"
or "named"). But the possibility of belonging always triggers an
ontological malaise, as Redonnet's embryonic beings seek to construct an identity for the future. Paradoxically this identity must
be predicated on the past, even if, Mélie warns, "one must not mix
the old and the new" (96), at the risk of remaining in the father's
shadow forever, like the narrator of *Hôtel Splendid*.

Choosing the fairy tale—a genre that has traditionally reinforced patterns of male authority—to articulate a new "feminine"
poetics, in the wake of Marguerite Duras and Julia Kristeva, was a
rather unusual move, but one that allowed Redonnet to deconstruct
and reconfigure her own "patrimony."[32] Besides the influence of
Beckett and Duras, and that of minimalist art, Redonnet has also
borrowed her narrative economy from fairy tales, eschewing long
psychological descriptions and concentrating on facts—the acts or
non-acts of the heroine in her quest. "The fable compensates for
the poverty and rigidity of its fundamental scheme by using repetition along all possible imaginable principles of connection," states
Claude Brémond, defining a narrative scheme that is regulated by
one or several of the following: degradation-amelioration, merit-
reward, demerit-punishment.[33] The only constant of the fairy tale,
Brémond adds, is degradation-amelioration, which ensures the
satisfactory closure of the tale.

Redonnet's subversion of the narrative unity typical of the fairy
tale—all of her texts, including *Rose Mellie Rose*, end in degrada-
tion and thus inconclusiveness—is most effective against a genre
that predicates its moral code on the rigidity of its narrative matrix. Besides unmaking the narrative totalitarianism of fairy tales,
Redonnet chooses only female protagonists—with the exception
of a few male protagonists in *Doublures*, and one other in *Nevermore*—changing the traditional hierarchization of sexes and
gender roles that the fairy tale presupposes and that Yvette Went-
Daoust has called, "from a feminine standpoint, the most anti-

emancipatory and frustrating genre there is, since women often end up with roles that are either passive or active, but secondary and baleful."[34]

Overall, though, Redonnet's novels diverge from traditional concepts of the "tale" and "novel," a fact that has put her various editors in an awkward position. For Jérôme Lindon, Minuit's late editor-in-chief, Redonnet's three early texts—her least novelistic ones—were novels, whereas *Silsie*, which took more liberties with the early fairy-tale aesthetic inaugurated with *Hôtel Splendid*, was presented as a tale (*conte*) by Gallimard's editor. Hence the transition from fairy tale to novel seems, at least from the standpoint of nomenclature, problematical, even though Redonnet's texts have tended to evolve toward a form more compatible with that of the novel and less with that of the fairy tale, though the tension between realism and fantasy runs throughout her oeuvre.[35] In fact, her most compelling opuses are those in which some equilibrium is reached between these two poles, namely *Rose Mellie Rose* and *Silsie*, whereas earlier works (*Doublures, Dead Man & Company*) tend to be stifled by the weight of their own narrative structure, and later texts (*Candy Story, Nevermore*) falter hesitatingly toward a more openly novelistic style, less driven by the formal imperatives of the tale. It should come as no surprise then that when it comes to the production of her plays, Redonnet wishes for actors "who are able to play abstraction and reality, both," since in her texts reality and fantasy coexist in the same paraxial zone, each shadowing the other.[36]

Beyond the fairy tale Redonnet's texts also engage autobiography as a genre. For the better part of the twentieth century autobiographies have imposed themselves as one of the century's foremost literary genres, and many authors, from Alain Robbe-Grillet to François Bon, through Georges Perec, Nathalie Sarraute, Marguerite Duras, Hervé Guibert, Annie Ernaux, Philippe Sollers, and Andreï Makine, have contributed to it. Speaking of the autobiography's utopian aim, Georges Gusdorf argues that "one of the justifications for autobiography might be a nostalgia for comprehensiveness of meaning," a nostalgia that only writing may begin to recall.[37] Jean-Philippe Miraux adds that "autobiography is a rebirth, an initiative that supposes the conditions for an eventual recovery of oneself, a reconstruction, a reconstitution."[38]

Indeed, in Redonnet's dystopian world reconstructing the past, be it personal or collective, implies that the narrator must engage the role of the speaking "I" in the narration of memory. For Gerda Zeltner the use of first-person narration in the triptych—and in all subsequent texts, until *Nevermore*—doesn't connote Redonnet's subjectivity, or what Gérard Genette would call "self-presence" (présence à soi): "Three novels follow, that go together. They are told in the first person: by an 'I' which is not one, although it says so, an 'I' that refuses autobiography and self-imagination as well as introspection."[39] Told in the third-person singular, *Nevermore* denotes a shift in narrative patterns, but the passage from first- to third-person narration does nothing to suggest a decrease in autoreferentiality, simply confirming the privileged position the fictional occupies in the text, given that Redonnet's narrative texts can hardly be read as first-degree autobiographies and that their narrative mode is not merely autotelic.[40] Even openly autobiographical pieces like "Redonne après maldonne" and "Redonnet, Marie" can't simply be used as keys to decipher Redonnet's fictional work. Rather, they foreground the structural and aesthetic developments of her novels and plays, not in metatextual but pretextual fashion. For Redonnet autobiographical prologues, and preludes, don't serve to tell the reader how to decode her archetypes (the dead, the dwarf, the king, etc.)—even though they do that—so much as they point to the privileged position that writing the self occupies in her fiction and, as Robbe-Grillet argues in his own autobiographical trilogy, potentially in all writing.

If for Philippe Forest "autobiography must affirm its fictionality, and assume that contradiction,"[41] conversely Redonnet's texts go to show that fiction must acknowledge its autobiographical nature and must signify within that tension. "The roots of the fool's words are too long" (the fool being the king's jester, but also, in

Redonnet's personal mythology, the father's daughter and, in both cases, the rebel against discourses of authority), Redonnet warns from the outset (*Dead Man & Company* 69), taking to task the constitutive paradox of autobiography and the problematic writing of history. Calling upon the emblematic figure of Kafka, Redonnet speaks of "the proximity between reality and an imaginary world, the reality of his story and History, the fiction of one opening the other, both becoming one, tragically linked."[42]

In that torsion between what is both the extratextual and the textual—which Serge Doubrovsky designates as "autofictional" and which Redonnet dubs "the border game with the real"—the father himself does not endorse the role of main character, but memory does, memory of the father, to be precise, and of the past.[43] Redonnet's allusion to borders becomes particularly significant in light of her own legend making, her maternal genealogy being, by her own account, "borderline" (frontalière).[44] Landmarks and thresholds then come to occupy a privileged position in Redonnet's imaginary topology, charting limits that may not be traversed without harm. In this sense *Dead Man & Company* inaugurates Redonnet's recounting of the past, its mourning and its fictional transformation, its staging, as the title's "Company" alludes first and foremost to the poetic transformation of the real. "Company" should then be read primarily as a reference to the world of theater, to the reinscription of the past into the text and its poetic renovation. "For me now, Sise is only *Sise Memories*," concludes Mia (*Candy Story* 44), the author of the aforementioned novel, a chronicle of her life in Sise, when she is leaving the city (65). The city and its past have become "a novel based on real people" (83), and reality finds itself disseminated throughout the various novels that appear in the course of the text. "[It's] pure fiction" (96) ("[C'est] du roman" [137]), complains Curtz, one of the several writers of *Candy Story*, after being inappropriately portrayed in somebody else's novel, unaware that the facsimile has become more real than the original.

"One may detect in what I write the theme of the initiatory

quest for memory," says Redonnet.[45] In what appears as both a metatextual and an autoreferential comment Redonnet says of Genet that for him "creating . . . was always talking about childhood. His failed childhood that his legend intended to reinvent as a definitive image, as mythical as it was real."[46] If Genet's work tends to be shadowed by his own myth, Redonnet's project for a memorial fiction also proposes to blur the boundaries between personal history and fiction in order to construct "a legend, that is to say . . . a mythical image that has a subversive effect on the real by inscribing itself poetically in History."[47] Both Genet and Redonnet hail the Greek notion of the poet as maker but also celebrate the death of a certain form of literature, with all the pomp required by the occasion (*Pompes funèbres*), or in a less ostentatious but no less seditious manner (from *Dead Man & Company* to *Nevermore*). "Here, there only are false witnesses," announces one of the artists of *Le cirque Pandor* (57), in a scene that plays like a *mise-en-abyme* of Redonnet's saga. If life is a novel, necessarily false, characters should embrace this falsehood, and bear false testimony, in order to stay true to themselves. Thus Mab, the illiterate bedridden wife of Mub, whose survival is directly linked to the letters sent by Tir and Lir, her children, tells her husband that he writes "just like in the novels" (comme dans un roman [*Tir & Lir* 76]), whereas Mobie, stranded on a small dinghy with her husband, Diq, wonders about the implausible turn their life has taken: "What a dramatic story, Diq, the kind of story that happens only in the theatre" (*Mobie-Diq* 16). In fact, Mobie and Diq owe their survival to her ability to amalgamate life and fiction. As the play begins the boat on which Mobie and Diq have embarked—-the *Tango*—-is sinking. In order to save herself and her husband, Mobie hits an old man who was fighting with her husband for the last lifeboat: "When I struck the old man on the deck of the *Tango* so he wouldn't climb aboard, I told myself I was in the big scene in *Tango*. That's exactly what gave me the courage to strike. . . . If I were a bad actress, we would be sinking with the *Tango* right now" (13) Diq then tells his wife that she behaved like a true theater heroine (13) and confirms that what he sees in real life seems to be taken from the pages of a novel: "what I see now, that's exactly what you would have seen on the screen" (15).

Under Erasure, Under Closure

But there is more to Redonnet's autofictions than the desire to rebuild memory or stop time. In fact, the simplicity of her style, the seeming naiveté of the autofictional prologue, the insistence on psychoanalytical tropes and figures, all testify to the manipulative intent of the author, to the point at which the analyst-analysand configuration (which allowed the text to emerge, by Redonnet's own account) is replicated in the scriptor-reader relationship, the text then becoming the manifestation and the space of neurosis. Hence the significance of Freudian and Lacanian topoi (the primary scene, the name of the father, the Oedipal complex, the castration complex, the mirror stage, the crucial role of bereavement) increases as the reader progresses into Redonnet's textuality. In fact, the autobiographical prologues serve precisely to orient the reader in this interpretive direction. By borrowing from the confessional style with which writers and readers of journals are familiar, they eschew any freedom or carelessness of style and aim to set the stage for a psychoanalytic reading of the text. If Warren Motte mentions Redonnet's "sustained metaliterary discourse, [her] reflection upon reading, writing, and the uses of literature,"[48] this is because her narrative strategies betray her intention to deploy her own imaginary through a palimpsestic *literary* reading of the past.

No wonder then that Redonnet's autofiction strikes the reader as uncanny: it discloses and dissimulates in the same move, as the text imposes its own rules; its own metaphoric and metonymic apprehension of the real; its own "true lying" (mentir vrai), to quote from Aragon; its own condensation and displacement, beyond that of the unconscious.[49] Still, if Redonnet's autofictional mourning (*Trauerarbeit*) occupies center stage, it also suggests that the real must be erased before its fictional reconstruction: "I wrote about mourning (for the revolution, but also for one's own story). I did not write about which new utopia one should invent, I wrote the loss of such a belief. . . . I wrote about its loss, its amnesia, about the void. I wrote to restore the account of domestic and historical bereavement."[50] For Bernard-Marie Koltès fictionalizing oneself and others entails their "murder" (mise à mort),[51] as if autofiction always signals an absence, a void, but also predicates its necessity as the chasm that constitutes the text. Commenting on the need for the author to disappear, Mallarmé argued that poetry is a sacrifice, Blanchot adding that "the book . . . needs the writer, insofar as the writer is absence and the space of absence."[52] In Redonnet's case all that is left are traces, not clear signs pointing to a pretextual reality, but ghostly figures that haunt the text and allude to the chasm within.

In her study of Genettian mythology Redonnet explains that Genet's creation revolves around "a hole with everything around it" (un trou avec n'importe quoi autour); it is out of this onto-logical void at the center, out of this vortex, that the book finally emerges.[53] Far from being an anthropological enterprise (in the sense of a personal anthropology), Redonnet's own autofiction al-ways initiates something, bringing order out of chaos.[54] Quoting from Félix Guattari, and commenting on Genet, Redonnet argues that "he deterrioralizes himself, and invents a new reality."[55] But Genet's "deterriolization"—a portmanteau word: *deterritorializa-tion* compounded through *deterioration*—is very much like Re-donnet's own deterriolization; it's a new universe born out of the decomposition of the old. In fact, Redonnet's work, or song, ar-ticulates itself on the dual process of dissemination and reorgani-zation, "[through] the scattering force of space and the collecting power of the rhythmic process."[56]

Hence in *Nevermore* Cassy Mac Key aims to expel the unspeak-able—war, death, the sexual exploitation of women—from her memory if only for an instant and transform it through the me-dium of song. "Only song," says Michel Corvin, "will give intimate truths (those that can't be demonstrated) a positivity likely to establish the being of nothingness."[57] If for Redonnet the figure of the poet foreshadows "the violent, vibrant passage between two periods" (*Nevermore* jacket notes), this is because of her "therapeutic belief in the power of the symbolic."[58] For failing to master language can have devastating consequences, as the murder of the first Silsie makes evident. It is the first Silsie who never managed to understand poetry—that is, the reorganization of the symbolic order—and could only pass on a journal with blank pages to her (twin) sister, the new, fictionally transfigured and empowered Silsie (*Silsie* 95).

One may argue that Redonnet's global project resides in the writing of the self into the symbolic; if spatial and temporal cohesion are extreme in Redonnet's Minuit triptychs, this is because only the most rigorous control of the chronotope can allow the poet to contain the chaos that threatens to wedge its way in. And it is that chaos, that white noise, which intrudes upon the poet's consciousness, which the soldiers from Ruido's army (literally the army of noise—*ruido* in Spanish) embody, as they slaughter everyone in sight (*L'accord de paix* 25), standing, allegorically, as a reminder that noise (that is, the voices of the past) always threatens to destroy the fragile balance of the narrative and the mental stability of the narrator. Thus the action of *Hôtel Splendid* remains mostly contained within the walls of the hotel, while each encroachment from "offstage" results in the growing decomposition of the center (diseases from insects and rats, humidity from the swamp). As Redonnet puts it: "When one sees the universe of Hôtel Splendid, that sort of devouring chaos, that mortiferous power, that swamp—for that power to be expressed in a nondestructive manner, I had to build systems, machines, tight controls, obsessions. It's true that my books contain very mathematical, controlled, defensive systems; maybe this was the only way to contain that force, the dangerous force of the swamp, and turn it into an imaginary metaphor, so I could speak."[59] Likewise characters' movements in *Forever Valley* stay confined within a geographical zone delimited by two borders that they can never cross. In *Rose Mellie Rose* the action takes place on an island—the island of Oat—while characters only report what they did or saw elsewhere; Mélie knows that she can, and will, never leave Oat (82). Only after *Silsie* do borders become more porous. When the eponymous heroine of *Silsie* goes toward the center of the sea, she leaves the "old" world, and the old psychological envelope, behind. Mia, the protagonist of *Candy Story*, travels across the world like several other characters (Witz, Curtz), but geographic—as well as personal—emancipation plays itself out on a more local level. Between the archaic Mells-le-Château and the freedom that Paris exemplifies for Mia, the town of Mills-le-Pont is a cratylic bridge, a nodal point toward an elsewhere. But bridges may collapse, neuroses flare up again, and in *Nevermore* all bets are off. Of course the two detectives of this novel (Willy Bost and Commandant Burke) do travel freely across the border between San Rosa and Santa Flor, but all they ever discover is that corruption prevails on both sides, as if chaos had spread throughout the world.

This containment of space has its corollary in characterization. Characters saunter on like puppets in the early triptychs, even though they tend to gain more independence in the post-triptych works. In Redonnet's latest writings they appear to be shaking off the weight of the original fate, to be swerving from the overly determined symmetry of the early texts. Yet if the narrator of *Hôtel Splendid* complains of her "misfortune" (malheur [46]), the young detective of *Nevermore*, five novels later, still suffers from an identical fate. "But what has he been until now, if not the slave of those in High Places?" he wonders in a rare moment of lucidity (86), only to succumb once more to the same atavisms that benumb each and every one of Redonnet's characters, the mysterious "High Places" having the last word, as in Kafka's tales. That characters should always have to face the same atavisms, the same cultural and psychological determinisms, shows that history, in Redonnet, functions like a linear system, imposing its tragic teleology on the narrative.[60] Finally, for Commandant Burke and his assistant "it will be San Rosa right up to the end" (*Nevermore* 6), for few can escape this Sisyphean fate.

It may seem at first that some of Redonnet's characters, notably Mélie in *Rose Mellie Rose*, Silsie, Mia in *Candy Story*, and Cassy Mac Key in *Nevermore*, have succeeded in breaking the yoke of the past. For Yvette Went-Daoust Silsie's final vision at the center of the sea recalls Rimbaud's "Bateau ivre," giving the measure of "the creative jubilation and writerly freedom that she [Redonnet] anticipates." Went-Daoust further states that "'the center of the sea,' which is also the maternal bosom, naturally [becomes] a new point of departure, as we know, for the work that the writer envisions."[61] For Elizabeth Fallaize the maternal spaces of *Rose Mellie Rose* allow for the same type of emancipation from the law of the father. But no maternal space can obscure the tyranny of the father here, nor is it supposed to do so. Rather, the ghostly presence of the father provides the necessary counterpoint to the heroine's undertakings. In each and every case of alleged "emancipation" the acts of the female protagonist do not take her anywhere, and, in the case of Silsie, certainly not to the center of the sea or to the new continent. Instead Silsie ends up adrift, on a small dinghy (148). As she states matter-of-factly, "I have no goal in life" (151). Silsie's statement is most definitive, for she may have no more past, but she has no future either. All she owns is a suitcase, and reaching the center of the sea remains, in the best case, a vision, projected beyond the reaches of the text. However, if the two earlier castaways of *Mobie-Diq* end their days in the belly of the white whale that they drift into, the later *Silsie* does open up a more hopeful perspective, albeit unrealized and deferred.

Here one should not forget that the sea, in spite of the generative role it plays in feminine cosmogonies, remains an entropic force in Redonnet's fiction, a presence that is devouring and destructive. Yem (the sailor) never comes back from his journey of discovery in *Rose Mellie Rose*, like Onie, who lets herself drift away in *Seaside*, while Cassy Mac Key and Willy Bost, the two star-crossed lovers of *Nevermore*, disappear in an underwater cave, ending their days in contemplation of the skeleton of yet another white whale, old as time itself. As for lakes, other bodies of water, evocative of the feminine principle but, on the surface, less agitated than seas, they bring their own lot of misfortunes. The village of *Forever Valley* ends up flooded beneath an artificial lake; in *Silsie* Dill, a young child plagued by a "hereditary defect" (74), drowns himself in another lake, at the bottom of which lie the underwater ruins of the same old castle.

Fuzzy Doubles

Nevertheless, the "deadly, nefarious inheritance" (the name of the father) that plagues Redonnet's characters does not rule unimpeded,[62] finding itself countered by one specific figure, that of the double, as if the dissolution of the self, through its partition between two twins or namesakes, is the only thing that might counter the inexorability of the one. This is a crucial component of Redonnet's poetics, and the unique instance of emancipation in her work, even though this emancipation does not serve any of her individual protagonists. Rather, emancipation exists only in its perpetual deferral, in the promise that it might come to pass from one double to another. For Redonnet the figure of the double—evoked primarily through twinning and homonymy—evokes a formal constraint that translates the obsessions of the author and her characters. "The fool's jars are always changing labels," states one of the permutational haikus of *Dead Man & Company* (87), illustrating, in metatextual fashion, how Redonnet proposes to counter formal (and mythopoetic) closure. In spite of its seemingly random placement in relation to the text as a whole (it sits in the middle of the book), and its cryptic message that borrows some of its tropes from medieval iconography, this particular stanza announces Redonnet's primary strategy: to use the double in a conflictual and creative dynamics in order to subsume the fatality of the one. For Gilbert Alter-Gilbert the formal structure of *Dead Man & Company* leaves no doubt as to its aesthetic and, I would argue, literary intentions:

Four hundred and fifty-six three-line stanzas detail
the exploits of these characters who turn up, time and
again, in ever-new and ever-surprising juxtaposition to
one another. Situations dissolve and reconstitute, and
seeming finales are marked by a false finality—what one
commentator has called "never-quite-ending endings."
Experiencing each new stanza is like being dealt a fresh
hand of cards, or pulling the lever of a slot machine, and
watching the fruit come up in different configurations.
Each stanza of Dead Man & Company *is a self-con-*
tained story. Some may convey oblique and parabolic
morals; others, more elusive and elliptical messages.
With each roll, the dice reveal novel combinations.[63]

After *Dead Man & Company* Redonnet adopted a similar scheme
for each subsequent text, along with the same open-ended permutational games and the same "false finality," while laboring to
offset the monadic presence of the father with an overlay of dyadic
configurations.

If the father remains the ultimate signifier in Redonnet's symbolic order, the use of doubles produces what Raymond Bellour
calls "an organized drift of the novel"; in other words, it offers a
calculated adjournment of closure.[64] As long as the permutational
games that Redonnet plays endure, as long as she does not exhaust
their combinatory possibilities, her protagonists still have another
shot at escaping the fatality of closure (both formal and semantic).
Doublures, her earliest work in prose, sets the tone for her entire
opus. The book tells the stories of twelve characters—Lia, Lii, Gal,
Gil, Gem, Gim, Sil, Sim, Lam, Lim, Nel, Nil—"twelve machines of
failure and death." Yet for all their physical deficiencies and professional limitations, these homunculi know one saving grace: they
exist not as individuals, but within a dynamics of exchange. They
are, in Redonnet's own words, "twelve proliferating and protean
doubles" (jacket notes); that is, they are fuzzy figures that herald
the proliferation of duplicates in upcoming texts. *Doublures* con-

sists of a series of twelve tragic fables that are all marked by the inexorable presence of disease and death, and out of the twelve protagonists, only one survives. And yet, in spite of the chrono-metric incidence of disaster in the text, I would argue that *Dou-blures* falls short of being a tragedy, in the traditional sense of the term. Whether the book is "tragic" is not in question. What mat-ters is which exit window Redonnet writes into the text, not only in *Doublures* but in the rest of her oeuvre. In this particular fiction it appears highly significant that, in the end, an actress (Gem) finds herself the lone survivor of the long string of catastrophes, for it appears, from the very beginning of Redonnet's cycle, that only an artist may envisage (textually and metatextually) another life and escape the fate that befell all others. It is equally important that, while Gem may escape her fate, another character—her almost identical namesake and understudy (*doublure*), Ger—becomes Gem's sacrificial lamb and takes the fall for her. For in so doing she must deal (*gère*) in Gem's place with life's drama, while providing the artist with a vicarious other and a way out.

Likewise in the monolithic world of *Hôtel Splendid* Ada and Adel, the narrator's crippled sisters, must carry the burden of an original si(g)n (once again the legacy of the father's presence). And even though the narrator never leaves the hotel, and even though life may not be livable anymore—if it ever was (90)—she does not die, but Ada and Adel do (105, 107). Sacrificed to the inhospitable presence of the father, and dying—literally and metaphorically—within his name (hostel-hospital-hospitalier), they allow the nar-rator to continue her laborious enterprise until the end, providing her with the images of disease and decay that she needs to begin her exorcism of the paternal ghost. Picking up the task where her predecessor left it, the narrator of *Forever Valley*, a young woman who lives with an old priest (another [compound] incarnation of the father), only lives to look for the dead that must be buried nearby. Of course it is in the father's garden that she launches into her grand project, a garden that will ultimately yield no corpse, only fresh graves where the old father and Bob, a "*probationary* officer" (douanier *stagiaire*), will sleep forever (110, 115). Bob's death follows close after the father's, doubling it, but his physical and professional deficiencies—he suffers from a heart condition that prevents him from doing his job or from having sexual relations with the narrator—also echo the narrator's own sense of destitution. His death, however, provides the only cathartic episode of the text: the narrator cries for the first—and the last—time on Bob's grave (116).

Rose Mellie Rose is the first novel to bridge the gap between the dead and renewal. Mélie, the young narrator, the daughter of Rose, gives birth to a baby girl whom she also names Rose, superimposing the name of the mother over death. But Rose is not the only split character in the novel. Mélie also has a double, an old ex-Madame, a *coquette* (41) who calls her Rose and for whom Rose senior—Mélie's mother—presumably worked, along with several other "Roses" (43), in the appropriately named *quartier des charmes*—a red-light district.[65] With Mélie senior's death—unreported by Mélie—the young Mélie can also sever the link with her mother's fatal past and abandon prostitution—into which she was initiated by another mother figure, Mademoiselle Marthe. "I was trained by Miss Martha," Mélie admits (71), but she knows that "you must not mix old and new" (74), a sagacious observation indeed, after the "shameful" death of Mademoiselle Marthe in the toilets of Le Bastringue, a seedy cabaret (124).

In *Silsie*, as in *Rose Mellie Rose*, Redonnet blurs the lines among characters. At first the narrator (Silsie) tries to escape the destiny of her dead twin—also named Silsie—a young prostitute probably murdered by one of her customers: "Since Silsie died, it's as if I was twice as old, my age plus Silsie's," she says (32), as if the surviving Silsie were dragging both their shadows behind her. In the course of the novel she runs across a child, Lonie, who becomes her adopted daughter, another dyadic part of herself. Lonie is murdered, however, allowing Silsie to sever the umbilical link with her own childhood. After the little girl's death Silsie goes back to her sister's grave to finally grieve her old (divided) self: "When I stand before the tomb at the end of the cemetery, I think about nothing. It's as if it was my tomb, and I was another" (114).

In *Silsie*, as in the rest of Redonnet's texts, naming interferes with meaning, or rather diffuses it. Names put characters and readers in a zone of differing and difference, or fuzziness, where identities are erased through the heterodoxy of names and through permutational manipulations. Because identity is a verbal construct in Redonnet's texts, a schizophrenic motion, exchanging names also implies exchanging bodies. Punning on the notion of "body" (both the physical body and a kind of undergarment in French), the narrator remarks that "Silsie and I, we exchanged our bodies" (39), in a précis of Redonnet's perpetual movement of symbolic substitutions. No wonder then that *Doublures* should open with the story of Lia (literally "linked"), a prototypical tale that ties into the stories of Lia's eleven doubles and successors and, intratextually, into the lives of the rest of Redonnet's pantheon. Further on *Candy Story* offers an even greater plethora of doubles, Dilo and Lou, Marion and the commanding officer of the fort, Ma and the commanding officer of Rore's fort, Madame Alma and the lighthouse guard, Mia and Kell, Mia and Enz, Lill and Witz, Line and Will. This first series is doubled by a series of doubles and triplets (Ma and Mia; Madame Alma and Madame Irma; Madame Anna and Madame Irma; Madame Irma and Erma; the two commanding officers; Lind and Lina; Wick and Witz; Yell and Kell; Luira and Luiji; Line, Lize, and Lill; Witz, Curtz, and Rotz), which is itself doubled by mother-and-child pairs (Lina and Li, Ma and Mia). At this point the multiplication of dyadic units comes to threaten the metonymic chain with implosion.

But no such thing occurs, for this would spell the end of the movement Redonnet initiated with *Doublures*. At the end of *Candy Story* Mia decides to write a novel entitled *Candy Story*, one that geminates upon the framing narrative and deactivates its malignancy at the same time. By crossing into the imaginary, into her own song, Mia (Spanish for "mine") saves herself, unlike her lover, Kell (or "quel," as in, "which one?"), who falls prey to his

own atavisms and perishes because he is unable to swerve from his
fate: he is killed in the same lighthouse where his mother was murdered, probably by the same person, or by his double, after failing
to solve the mystery of her death (137). But Mia's song, like Silsie's
voyage, only succeeds in suggesting the unknown, and the novel
closes on Mia's terse statement: "After that, I don't know" (97).
The speaking "I" ignores what or who she is, where she comes from
and where she goes, only knowing that, to survive, she must necessarily become another, her own double, her own twin, in a game
of permutations that recalls the metaphysical angst experienced
by Oscar Wilde's protagonist in *The Portrait of Dorian Gray*. Unlike Gray's portrait, however, the portrait-reflection of Redonnet's
protagonist must merge with the original, making peace with her
tragic beginnings, before breaking away, like Silsie with her twin,
and thus pervert the specular relation, instead of dividing the self
from its specular object.

In other words, in Redonnet's fiction the portrait is not destroyed
at the end, provoking the death of the subject. It may fade away,
like the painting of Rose senior in *Rose Mellie Rose*, allowing the
other part of the dyad to survive or not, but if anyone survives
in Redonnet's texts, it is only thanks to, and through, the other.
Interestingly *Nevermore* fails to cross the threshold inaugurated
by Mia's question at the end of *Candy Story*. Iconized in the title
(never more), the past still beckons the narrator, who wishes to
break away from it, just like the lone melancholy mourner of Poe's
"The Raven." The action of *Nevermore* takes place next to a border, across which two towns face each other (San Rosa and Santa
Flor) like mirror images, like two flowers exhaling the same poison, "as if San Rosa and Santa Flor were two become one, and as if
everything was mixed together there contrary to all appearances"
(51). In this dual space paired elements complete the picture, like
the *Moby Dick*—Gobbs's ship, a key participant in the "traffics"
that make up the basis of the novel's (and the towns') mortiferous
economy—one that points to the corrupted remanence, and proliferation, of the past. The copy of an ancient ship whose crew was

decimated by the plague, and ultimately burned, the *Moby Dick* is also the mirror image of Dora Atter's ship, the *Salve Regina*—the other part of *Nevermore*'s diabolic dyad—as well as an intratextual trace (of *Mobie-Diq*, Redonnet's second play).[66]

Other fated icons from the past resurface throughout the novel (the white whale, the whorehouse, the circus, the border), and duplicate atavisms also reappear, like recurring neuroses, all referring to cognate elements up the chain. If the whale appears in *Mobie-Diq*, the whorehouse is a key element of *Forever Valley*, *Rose Mellie Rose*, and *Villa Rosa*, and prostitution is explicitly referred to in *Hôtel Splendid*, *Candy Story*, *Tir & Lir*, *Fort Gambo*, and *L'accord de paix*. *Le cirque Pandor*, as its name indicates, tells the story of a circus, while there are references to the world of the circus, or to the performing arts in general—dance, theater—in *Doublures*, *Seaside*, *Hôtel Splendid*, *Candy Story*, and *Villa Rosa*. As for borders, they are omnipresent in Redonnet's texts. Survival, though, must not be mistaken for liberation. Once again protagonists who manage to free themselves from the tyranny of the narrative matrix, and the symbolic order it predicates, are not empowered by this move. *Nevermore* closes on these words: "We will never know what happened between Cassy Mac Key and Willy Bost in the grotto. Ever since Mattie's death, Angel Cove (next to which the sea cave is located) has become a cursed place, which everyone wants to forget, and where no one ever goes" (123). Once again forgotten, and damned into oblivion, the protagonists must wait for other reincarnated selves, serial successors, in order to revive their memory (and their forerunners' memories). "I would like to leave traces behind me, so that I'm not forgotten," says Martin, the storyteller of *Le cirque Pandor* (48), a sentiment that is reiterated by Judie, the puppeteer: "I have no more heritage" (53). But though this loss of the past and serial transference of the double may signify a new beginning, it also reveals the lack on which the text is predicated.

Failure does beckon most of the protagonists and their doubles, for doubles and mirror images always retain—even with some distortions—the features of the subject they reproduce. The original malediction is transferred to the doubles who inherit it, almost congenitally, as in *Tir & Lir*, in which the father's gradual atrophy passes to the son, who will lose both his legs, while the mother's venereal disease becomes the daughter's own. In fact, the double stands for the very stigmata of the malediction, for it iconizes the loss of ontological unity. The original curse is, by the very process of doubling, inescapable, always traceable, always there, emblazoned in the original name, and places—like people—suffer the same fate. When in *Rose Mellie Rose* the *quartier des charmes*—a former red-light district—is rebaptized the *quartier des pêcheurs*, the original sin does not fade away but remains engraved in the name, with only the slightest diacritic modification, from *pécheurs* (sinners) to *pêcheurs* (fishermen) (125). "The fool always digs the same hole," warns Redonnet in *Dead Man & Company* (113), for the poet is tied to her genealogical palimpsest like Prometheus to his rock.

The protagonist's final redemption, as envisioned by some critics (maternal space, women's time), fails for want of a space untouched by corruption and because these redemptions must be narrated over and over again to be remembered.[67] *Rose Mellie Rose* is a Bildungsroman that begins with the departure of Mélie from the cave where Rose—the surrogate mother—died and ends with the birth of Mélie's child, baby Rose. Yet the novel does not close on Mélie's return to the cave—the womb, in psychoanalytical and mythological terms—where she delivers her baby, nor does it end on her last picture—the twelve photographs that she takes with her Polaroid that iconize her gradual emancipation from the symbolic. It ends on the beach where she dies, facing the unknown—the sea, and beyond it the continent—which she refuses to enter, this exoteric space where her husband (Yem) vanished earlier in the book. For such is the perverse effect of Redonnet's fairy-tale matrices—the return to the same—even if she subverts their traditional ideology. The choice of the fairy tale always implies, somehow, that the protagonist is bogged down in narrative teleology, condemned like Sisyphus to repeat the same moves. Eventually the same cards are dealt again (*redonnées*). Even the later texts, which depart from the triptych's rigorous architectonics, take to task the possibility of literature proscribing the figure of the dead. Like recurring neuroses, Redonnet's post-triptych texts only mold themselves around an entropic figure that has been in place since *Dead Man & Company*.

For Redonnet Kafka and Beckett dramatize at its highest point the disincarnation of literature, the stripping away of the old paradigms, but also the end of a story. Writing after these two figures of the dead, she attempts to deliver herself, and literature, from this myth: "I wrote about an ending that both of them incarnated, in a project of rebirth and passage. To give back some life to literature, in a way, by rediscovering the character, the imaginary, and poetry, History. Trying at least."[68] Dealing again occupies a crucial place in Redonnet's work; her characters testify to this, while attempting desperately to write themselves out of the old order and into a fledgling one. "The dwarf leaves the kingdom with an empty satchel," writes Redonnet in *Dead Man & Company* (177), stressing the need for the artist to begin writing from an exoteric position.

Last Rites of Passage

But the poet can never start with a tabula rasa, and the schoolbag, though seemingly empty, ties the dwarf to the tutorial figure of the dead. Thus the passage from the old to the new—Redonnet's texts can be described as rites of passage—solely signifies within a thanatophilic perspective, not after death.[69] It is death itself that is redemptive in Redonnet's texts, not an elusive deliverance from symbolic preordination. It is the passing of the baton—from one twin to the other—that ultimately saves Redonnet's characters, through the transmission of memory and history. If death provides the only space of freedom for the artist, this is because today, says Jean Baudrillard, death is a deviance, a mark of ultimate marginality.[70] Like Mallarmé's, Redonnet's texts are self-consuming. "I created my work only by *elimination*," remarks Mallarmé, "and every acquired truth was born only from the loss of an impression that, having sparkled, was consumed, and allowed me, thanks to its liberated shadows, to advance more deeply into the sensation of Absolute Shadows. Destruction was my Beatrice."[71]

Indeed, throughout Redonnet's work characters exhaust themselves in meaningless outputs of energy, machines break down, and architectural structures teeter on the verge of collapse, if they have not crumbled already. Her fictional chronotopes bespeak an entropic model, modeled on the second law of thermodynamics, that states the irreversibility of processes. Eleven characters out of twelve die in *Doublures*, two out of three in *Hôtel Splendid*, two in *Forever Valley*, five in *Rose Mellie Rose*, eight in *Silsie*, sixteen (out of forty) in *Candy Story*; twelve nuns are raped and killed in *L'accord de paix*, and five characters meet an unfortunate end in *Nevermore*. Short of extinction, characters must confront paralysis, in physical and professional terms. Hence the customs officer of *Forever Valley* "wants to show that he is not done for" (42), while others (the father, Massi, and the narrator herself) succumb to physical torpor by slow degrees or fall into apathy. The engineer of *Silsie*, whose lungs have been exposed to the poisoned air of the mine shaft, dies of blood poisoning, although his mind seems to have been equally affected by this disease—he rapes Silsie in an excess of delirium (102). As for Willy Bost, he is "soaking wet" (*Nevermore* 4) from the very beginning, melting, as it were, from friction with the past. Unable to "take the heat," the young detective ultimately fails in his autobiographical enterprise. His fate is left open, though, which is not the case for Mélie, unable to breastfeed her child (*Rose Mellie Rose* 133), and hemorrhaging (134), until she dies alone on the beach. Conversely Ada, the failed actress of *Hôtel Splendid*, retains liquids—she suffers from rheumatism and has a goiter—but the end result is the same: she dies from an inability to process inner and outer fluids (here the humidity of the swamp).

Like the characters that use them, the bathroom installations of the Hôtel Splendid, which transport liquids in and out of the building, are described at one point as "a perfect breeding ground for . . . disease" (79). For nonfunctionality also affects mechanical devices, as if no object that processes energy of some kind or other could avoid entropic evolution. Liners sink in *Mobie-Diq* (15) and *Silsie* (148), leaving protagonists adrift on old dinghies; cars break down in *Seaside* (12), *Rose Mellie Rose* (123), and *Nevermore* (10); rickety trains patter on antiquated railroads in *Silsie* (18) and *Candy Story* (23), when rails have not completely sunk under their own inertia, as in *Hôtel Splendid* (107). Hotels barely hold against decay (*Hôtel Splendid*), if they have not caved in to erosion (*Candy Story* 65); if they stand up they are abandoned or do not attract the customers they need, as in *Hôtel Splended* (122), *Silsie* (36), and *Candy Story* (53). The power needed to make these architectural structures functional and livable is also lacking, as in *Hôtel Splendid*, where the wood fails to give off heat (25, 77). Energy might leak out and provoke power outages too (*Hôtel Splendid* 104; *Rose Mellie Rose* 98), plunging a whole city into darkness: "Dolms is in the dark. There was an unpredictable power failure at the plant, and the technicians were not able to fix it on time" (*Silsie* 98).

The failure at the power station, unpredictable though it may be for the narrator of *Silsie*, partakes of the general collapse of the center. For to rid herself of the figure of the dead that sits enthroned at the center ("the king" in *Dead Man & Company*) the poet must provoke the "central collapse" that Willy Bost, the young detective of *Nevermore*, experiences when he attempts to investigate the past. "His words lead to nothing but a black hole," says the narrator (115), to the black hole of memory, a "hole with anything around it" (un trou avec n'importe quoi autour). For Redonnet Jean Genet "writes his legend like a tomb where he would entombed, . . . so he may come out with a living image."[72] Vamping the Genettian legend to make it her own, Redonnet has built her own mausoleum to memory over the course of thirteen texts.

But as Willy Bost soon realizes, "what makes his book so difficult to write is that it is a book of memories written in the absence of memories. He invents his memories as he writes" (109).

In this thanatophilic perspective beginnings, not ends, become the vanishing points of the text. Rather than articulating what Jordan Stump calls "a struggle between life and death," Redonnet's texts illustrate rather a struggle for life *in* death, in a never-ending, perpetually fuzzy, syntagmatic chain.[73] Hence in *Nevermore* the dead of the past still beckon the protagonist. "It is forbidden to remember the past," scribbles the detective in his notebook (3), but only the lifting of the taboo—here the Final Solution, or the genocidal magnification of the figure of the dead—and its transgression can allow the poet to reinvent memory. By focusing on the past Cassy Mac Key, the other protagonist of *Nevermore*, attempts to prevail, for naming one's future depends in large part on being able to face and rename the past. Life, that is, continuation, depends on reconciliation with the abject, with the (partial) resolution of the love-hate relationship: "Like a ghost, like the specter of death, the disavowed past comes back," Gerda Zeltner writes of *Nevermore*, but she adds, "Only those who look back and accept the past may celebrate the future."[74]

The poet writes "to be in mourning," says Redonnet, adding, "I am in mourning in the Freudian sense, which implies a loss, but also the salvation of memory through the symbolic transmission of your heritage, through the symbolic action of mourning."[75] Ends tend toward beginnings and, conversely, beginnings toward ends, and if narrative desire is desire for the end, as Peter Brooks says, it is also desire for origins in Redonnet's texts.[76] Her texts start from that final point death represents and work their way backward. "The Splendid is not what it used to be since grandmother died," laments the narrator of *Hôtel Splendid* (3), before proceeding to recite her twenty-three-song eulogy to the father's memory. As *Dead Man & Company* underscores, the dwarf (the poet) can only open the gates (of memory) for the dead. "The roof of the church finally collapsed," observes the narrator of *Forever Valley*

(3), electing to stay in what will become her Golgotha (four tombs dug at the four cardinal points around a ruined church, the general pattern forming a cross). *Rose Mellie Rose* begins with an account of Rose's death, and *Silsie* opens in Camus-like fashion on "Silsie died a year ago." As for *Candy Story*, it begins with the colonel's project of writing his memories, "[a] plan for the future," the narrator comments (7), one that replicates her own (*Sise Memories*, Mia's first novel).

Reinscribing the past into the present has its dangers, though, and memories of the past sometimes become the chronicles of a death foretold, as when Line forecasts Lou's and Dilo's deaths from the abandoned journals of long-dead sailors (*Candy Story* 57). Conversely the death of the Commandant in *Nevermore* corresponds to the disappearance of the archives that might have exposed San Rosa's fatal past (138) and closes the book on the memory of the Commandant's predecessor—"who was obsessed with files and wanted to leave some mark of his existence behind him" (6)—and on the Commandant's (professional) genealogy. Graveyards—reprieved signs, but also markers of deferral—are caught up by the past and erased, back to dust or to primordial matter: the swamp in *Hôtel Splendid* (48, 62). This induces the narrator to note "how perishable everything is" (51), as bodies keep evolving and changing, even in death, until the names that are—literally—inscribed on them fade away. For this reason the swamp swallows Ada's and Adel's tombs, while their names become gradually erased, fading at the same time from the narrator's memory (117).

Finally, finding tracks is as difficult as leaving them, as with Monsieur Codi, who has lived with "a memory whose reality exists no more" (*Silsie* 33). In this game of mirrors, where bodies appear and disappear, the book becomes a tomb, a place of mourning, whose threshold one must cross (*Silsie* 134). "His memories were invented by his bad memory," says Silsie of Monsieur Codi (106), warning that remembrance cannot be undertaken lightly. Such is the case of Lend, who writes "a dead woman's journal" (*Seaside* 53), or, in other words, the wrong story. For the past is deadly and deceptive. The characters' futile attempt in *Mobie-Diq* to probe the ocean's depths is but one of the many physical examples of collapse in Redonnet's fictions, leading to a dead end. "There is no more Stork Street," says Mélie (*Rose Mellie Rose* 107); the old world of myths and fairy tales (and life—"stork") is gone, leaving nothing in its place. Still Mélie insists that the site of Rose's death has disappeared from memory—"people must be forgetting about the site" (3)—that is, it has been erased before its symbolic rewriting, just like Cassy Mac Key, who misses "an inheritance and a memory" (*Nevermore* 121). Only in the ruins of literature, among the stories and archetypes of old, will the poet find them, if she attempts to reinvent history and its memory in a new poetics of transmission, "final and radical, deadly, like the reality it is uncovering":[77] "Between the plants and flowers that invaded the ruins, a curious visitor might have discovered, all over, pieces of frescoes and paintings, with bright colors. And, on a section of wall that was still standing, hiding behind a growing rosebush, he would have found the portrait of Rosa Bell, intact, a pure wonder. He could have dreamed then about the Villa Rosa as it probably was before it fell in ruin, and reinvent its history so as to save its memory" (*Villa Rosa* 81).

5. Antoine Volodine
Inside Wars

And as I turned to toss my stole aside
My feathered shoulders were a pair of wings,
And feathers struck their roots within my flesh,
Nor could I beat my naked breasts with hands,
For both had vanished.

Ovid, *The Metamorphoses*

An Aesthetics of Deceit

In his magnum opus Sun Tzu describes the art of war as the capacity to deceive the adversary, arguing that military victory does not ultimately depend on sheer strength and numbers, but rather on one's ability to mislead opponents. To be sure, this unconventional approach to warfare gives firm precedence to strategies of containment and would seem to run contrary to the experience provided by centuries of military carnage, where military might normally makes right. But the wisdom of Sun Tzu's war treatise is not lost on Antoine Volodine, who has endeavored to construct an oeuvre organized around the coextensive notions of containment and misdirection. Working with a general backdrop that incorporates all the war-related calamities that have plagued the twentieth century—from the horrors of Auschwitz and the Kolima, to protracted ethnic conflicts and stillborn revolutions—Volodine's work engages one of the key axioms of modernity and suggests that war, not scientific progress and the belief in reason, constitutes the defining paradigm of contemporary societies. For Infernus Johannes (one of Volodine's heteronyms) the world—like language—is "a *battrelfield*" (un champ de *batraille* [*sic*]).[1] Volodine's narratives may not propose a sociological typology of belligerency, but, in keeping with Sun Tzu's *ars belli*, they transform the art of narration itself into a praxis of deceit, and language into a warlike—or terrorist—ritual, so that misleading and misreading inform much of Volodine's narrative rhetoric.

Drawing on the title of the first fragment of Volodine's third novel, "Rituel de l'esquive" (Rite of evasion), Frédéric Briot confirms that in these novels, "there is no other rite than literature, and no other ritual art than evasion."[2] Elsewhere Volodine insists on the related notions of ritual and evasion (*esquive*), as with the title of the tenth fragment of *Un navire de nulle part*, "Splendeur de l'esquive" (Splendor of evasion), and the title of Volodine's third novel, *Rituel du mépris* (Rite of scorn). Often Volodine favors interrogation scenes in which inquisitors or prison guards attempt to extract (with varying degrees of violence) narrative confessions from their prisoners, would-be terrorists who in turn (re)construct elaborate narratives, woven from truths and lies, and try their best to dodge questions and dissimulate information. Of course, when interrogated, one always confesses, as do the terrorists of "Justice est fête," but the question concerns not so much what one says but the fact that one exists in a dialogue, although that dialogue is framed in lies and dissimulation. Thus the prisoners of Volodine's stories may be the state's political opponents (*l'ennemi*), but they are, first and foremost, its verbal nemesis, and one of the poles around which discourse is constructed (and without which dialogue would not occur), as they displace meaning along lexical and

syntactical lines and deconstruct a reality that is, ultimately, mediated through language:

> *On the second Wednesday of the New (or Ninth) Year,*
> *men came in, and accused us of spreading scandal. We*
> *had, it is true, spread some phlegmongerings about the*
> *imperial family. . . . As the funnel and the gauntlet had*
> *been applied to our carcasses, we acknowledged that,*
> *in the wee hours, we had set a few podgy kegs of anar-*
> *chist powder that sang in the alcoves, night after night,*
> *and hurled among the velvet drapes the king's favorite*
> *sirloins and some duchesses' thighs. Infernal machines*
> *had painted dark red the lower portion of the chapel; we*
> *confessed to the deed. We said we had helped the enemy*
> *tread upon the border's wild thyme, we did not conceal*
> *we were the enemy. . . . Soon, we gave in, greatly dis-*
> *jointed and excoriated, but still dreaming of pirouettes*
> *and twaddle.*[3]

Even though this is one of Volodine's earlier published texts, a
crucial syllogism emerges, one that will shape the rest of his oeuvre: (1) people are bound to engage in dialogue; (2) dialogues are
fraught with lies (and framed by poetic license); (3) people are liars
(and must be in order to survive and coexist). So, taking a page
from the chronicles of Vichy France or Soviet Russia, the actors
of Volodine's tales grow to be collaborators, for in this case collaborators are not only survivors but control (to some extent) the
narrative of their own oppression.

If the fuddling of things only concerned the pas de deux between
narrator and narratee, readers might still feel that they could get
a sense of what's going on, of who's telling the truth or not. But
the reader is an active principle of interpretation, Umberto Eco
tells us, whose "rate of initiative" plays a critical role in the cultural and linguistic encoding of the text.[4] Indeed, a few lines into
a Volodinian text readers find themselves already in an odd position. Though invited into the story, they are asked to function as

intruding critics, as doubles of the investigator whom the narrator seeks to disconcert and from whom he or she withholds information. Yet if the text implements strategies of deception, confusing the reader and diffracting meaning, Volodine's goal is certainly not to construct textual mazes in the form of Borgesian labyrinths and riddles. The blank spaces of the narrative are not meant to be decoded but are left open to contingent interpretations. For Volodine the text must remain (partly) encrypted, or else it would merely resolve into autobiographical fiction. Instead, and because of its hiatuses, Volodinian fiction calls for the reader's active participation in its poetic elaboration, although, from the incipit onward, the interchange between the readers and the text is fraught with uncertainty.

For Breughel, the narrator of *Le port intérieur*, "there's always an unfriendly ear lingering behind the walls. A hostile intelligence." To which Kotter, Breughel's opponent and professed expert on counterintelligence warfare, replies: "That's true. . . . You must encrypt things."[5] Challenged into reading "through" the text's aporias—an impossible performance—readers are placed in the position of the "adversary," that is, both opponent and prosecutor. (In the Hebrew tradition the "adversary" was the prosecutor in a trial.) Occupying an adversarial position does not mean, however, that readers should feel hostile toward the text, but that meaning is never completely accessible, and then only through confrontation. "In the end, utter confusion creepy-crawled in" (A la fin, la plus grande confusion se mit araignée), quips one of the literary investigators of *Biographie comparée de Jorian Murgrave* (10).

However dispirited this statement, meaning is not absent from the Volodinian text, though it is deferred. Its logic is displaced, elsewhere, and articulates itself along a logic of fuzziness. As a consequence the text itself is necessarily other than the reader projects it to be and becomes an alien and alienating environment, a fiction that embraces fuzziness on both aesthetic and formal levels. Manipulated by the narrative instance, through the encryption of literary genres and codes, readers have no other choice but to become an intrinsic part of the bellicose strategy that the text develops. Episodically the narrative may refer to the literary typology that frames it. But its terms remain "vaguely" familiar, including false friends like *shaggå, narrat poétique, narrat lyrique, romånce,* and *féerie.* Wherever these terms appear in the body of the text, they only hinder topological elucidation, even though they call to mind a lexicon with which readers are familiar (saga, poetry, lyric poetry, romance, and fairy tale). What is important then is that these neologisms only function intratextually, within a closed signifying economy, only looking as if they were dead—not empty— signs to outside readers. Only the text's narratee may see beyond topological fuzziness.

If the terrorists of "Justice est fête" do not exactly "lie" to their captors (that is, they do not make statements that the reader and/ or addressee know to be patently untrue), this is probably because they are in no position to do so. Yet they still carnivalize the system by turning justice into a game (*fête*), and thus into a system whose rules can be modified, if not amended or upended. As a consequence lying comes to occupy a privileged position among the subversive tactics developed by Volodine's narrators, one whose purpose goes far beyond terminological inexactitudes or the substitution of one verbal object for another. Rhetorically speaking, lying offers a rich palette of narrative moves, like forgery, counterfeiting, falsification, and misrepresentation, all of which are used by Volodine's terrorist narrators. It is telling that for Ingrid Vogel the creation of neologisms—or lexical sabotage—partakes of a more general "spiritual gymnastics of falsehood" (*Lisbonne* 49). "I had started lying again," confesses Golpiez, the protagonist of *Le nom des singes* (*Naming the Jungle*), to his psychiatrist, who urges Golpiez to proceed with his story, after realizing that confession is worthless as an admission of guilt, since a confessional narrative, like all narratives, partakes of its own fabrication (13). Beyond truthfulness and falsehood, Golpiez's confession and/or deceit can only be read as an X marking the spot, that is, the beginning of the narrative trail, the start of the story.

If lying corresponds to one of the most discernible manifestations of narrative fuzziness, every facet of the Volodinian text actively incorporates some degree of vagueness. To wit, the multiplication of characters and their overlapping in the process of character-ization—several may share one voice or exchange physical traits or personalities—hinders or completely prevents identification. In *Jorian Murgrave* the reader encounters forty-one named charac-ters, and more remain unnamed. There are thirty-seven characters in *Un navire de nulle part*, thirty-three in *Rituel du mépris*, fifty-one in *Des enfers fabuleux*, sixty-one in *Lisbonne, dernière marge*, twenty-four in the 126 pages of *Alto solo*, a more manageable nine in *Le nom des singes* (*Naming the Jungle*), five in *Le port intéri-eur*, seven in *Bardo or not Bardo*, before the number goes back up to thirty-six in *Dondog* and a whopping forty-nine in *Des anges mineurs* (*Minor Angels*). And yet even the dearth of characters in some texts doesn't aid toponomical legibility. Rather, the greater legibility that a smaller cast would normally provide fails to ap-ply within the Volodinian archive, because of the unremitting fu-sion and permutation of the characters' identities (names, physical traits, personalities, narrative voices). In this ever more dizzying game of musical chairs, one Fabian Golpiez interfuses with Gon-çalves, Manda with Leonor Nieves and Maria Gabriela (*Naming the Jungle*), whereas a Breughel bespeaks a Machado and a Kotter, who in turn devolves into a Breughel (*Le port intérieur*), without the reader being at any point the wiser concerning the real or defi-nite identity of any of these characters.

And to make matters more unfathomable, the names of charac-ters seldom function metaphorically, and even less so in Cratylic manner. (Okhro [Fangs], a guard, is a notable exception, but in this case the onomastic analogy is so obvious that it defuses its own symbolic value.) Neither do they symbolize a clear, specific sociocultural status or geographical origin. Instead linguistic het-erogeneity charts an unspecified space, a semantic Babel, where the defamiliarization engendered by toponymy generates, for the reader, an estrangement from (linguistic and cultural) familiar-

ity. Dojna Khatoun, Hakatia Torénégué, Slobodan-Kateth Mi-
nahualpa, Istvo, Astvo, Charco, Gros-Tas, Pied-de-boeuf, Tyran,
Sachemarde, Jacquou-Nécromane, Jérôme-Emporte-pièce, Sylvain
Névroptère, Vassili-le-chancelier, Bloom, Toghtaba Ozbeg, Tregar-
Molop, Greblöh, Darwâya, Meyerberh, Ash-Duan, Chaïm, Oural,
and Ilhel-Dô all belong to *Jorian Murgrave*'s motley cast, but the
only thing they make plain is that naming fails to denote, rather
interfering with and diffracting meaning through the permutation
and fuzzying of idioms, so that in the end names can only function
as loci of disruption.

Toponymic disruption is not only taxonomical but also phonetic. The Gortmank, Grölwesh, Gaïehel, Gazhoffk, Gyyzden,
Guéeph, and Guyïep of *Rituel du mépris*, the Holthadjayk, Rak-
kodyradja, Byleer, Phrango, Ronghra, Wohrad, Sonwoo, Olthad-
jayk, and Ronghradja of *Des enfers fabuleux*, the Sarvara Drajdia,
Tchaki Estherkan, Dimirtchi Makionian, Ansaf Vildan, Mourtaza
Tchopalav, Kaanto Djylas, Danylo Tagrakian, Sevasti Palataï, Na-
ïsso Baldakchan, Tamian Ichkouat, Kirghyl Karakassian, Bieno
Amirbekian, Iakoub Khadjbakiro, Dojna Magidjamalian, Hakatia
Badrinourbat, and Vassila Temirbekian of *Alto solo*, and the Dondog Balbaïan, Toghtaga Ozbeg, and Djanniya Otchoïan of *Dondog* refer to something (unknown) and may seem unpronounce-
able and illogical from a phonetic and etymological standpoint. If
not, they still seem illogical due to the incongruous collocation of
a name and a surname of different cultural origins. In both cases
they tend toward complexity. Either the reader confronts the enunciative difficulty and understands that names fail to create meaning, literally or figuratively, and partake of the text's fuzziness, or
the reader simply passes over the aporia that the name presupposes, mispronounces it, and goes on with the story itself. But in
this case the reader's unwillingness to "sound out" the names, to
take to task the enunciative difficulty, might well signal the first
manifestation of a xenophobic attitude that begins with phonetics
and extends through semantics and ideology.

Another aspect of Volodine's aesthetics of deceit concerns the

uncertainty of space (unfamiliar or defamiliarized locations, sometimes recurring in different episodes), which translates retrospec-
tively to the notion of place, so that the several references to Mon-
golia, Slavic countries, Southeast Asia, and the Lusophonic world
that crisscross the text cannot be exploited by readers to elucidate
its aporias. The towns of Kolombo, Tchikagow, and Lissabonne
(*Un navire* 23) do not map out the fuzzy space of Volodine's novels any more clearly than Colombo, Chicago, and Lisbon; nor do
Schrapool (*Rituel du mépris*), Chamrouche (*Alto solo*), and Puesto
Libertad (*Naming the Jungle*) locate the action in a recognizable
Central European or South American locale. And if *Le port intérieur* actually takes place in Macao, it does so in the slums of
the city, where a Babelian maze of houses and alleyways reveals a
world impenetrable to the narrator, a world saturated by noise, by
a constant sensory and visual overload, utterly alien and alienating, where "intelligence . . . dilutes itself in vapor and noise" (30).
As for *Lisbonne, dernière marge*, while it does open on "Arsenal
Street, Lisbon, where gallows abound" (7), it closes on "We were
young then, and, to fight against the unforgivable absurdity of the
world, WE HAD WEAPONS" (245). Framed between incipit and explicit, Lisbon defines another Michauxesque *battrelfield*, unmark-
ing its own geographical margins, turning narrative space into a
battle zone where meaning is disputed by competing agencies. In
the Volodinian chronotope geographic markers only aim to evoke
traces of other cultures, which can be followed or not. They function like contingent referential walks that can be pursued by readers should they wish to do so; in hypertextual manner they open
other windows that branch out from the text's main frame, but
that are not indispensable to its signifying economy.[6]

The semantic contents of space are constructed like the semantic
contents of characters Mieke Bal outlines.[7] They include determina-
tion, repetition, accumulation, and transformation, making space
an acting place rather than a place of action. This is all the more
true since, in Volodine's novels, space diffracts signification by denying readers the right to imagine a lifelike picture of the environ-

ment presented. The shantytowns, ethnic ghettos, and industrial zones of Volodine's "postexotic" world may appear quite realistic, but they remain unlocalized. They are, in a word, "dispossessed" environments, which Marc Augé would describe as "nonspaces" (non-lieux)—that is, transitory spaces—and which Volodine identifies as "unrecognizable places for an unspeakable time" (*Jorian Murgrave* 15). Yet, rather than being a symptom of failure, the transitivity of space, we should note, constitutes an indispensable condition of textual activity (along with the transitivity of characters). In light of this, mapping the environment—mineral, vegetal, or animal—becomes a daunting and impossible task for readers, as the constant redefinition of borders turns space into an aleatory, ever-shifting element, or in other words, vague space.

"It was the day before, or after, depending on the point of view," Golpiez mumbles matter-of-factly in *Naming the Jungle* (183). Likewise Breughel, the narrator of *Le port intérieur*, confesses a "calamitous conception of the present" (121). For both characters time is not a category that allows one to make sense of the real (any more than space or names). Baiting and denying the reader's expectations of temporal order (through chronology), narrative time can best be described as cyclical in the Volodinian chronotope, even if the overlapping of micro- and macrocycles prevents readers from falling into a predictable rhythm. If there is some temporal progression, it can only be one that deconstructs notions of "now," "before," and "after." Actions repeat themselves, often through the gaze of different narrators, or through the conjunction of different gazes when several overlap, making the "authenticity" of facts and events at best a problematic notion, and at all times a fuzzy one. In fact, "that's enough to lose your sense of time," concludes an anonymous voice in *Des enfers fabuleux* (29). It often is enough for the wandering souls of Volodine's dead worlds, like the seven dead helplessly awaiting reincarnation in *Bardo or not Bardo*, adrift on the sea of time, between two lives, whose attempt to reincarnate Volodine dubs a "Bardo de la méduse" (105–33), a cheeky send-up of Delacroix's masterpiece. Similarly from one novel to the next there is no (chrono)logic that runs from *Jorian Murgrave* to *Dondog* and organizes events sequentially. Rather, the cyclic temporality of Volodine's novels invokes (quite specifically) Buddhist philosophy. Time, it would seem, can only be mediated through language and as such may only amount to the fuzziest of truths, one among billions of "shimmerings of reality" (*Des enfers fabuleux* 28).

Polyphonic Architectures

As truth finds itself mediated through fiction, relationships between narrators unfold in strongly agonistic manner, as voices fight for their right to speak, for the privilege to affirm their presence, their truth, like Lilith with Weyloomaja in *Des enfers fabuleux*, Golpiez with Gonçalves in *Naming the Jungle*, and again Breughel with Kotter in *Le port intérieur*. But taking the floor, and keeping it, proves a most difficult task. Textual fragmentation, the blending of stories, the overlapping and confusion of primary and embedded texts, all render narrative authority conditional and variable. "There is many a story to narrate, isn't there," whispers one voice to another tentatively in the opening pages of *Jorian Murgrave* (20). Such hesitation is understandable, for the multiplication of plots and subplots, of "episodic narratives and nest-of-doll stories" (27), only foregrounds the possibility that someone's narrative might always be framed within somebody else's, or that a framing narrative might lose its transcendent status through the intertwining of plots and subplots, as with the aporistic *mise-en-abyme* of the last chapter of *Lisbonne, dernière marge*.[8] Then to complicate things further some of the titles of encapsulated and encapsulating narratives are identical, diffracting narrative authority further, as is the case with "Des enfers fabuleux" (*Des enfers fabuleux* 9–69). Some of those that do not match should have been identical, like "Quelques détails sur l'âme des faussaires—*Einige Einzelheiten über die Seele der Fälscher*" (*Lisbonne, dernière marge* 26–245), had it not been for editorial changes.[9]

In a move clearly designed to make things even murkier, Volodine articulates the struggle for speech on both intratextual and intertextual levels and so develops a combinatorial principle on two axes, a vertical axis that I will call the axis of "possession" and a horizontal axis that I will call the axis of "transmutation."[10] The vertical axis extends from the orthonymous author, the single speaking voice at one end of the signifying chain, down through the metanarrators (*sur-narrateurs*), to the narrators, to the characters, and concerns the paradigmatic ordering of voices. But in this peculiar framework the orthonymous writer (Volodine—a nom de plume) acts not so much as the apex of the narrative pyramid as the pseudonym (*prête-nom*) that ties all the heteronymous metanarrators together. It should be noted that among the various heteronymous voices narrators are frequently named in the novels, whereas metanarrators remain anonymous voices that superimpose themselves on the narrators, in an unending fight between being and nothingness. Finally, down at the end of the first axis, each character functions like an Uber-marionette, now and again conscious that "threads are pulling him [or her] in directions that he [or she] thought they had chosen themselves" (*Des enfers fabuleux* 229).[11]

Indubitably enough, the dispersion of the Volodinian galaxy invokes the polyphonic oeuvre of Portuguese modernist Fernando Pessoa, first with regards to the general architecture of the texts, the proliferation of narrative voices. (Pessoa himself invented about fifteen different alter egos, all of whom wrote their own works in a style distinct from the others, three of them [Alberto Caeiro, Ricardo Reis, and Alvaro de Campos] achieving a higher degree of fame than the others.)[12] Second, Volodine also invokes the distinction Pessoa drew between "orthonym" and "heteronyms," that is, not the difference that critics traditionally make between "orthonym" (the author's real name) and "pseudonym" (a fictitious name, or pen name), but the distinction that exists between the fictitious author who serves as the coordinator of the poet's fictional universe and his coauthors. W. S. Merwin, in "Footprints of a Shadow," describes Pessoa's composite universe in the following terms: "Pessoa, in Portuguese, means 'person,' and in Pessoa's life it came to stand for a series of personae, an inner ring, and outer figures of various magnitudes and insistence, projected by and projections of Pessoa himself, whoever that was. 'The whole constitution of my spirit,' he wrote in 1910, when he was twenty-two, 'is one of hesitancy and of doubt. Nothing is or can be positive to me; all things oscillate round me, and I with them, an uncertainty unto myself.'"[13] Akin to the Portuguese poet in his penchant for depersonalization and simulation, Volodine diverges from him on the idea that each heteronym must remain a fully distinct persona. For the French writer heteronymy only applies partially, and in novels like *Jorian Murgrave*, *Lisbonne, dernière marge*, and *Minor Angels*, which are constructed of several texts or fragments from several authors, textual authority is challenged from the outset. "We're there and we begin," announces an undifferentiated voice in the first lines of *Des enfers fabuleux* (9). From this *on*, both "we" and "one," singular and plural, the narrative laboriously shifts to third person as the main narrator, Lilith, begins to assert her authority. Yet throughout this first segment—other voices appear in the other segments of the novel—Lilith interrupts the third-person narrative with questions directed at the other voice (the metanarrator's), warning him or her that it is she, Lilith, who has the floor: "Don't forget that I have the floor" (12). This narrative counterpoint runs the entire course of the novel, leaving the question of narrative influence open.

Like narrative authority, the name of the narrator often remains encrypted. Some of the few narrators named in the novels include Moldscher (*Rituel du mépris*), Lilith (*Des enfers fabuleux*), Infernus Johannes (qtd. in *Jorian Murgrave*, *Rituel du mépris*, and *Des enfers fabuleux*; in all likelihood the author of "Le montreur de cochons," in *Lisbonne, dernière marge*), Ingrid Vogel (*Lisbonne, dernière marge*), Iakoub Khadjbakiro (*Alto solo*), Golpiez (*Naming the Jungle*), Breughel, and (possibly) Gloria Vancouver (*Le port intérieur*); the forty-seven minor choir voices of *Minor Angels*; and finally the dogged and doggoned (his death is announced from the outset) Dondog (*Dondog*).[14] Unlike Pessoa's heteronyms, though, these heteronymous narrators tend to resemble one another stylistically. Even though some of them have resolutely distinctive styles—Iakoub Khadjbakiro (*Alto solo*) writes minimalist fiction, and Infernus Johannes (*Lisbonne, dernière marge*) goes from the violently lyrical to the most florid trash—most heteronyms share the same taste for multilayered narratives, complex polyphonies, and cryptic allegories, although all speak with an urgency and violence that belittle the accusations of obscurity and unreadability that could have been leveled at them.[15] Besides, as Kurt Wellenkind impresses upon Ingrid Vogel in *Lisbonne, dernière marge*, though they generate chaos, allegories serve to organize it as well (16–17).

The second axis (transmutation) concerns the syntagmatic recycling of characters and narrators. The eponymous protagonist of *Jorian Murgrave* possesses a number of pseudonyms that cross and subvert gender and cultural lines, including Myriel Moïsche, Thü, Bloom, Borshoïed, Stevän, and Gogley. Tula, the witch of *Un navire de nulle part*, is known under two different identities and owns two different names (Tula and Sayya de Tazrouk ou d'Essendilène). Her first name, Tula (*tu l'as*: "you've got her"), comforts her Bolshevik lover, Mamoud, in the certitude that indeed he *has* her, that he knows her and controls her. But when Tula reveals her duplicity, what was singular reality becomes plural— Sayya de Tazrouk ou d'Essendilène—and refuses to be decoded or translated into one single reality. "Learn my name," Sayya tells Mamoud (21), but the latter can only flee, "drunk with fear," before Sayya's polymorphous and devilish presence (22). *Un navire de nulle part* is a magical realist novel that tells the story of a Russia that counterrevolutionary sorcerers have transformed into a jungle. As the jungle slowly gains ground and covers the entire country, the actors of the revolution (the Bolsheviks), as well as its memory, begin to be "gangrened," to use Volodine's metaphor. "It seems obvious that the memory of the revolution has been gan-

grened by the malignous fevers of the tropics," states the cover
of *Un navire de nulle part*. For his part Dondog, the eponymous
narrator of *Dondog*, flatly admits that his memory is not credible
(95).

But those in the opposition are not the only ones to use magic.
Tradition teaches that a magician is one who has occult powers
(*magu*, in Latin), but also one who can interpret dreams (*máyos*,
in Persian), and that the ability to control dreams enables one to
shift between identities. Conscious of this threat, Wassko Koutyl-
ian, head of the "Cheka" and leader of the revolution, decides to
fight the sorcerers on their own occult ground, changing identities
to face the shifting hazard that they constitute. But in so doing he
dooms any (illusory) prospect the powers-that-be had of inhibit-
ing political and narrative heterodoxy. Under the name of Mou-
raddek d'Essendilène (138)—a counterpart to Sayya—the Cheka
boss does finally succeed in infiltrating the counterrevolutionary
organization, but the novel ultimately remains open and the Bolshevik victory more elusive than ever. In the end Wassko has become Bloom, a Joycean ghost who haunts a bombed-out area of
Petrograd, extorting money from other ghosts and living among
the corrupted souvenirs of the revolution, the echo of a man reliv-
ing the last broken-down memories of the insurgency.

Volodine uses heteronymy even more systematically in *Lisbonne, dernière marge*. In the uchronic Germany described here
oppositional writers operate within (purportedly) autonomous
cells; for these cells changing faces and names means staying alive
and avoiding being brutally murdered by the state's political police. Among these the commune Elise Dellwo practices literature
like one would counterintelligence warfare, ceaselessly changing
locations and identities, appearing nowhere and everywhere at
once (130). When the police think they have eradicated the commune (134), other heteronyms appear: the *colonne* Waltraud
Pohle (132)—also a pseudonym for Ingrid Vogel; the *patrouille*
Anna Fritzsch (161), which at first gave every indication of being
a progovernment cell; the *détachement* Infernus Johannes (160),

which authored the subversive "Montreur de cochons" (Pig master); the *patrouille* Detlev Viett, which wrote "Filières et poubelles de la sociale-démocratie" (Channels and trashbins of social democracy), a scorching pamphlet against Renaissance ideology (161); the much more mainstream *collectif de linguistes* Hedwiga Koday, which put together a "Psycho-analyse de l'énumération du Ier au IIIe siècles" (A psychoanalysis of enumeration from the first to the third centuries) (175); and finally the commando Ulrike Siepmann, its most destructive heteronym (228).

This last incarnation goes to show that transmutation is textual as well as intratextual. Ulrike Siepmann may be the final incarnation of the constantly reborn Elise Dellwo commune, but Siepmman's violent activism is more directly evocative of the radical rebellion of a character from another novel: Ulke/Ulrike, the young anarchist of *Des enfers fabuleux*. Across the Volodinian oeuvre pieces of the characters' complete semantic puzzle find themselves recycled from novel to novel, like attitudes, opinions, and even names, but transmission of these semes is never patent, and at best readers experience a certain feeling of déjà-vu. Among the many examples of character recycling, one may mention Breughel, who is the narrator of both *Le Port intérieur* and *Nuit blanche en Balkhyrie*, albeit a different individual in each case, or again, Vassila Temirbekian in *Alto solo* and *Dondog*, also different characters who, besides their homonymy, may share only a few physical or psychological traits. This is also the case with Dojna Magidjamalian and Hakatia Badrinourbat, two women who are both former lovers of *Alto solo*'s primary narrator: "Iakoub Khadjbakiro had loved several women over the course of his life, and in particular, Dojna Magidjamalian, Hakatia Badrinourbat and Vassila Temirbekian. As in a theater, Dojna, then Hakatia and Vassila entered the desolate set of the last scene, one after the other. . . . Iakoub Khadjbakiro wished them to go at one end of the picture, and then, he wanted to bow . . . before their faces, each different from the next, but somber and beautiful, these three women's faces, transfigured by their trials" (34). That these two women (Dojna and Hakatia, both artists) should be joined together, along with a third woman who is already dead when the story begins (Vassila), is no coincidence, since the same couple of characters appear in *Jorian Murgrave*. In that earlier novel Dojna Khatoun and Hakatia Torénégué are literary investigators on the trail of the mysterious Murgrave; it is telling that for the narrator they appear as "two images that came out of the mystery of mirrors facing one another" (93). Like their counterparts, they appear on the scene, summoned by the magister ludi, "transfigured faces," refracting each other infinitely. As mirror images of each other, they emblematize the cyclical reappearance of characters across Volodinian space, their alterity and infinite fragmentation.

"There were moments when I confused Eliane Hotchkiss with Eliane Schust," the vengeful Dondog confesses in his monologue (*Dondog* 295), not knowing whether he should punish one of the two Elianes for being a victim or an executioner. But as Dondog's memory fades in and out of consciousness, and his grip on reality slips ever further away, only one certainty remains: each and every character is caught in a dynamics of exchange, forced into a collaborative process in which individual identities melt away and fuzzy overlaps are substituted. It is no small wonder that the collaborators of *Dondog* should be called *schwitt* by the hero (*schwit* referring, in German, to "sweat" or "ooze"). For characters literally and metaphorically melt into other characters, as their physical and psychological borders dissolve, in the manner of fuzzy subsets, preventing both the narrator and the reader from seeing through the proliferation and fuzzification of personalities. Individuals do not disappear, or cease to matter; they simply become interchangeable, exchanging roles, trading names, but in due course they allow the story to be told.

Literature as Revolution

Volodine's novels illustrate the substantive alterity of literature when confronted with the readerly gaze, as they interrogate the nature and function of post-Beckettian fiction and underscore its

"grayness," its partial and manifest unaccountability, and ultimately its duplicity.[16] Following Maurice Blanchot's suggestion,
Volodine's fuzzy text grows to be the nocturnal inverse of reality
and inscribes itself *en porte-à-faux* of language and literary forms,
in a resolutely marginal position.[17] Such chaotic textuality not
only endeavors to disconcert and challenge the reader but also engages the determinisms of mainstream literature, its ideologies and
formal paradigms. For Volodine, though, ideological awareness
does not square with the erstwhile ideological project endorsed by
littérature engagée:

> *One must distinguish "political sensitivity" (the op-
> posite of an apolitical attitude) and "political engage-
> ment." It's obvious that all my characters voice feelings
> of rebellion, a rebellion fed both by the memories of the
> atrocities of the twentieth century and the spectacle of
> the equally atrocious present. . . . However, that rebel-
> lion is always brought back to its individual and indi-
> vidualist dimensions. Since there's no [political] party,
> there's no engagement. . . . Political parties belong to the
> real world, ideological convictions relate to the world of
> fantasy.[18]*

In common parlance *littérature engagée* is a staple of pre- and
postwar French literature, extending from surrealism to proletar-
ian fiction and existentialism. At the end of the 1950s, though, the
urgency of engagement was exhausted. Already in 1946 Benjamin
Péret had railed against the capitulation of literature to ideology
in *Le déshonneur des poètes*. For him "the poet's task is not to encourage in others an illusory hope, celestial or human."[19] Instead
the poet's action can only be meaningful if it remains aesthetically
blasphemous and formally innovatory. The revolutionizing of poetic forms should remain distinct from political revolution, wrote
Péret, even if the poet's sympathies or personal engagement lie with
revolutionary ideals. Forty years later Volodine's narratives pick
up Péret's cue, examining the need for new and resolutely marginal

forms of revolutionary literature in a postmodern environment, in which transnational capitalism (globalitarianism) has effectively deprived national struggles of much of their revolutionary potential, when "network power . . . includes as its primary elements, or nodes, the dominant nation-states along with supranational institutions, major capitalist corporations, and other powers."[20]

No wonder then that Ingrid Vogel, the breakaway terrorist of *Lisbonne, dernière marge*, should point out her ideological disenchantment. For her, besides the military-industrial complex, the entire society, its margins included, has fallen into "an ideological wallow" (la bauge occidentale [150]). For Volodine, faced with the general rout of the socialist option and the economic and political marginalization of growing segments of the population, the poet must more than ever carry on the role as *maudit*, as literature should remain the only revolutionary space not yet occupied by the enemy, which leads Frédéric Briot to describe Volodine's writings as "fictions about politics (and not political fictions)."[21] In the predominantly apolitical and intimist *Zeitgeist* of today's French fiction Volodine's work may look heretical in more ways than one.[22] Though seemingly minimalist at times (witness the economy of means in *Alto solo*, *Le port intérieur*, and *Minor Angels*, for example), it has but few similarities with the texts of other committed minimalists like Marie NDiaye, Jean-Philippe Toussaint, Christian Gailly, and Marie Redonnet.

Standing apart from the works of other contemporary novelists, including fellow writers from Minuit, Volodine's novelistic cycle constitutes a *sui generis* category, a Pessoan polyphony that affirms its outlandishness, complete with an orthonymous author (Volodine) and seventy-two heteronyms (narrators and metanarrators). The question remains, however, whether it can succeed in charting out a dissident space, unremittingly distinctive from mainstream fiction and political power. Although Margaret Scanlan concludes that the Volodinian text "fails because it cannot occupy an uncontaminated pure space from which to offer a critique of power,"[23] it is precisely the narration of that failure—and not the failure of narration—that constitutes a new nodal point from which literature, having completed one entropic cycle, or revolution, can begin anew in yet unsuspected directions.

Therefore, although they remain distinctively dystopic in tone, Volodine's texts teem with images of renaissance, from the recurring topos of the phoenixlike passage through the flames that allows characters to travel and explore the universe in *Des enfers fabuleux*, to the constant intratextual recycling of characters' semes, to the cyclical character of time and space. The town of Puesto Libertad (Freedom Post), in *Naming the Jungle*, emblematizes this process of rebirth. Haunted by the dead bodies of fallen revolutionaries, Puesto Libertad marks the last hellish stage before oblivion. But far from freeing characters, Puesto Libertad, city of the dead, grinds them into a pulp, like so many homunculi that will reemerge in subsequent works, in other fallen, bombed-out wastelands, lost at the end of nowhere. If the city only leads back to other versions of itself, this is because the text itself is a matrix, a linguistic matrix, an intertextual matrix, and a revolutionary matrix. Thus Volodinian novels do not end, but branch out to other related texts that recycle some of their narrative elements (time, space, characters, narrative voice). Each novel contains to some degree the other novels of the cycle, like so many fuzzy subsets, though this degree remains unknown to readers, who can at best recognize certain elements resurfacing from one text to the other. However, the point is not to create recognizable links between the texts, but rather to blur the borders between them, to substitute for "authorial" authority over one text the dynamics of narration as an interrelated construct, as palimpsestic revolution.

Volodine's rebellious intention does call forth the effervescence of revolutionary art in the two decades preceding World War II, and more generally the surrealist engagement of the 1930s. Early in his career Volodine became interested in the Association des Ecrivains et Artistes Révolutionnaires (AEAR), founded in 1932 by Paul Vaillant-Couturier and joined by many surrealists in order to constitute a united front against fascism and war. Comparing the dynamics of his own constellation of narrators to the dynamics of the AEAR, Volodine has confessed: "It is certain that the type of engagement of the AEAR militants, their vehemence, the relation they formulate between writing, sociopolitical action, and attachment to the dream (revolution) + dreaming about reality (Stalin's USSR), all correspond to a scheme that readers could find (with some nuances) in many of my narrators."[24] It comes as no surprise then that Volodine's early prose poetry, published in the very surrealist and factional *Cahiers du Schibboleth*, puts the reader in mind of René Char's militant poetry.[25] The paroxystic violence of his language, his refusal to make concessions to the watchwords and anathemas of the day—including surrealist slogans—and the jinglelike quality of his prose signal a Baudelairian *correspondance* between Char's work and Volodine's. For Char, as for Volodine, poetics and ethics are cognates. The poet must seize the convulsive beauty of chaos while confronting the chaotic violence of history. In "Les apparitions dédaignées" (1968) Char invites the poet and the reader to seek emancipation beyond the modus vivendi: "Half a freedom for the insect that sleeps and waits in the chrysalis. A ghost, barely a memory, and freedom in the midst of riot. Freedom was at the top of a mass of hidden obediences and acknowledged conventions, behind the traits of an irreproachable deception."[26] Gloria Vancouver's "Rêve" (Dream), a nine-episode story divided into two segments (50–66, 152–73), one of the fragments of *Le port intérieur*, tells the story of a deserter who fled the pogroms of a brutal conflict only known as "the black war" (51), whose excesses strangely recall the savagery of current postcolonial conflicts, from Chechnya to the Congo. Yet in the midst of combat and exactions the soldier decides to live for the woman he loves (Gloria, another double of the author), and in order to do so he kills those who cross his path "with dirty, lightning-fast techniques" (171), until in the end he himself wanders "on the path to mass murder" (166). But his attempts to find love fail in an enemy assault that results in a complete massacre, mixing the killers and their victims, the living and the dead. If there is no avoiding war, then for Char the choice only consists of "subordination or terror, then both at once, the totalitarianism where everything converges."[27] For Gloria Vancouver, who has arrived "at the last degree of her suicidal combustion" (149), verbal vehemence and ideological nihilism point to the same urgency and disillusionment: "FOR A SCRATCH TO ONE CHRYSALID, SEVEN SAILORS ARE BURNED TO THE MARROW" (81); and again: "FOR A BESIEGED CITADEL, A THOUSAND SEAMEN WITH THEIR THROATS SLIT OPEN! FOR A WOUNDED CHRYSALID, THREE . . . CARGO SHIPS BURN ON THE HIGH SEAS" (109–11).

Like the butterfly for Nabokov, chrysalides are crucial recurring figures of Volodinian poetics, iconizing the gestation and eventual emergence of other orders of reality from the chaos of existence, as the chrysalis destroys the old in order to re-create another, just as entropy precedes negentropy. Hence the "alien" chrysalides of *Rituel du mépris* absorb and destroy human communities piecemeal in an effort to "fragment the old authenticity" and weld the futures of the different communities together through the inferno of war (179–80). As for the participants in the conflict of *Le port intérieur*, they trade massacre for massacre, pogrom for pogrom, with human communities: "FOR A CITADEL BESIEGED ON THE HIGH PLATEAU, THREE CARGO SHIPS BURN ON THE HIGH SEAS" (168). But the end result is once again the extermination of all antagonists, so their offspring, "irrepressible race," may take possession of the earth (*Rituel du mépris* 153), even though such a prospect is clearly couched in utopian terms and projected beyond the limits of the text. For Ingrid Vogel, the archetypal terrorist-narrator of *Lisbonne, dernière marge*, oneiric exile will ultimately allow her to reemerge from her "chrysalis shape" and strike again at the soft underbelly of German social democracy (22), only to begin the cycle anew.

It should be pointed out that Volodine's novels and short stories resonate within an intertext that incorporates not only militant literature but more generally fabulist fiction, in particular the texts of Mikhail Bulgakov, Boris Pilniak, Andrei Platonov, Lewis Carroll, Fernando Pessoa, and Machado de Assis. Two significant paradigms emerge from the Volodinian intertext: the importance of fantasy and the need for literature to be, as Evgeny Zamyatin puts it, in "perpetual revolution."[28] Here revolutionary nostalgia fans the flames of characters' acts and discourses, yet in the end only amounts to a tautology, as revolution always points to its rearward inclination. By and large, history's revolutionaries have taken dramatic steps only to re-create a moment of political grace, to recover an ideological Eden that was manifestly lost. History teaches that the radicals of 1789 actually planned on restoring the Roman republic, whereas the Communards of 1848 meant to resurrect the revolution of 1789, the insurgents of 1871 wanted to give the uprising of 1848 a new chance, and so on. For Mikhail Bakunin "revolution . . . becomes a sign of purity of the origins that were reconquered by humanity, marching toward its reintegration."[29]

As *Naming the Jungle* ends, the four principal characters—Golpiez, Manda, Gutierrez, and Gonçalves—leave the city and wander off into the tropical swamps that border Puesto Libertad, with the intention of settling a utopian commune for Indians or, perhaps, for monkeys and spiders. But this quixotic search for original purity that would have transformed the revolution into a utopian project flounders piteously, and the characters either die or are lost. What matters here, however, is that the ill-fated expedition plays out like an attempted and (predictably) disastrous return to the past, but an attempt whose utter failure forces the reader to consider alternatives. At this point one critical element distinguishes Volodine's revolutionaries from pre-Beckettian types. In Malraux's *Man's Fate* both Kyo and Tchen, the main two revolutionaries, do live out their romantic commitment to the Chinese revolution with the hope of succeeding, or with the painful realization that their acts are rendered pathetic by the absurdity of human fate. But in both cases the revolution's potentiality remains intact, and the revolutionary process still functions in a teleological manner, toward a moment of revelation. "Revolution failed," laments Zven in *Jorian Murgrave* (66), a feeling that other characters echo throughout Volodine's novels. The last remaining Bolsheviks of *Un navire de nulle part* attempt desperately to resuscitate "the shadows of a feudal past," which might as well be prehistoric, in the ruins of Petrograd (103), whereas *Dondog* evokes a postrevolutionary purgatory where the actors of interethnic conflicts relive their failures, while clinging to the shreds of their erstwhile political fantasies. "Revolution had died, once more," Golpiez confesses to Gonçalves, the shaman-psychiatrist, in *Naming the Jungle.* "I was ashamed of being a part of that mess," he concludes (7). "I don't react like I used to. Now, I can't cry well," concludes an unnamed narrator, one of the forty-nine voices of *Minor Angels* (9). Even tears, it seems, have been exhausted, along with dreams, ideologies, and hopes for a better tomorrow.

The perpetual revolution of Volodine's texts functions as a paradox, as the text articulates itself upon the tension provided by the conflicting presence of evolution and revolution. But this paradox, far from hindering narrative progression, incites it. Hence the impulse to restore the glory days of the October Revolution pushes the war-burned Chekists of *Un navire de nulle part* to reactivate old, nearly forgotten slogans and march on for the "attested values of the world" and against "bourgeois decadence . . . and nihilistic temper" and "counterrevolutionary thoughts" (15–16).[30] Even in the face of impending chaos, even if the "free" (that is, Red) world has been submerged by the jungle created by oppositional magic, even if Bolshevik patrol cars stray into vortexes of "turbulent magic" and are sent flying over the city (63), and Bolsheviks themselves have been driven back against their last stronghold, Petrograd's Winter Palace, they keep marching on.[31] "There's yet a long way to go until the final torpor," quips the ghost of Bloom, the ex-commissar (162), poking fun at the illusions of the "final fight." But the polymorphous figure of Bloom suggests that, through the Joycean quest for the differentiated same (Poldy, Polly, Henry Fleury, Sir Leo, etc.), the revolutionary impetus might well outlive itself.

In the revolutionary intertext that the text occupies Volodine's turbulent narratives evoke even more symptomatically the terrorist aesthetics of Bakunin and the Russian dissidents of the 1970s, from Vladimir Boukovsky to Leonid Pliouchtch. For Volodine a vital element of *engagement* lies in the radical disparity between opposition (*ob ponere*: "to place against") and dissidence (*dissidere*: "to sit apart"). Speaking at the First International Congress for the Defense of Culture in 1935, André Gide stated, "It appears to me quite impossible today that, in the capitalistic society where we still live, literature be anything other than oppositional literature."[32] Breton himself described the surrealists as "systematic opponents."[33] Yet oppositional literature—like surrealism in 1935—has a public voice, even though it is deemed ideologically subversive and aesthetically decadent, and oppositional works, from fiction to political pamphlets, find their way to publication in spite of censorship. In short, in their time surrealists and other oppositional figures like Gide and Malraux enjoyed a legitimate existence, not only for the intellectual community but also for society at large. Artistic opposition in the Soviet Union may have encountered more resistance, but nevertheless, artistic movements and factions endured, and a debate still took place. Indeed, Pilniak, Platonov, and Bulgakov all occupied a position essential to the system: Bulgakov worked in the Moscow State Theater on Stalin's recommendation, and both Platonov and Pilniak continued their literary activities until their deaths.

Dissidence, on the other hand, occupies a marginal space. Because dissidents had seceded from the official aesthetic of socialist realism in the Soviet Union, their works circulated outside of normal channels of publication and could only be published clandestinely (*samizdat*) or abroad (*tamizdat*), even though many dissidents ended up in a gulag. In the 1970s, because the system cataloged them as "social schizophrenics," the cell of the asylum became the dissidents' new sounding board. Excluded from public life, Soviet dissidence could only exist at the margins and give rise to what Gilles Deleuze calls a "minor literature."[34] Although Volodine's intention is clearly not to comment overtly on the theme of

Soviet dissident fiction, the particular experience of these (ghost) writers serves as a place from which a critique of the nepotism of today's new world order and a fictionalization of literary radicalism can be elaborated. Using the dissident's antagonistic relation with the outside world as a structuring—and destructuring—principle for his texts, Volodine has manifested his own rupture with the Western world-view. In this absolute and mutual exclusion of the center and its margins only a minor literature could mature, foreign to the world and exotic to the gaze of the nondissident other. Only in such a marginalized and alienated space, always partially outside the censor's gaze, and thus facing the distinct possibility of nonexistence, could writers be in the position to experiment with different forms of subversion. Finally, naming this minor literature, which intersects the concepts of artistic dissidence and cultural marginality, was critical in allowing Volodine to stake a place for the exotic other.

Before joining Editions de Minuit in 1991, Volodine had four novels published by Editions Denoël, in the collection *Présence du Futur*, exclusively dedicated to science fiction. Volodine's mystifying and uncharacteristic novels soon chartered a terra incognita in the world of sci-fi, having little in common with the formulaic productions of other writers in *Présence du Futur*.[35] His odd polyphonic novels challenged science fiction's orthodoxy, and the Volodine case soon degenerated in a new *querelle des anciens et des modernes*. Reluctant to have his novels bowdlerized into normality under a "safe" label (sci-fi, space opera, *le fantastique*, horror, fantasy), Volodine coined the term *fantastique post-exotique*, which in time simply became *post-exotisme*. Like *shaggås* and *romånces*, postexoticism was—at first—a dead sign that pointed to his ideological heterogeneity and aesthetic fractiousness.[36] Of course this alien and idiosyncratic terminology only added to the preexisting ontological malaise. Critics were unsatisfied, and while the quarrel was forgotten, it was never settled.

With the publication of *Lisbonne, dernière marge* by Editions de Minuit, the genre of Volodine's novels no longer perplexed and angered naysayers, although this fifth volume was as postexotic as the previous ones. But now critics contented themselves with the fact that Volodine's novels occupied a divergent space because Minuit traditionally published experimental literature. However, for Volodine the question of a label impinged upon the more important question of marginality, and a label was precisely what allowed him to display the paradoxical foreignness of his texts. Having traced out a new space for postexotic literature, he then set out to construct its own intratextual archive. His postexotic writers number seventy-two, and their works total 342, with dates of publication between 1977 and 2012; the comprehensive list of postexotic texts appears in *Le post-exotisme en dix leçons: Leçon onze*.[37] The novels and short stories published by Volodine, from *Jorian Murgrave* to *Dondog*, all belong to this corpus, but their titles differ from the titles that appear in the published list of postexotic titles, although there is some degree of crossover. It is important to understand that, according to Volodine, the novels that are printed under the name of "Antoine Volodine" must be read as collages of different texts, from various postexotic writers, and that it is in fact the titles of these individual texts, or fragments, that we find listed in the postexotic archive. In addition not all the titles on the list refer to the published novels. Some are virtual texts; others have been written but were left unpublished.[38] Likewise not all seventy-two postexotic authors have absolutely participated in the elaboration of one of the Volodinian novels, though this point is left unclear by the orthonymous author (Volodine).

Despite Fredric Jameson's claims about the impossibility of counterculture existing in the postmodern age, the postexotic list sanctions the appearance of a new form of fiction and the emergence of an alien organism within the body of mainstream literature.[39] Further, though Volodine does not intend postexoticism to be a manifesto, it still signals the existence of a potentially marginal territory for literature, resolutely subversive, unreachable by most, if not all, except maybe the author himself. To be sure, such extreme marginalization of the old romantic ideal of the poet as rebel might amount to literary suicide, and the charges of "obscurity" leveled against Volodine attest to the danger of literary radicalism. But by his own account Volodine seems, if not satisfied, at least resigned to live in the relative obscurity of "a small muddy corner, far away, closed and not closed, where one writes in French something xenoliterary."[40] But apart from the alleged opacity of Volodine's novels, his fiction does seem a long way from postmodernism's anti-ideological stance. In fact, Volodine's work goes to show that the deconstructive stance of most of postmodernism amounts to a reencoding of ideological discourses that (deliberately or not) ignores the effect of ideology in and through fiction.

In light of this *Lisbonne, dernière marge* offers a *mise-en-abyme* of the relations between minor literature and the mainstream. In this text the state has come to control literary production, including oppositional writings—even *shaggås*—though indirectly and through the manipulation of decoy organisms and figures (148). Only the debased "trash literature" (littérature des poubelles), condemned as violent and futile by the authors of the Renaissance, and described as "incoherent . . . , complicated with absconse allegories, without the slightest dramatic progression" (39), seems to provide a viable counterpoint to the state's hegemonic discourse. Trash literature becomes significant then not so much "because it is perverse and indecent, or because it violates the recognized aesthetic canons," Margaret Scanlan argues, "but because it is *autre chose*, something outside the boundaries of . . . official culture."[41] Emblematic of postexoticism's attempt to chart out something else, a *xeno-fiction*, a fiction that points toward fractiousness, dissemination, and constant reinvention, a "fuzzy" fiction, trash literature is necessarily other, to the point at which, for the official censors of the Renaissance, this impossible literature cannot be written by a human being, but only by a scriptor "of a different species" (150), not someone who exists as individual, but only a minor voice in a choir of voices, who alludes to other voices beyond the self, weaving a collective elegy against death.

Both a utopic and a uchronic project, the postexotic archive constitutes the structural backbone of Volodine's novels. Postexotic writers cite each other and engage in fiery debates with their peers, not so much to shore up their own argument but rather to supersede the individuality of the narrating self with the multiplicity of voices that (in)form and surround it. Their narratives are collective efforts, not only because literary cells produce them but because their meaning partakes of a communal dynamic. Each individual voice echoes other voices, and each text functions like a palimpsest to other texts, making the postexotic archive a doubly subversive mechanism, a debunking of the romantic myths of the writer as demiurge and of the uniqueness of the work of art, forcing readers to appropriate a resolutely alien text. To be sure, Volodine's novels are also intertexts insofar as other (non-postexotic) texts are refracted within them, but, as Kristeva suggests, only by means of dissemination, not by means of a traceable filtration.[42] References are rarely transparent and, more often than not, only suggest traces or residues of other hypotexts, other voices.[43]

Emblematic of this fuzzy referentiality, *Le port intérieur* stands as an ode to literature, a dense and uncertain network of correspondences. Breughel, the main narrator, lost in an inferno of his own making, recalls not only Dante but also the Flemish painter "Hell Breughel" (1564–1637). One of his many aliases, Goetz, brings into play two more figures of the artistic world: the German composer Herman Goetz (1840–76) and the German Don Quixote, Goetz von Berlichingen (1480–1562). Breughel's foe, and one of his many doubles, Kotter ("co-author") bears the heteronym of Dimitri, alluding to the false czar in Pushkin's *Boris Godunov*, yet another figure of the double. One of Breughel's companions, Machado, brings to mind Brazilian writer Machado de Assis (1839–1908), whose 1864 dystopic oeuvre, *The Crisálides*, echoes throughout the pages of Volodine's novels. But however instructive these cross references might be to the amateur critic, they fail to elucidate the passages in which they appear. If anything, the presence of additional figures from the endoxa doesn't give the novel an intertextual framework, but adds to the mirroring effect already at work in the text. As such, it diffracts meaning even further, compounding the fractionating of the unitary subject, not only jumbling identities but also hybridizing the individual into the seditious group, into the postexotic "fraction."

In literatures of exoticism the subjection of the racial, sexual, and economic other finds itself mediated through the discourse and desire of the colonizing self, whereas the cultural anxiety of the dominant group is reduced through discourses of racism, homophobia, sexism, and class discrimination. So in order to undermine the linguistic and cultural consensus Volodine's novelistic project borrows from the ludic combinatorics that characterize the literature of fantasy, from its recombination of semantic elements and its defamiliarizing effect. But it also proposes to go further than that. Fantasy, like parody, entertains a specular relationship with the real and thus accentuates the reflective articulation between the fantastic subject and the parodied object. The representational strategy of parody predicates in the same movement the ridicule of the parodied object, its undeniable presence, and its necessity, if only as narrative support. For Michael Issacharov intertextuality remains the indispensable condition of parody, as the intertext leaves in the text an indelible trace. And yet because of their fuzzy intertextual bent—intertextuality functions mostly "within" the postexotic archive, and even then it is highly suspicious—postexotic works display a more adumbrative type of specular strategy than traditional fantasy does.

Alto solo, Volodine's most seemingly satirical novel, emblematizes best this deconstruction of the traditional strategies of satire and fantasy. The story takes place in the imaginary city of Chamrouche, a city ruled with an iron fist by the neofascist *frondistes*, where public liberty hangs on by the skin of its teeth.[44] The head of the frondist nomenklatura, Baalynt Zagoebel, is but a second-rate incarnation of the Archfiend (Baal/Goebbels), who walks around dressed in a leather coat, surrounded by his bodyguards (38), like a B-movie ss impersonator. Though the fascist paraphernalia that scar the streets of Chamrouche recall the trappings of another thousand-year Reich, they only do so through caricature, and even though frondist militiamen round up foreigners and "decadents" for public executions, the killings become the highlight of a public show, complete with clowns and acrobats (115–16).

In fact, the picture the narrator draws of the fascist system that provides the political backdrop of the novel consistently appears too garish and transparent, not to be taken without some degree of suspicion. Even though Volodine's satire condemns the populist and murderous rhetoric of neofascism, the explicitness of the condemnation suggests that the satire's most interesting aspect resides in its deactivation. The novel, like Baalynt Zagoebel himself, is shifty ("ubiquitous leader" [108]), displacing meaning where the reader does not expect it. The frondist xenophobia, the thaumaturgic role of the leader, and the corruption of democratic ideals by the plague of *frondisme* all evoke the traditional tropes of antifascism, but the broad strokes of the allegory render the parody less significant in terms of narrative strategy.

The decoding of the traditional tropes of fascism and antifascism in *Alto solo* emblematizes a more general deconstruction of modernity's foundational tropes (self-other, past-present-future, life-death, beginning-end) throughout Volodine's novels. This erasing of opposites is not mere philosophical posturing on the part of the orthonymous author or his characters, but reveals a lack, which is the narrator's withdrawal or severing from the self. I do not mean that the narrator is absent from the text but that, as an indispensable condition of postexotic narrativity, the narrator is dead. Narrative deferral does not imply that narration is deferred, since that would mean the absence of narrative text: by definition the narrator begins speaking "at once." Here narrating is a postmortem act, a fact made obvious in novels like *Bardo or not Bardo*, in which each narrator is speaking from the limbo between death and reincarnation. And even though Ingrid Vogel is not physically dead, she affirms her intention to write a narrative after her suicide, in which she will express "the incommunicable thought of the dead, the memories of the dead, incomprehensible and coded" (17).[45]

In fact, the reader's initial contact with Volodine's first (published) work underscores the privileged position of death in his poetics. The figure of death is iconized liminally in Volodine's cycle—in the title, that is to say, in the first element of the initial text (or paratext) of Volodine's first novel, *Jorian Murgrave*. Indeed, Murgrave's name itself evokes death (the English *grave*), doubly so when one considers that one of Jorian Murgrave's heteronyms is named Gorbek and that a partial anagram of Gorbek is *grob*, which is Russian for "grave." The presence of death is double (*grave/grob*) and twice removed (translinguistically), in a move that is emblematic of Volodine's process of defamiliarizition. If the epigraph to *Jorian Murgrave* (from Infernus Johannes) is any indication, life, the semantic cornerstone of all Western philosophy, is a delusion, refracted through narrative mirroring, also deferred, *en souffrance*: "life is only the appearance of a shadow on a sooty reflection." At the other end of the spectrum *Dondog*'s dead-on-arrival hero must reach his goal (a revenge murder) before forty-nine days have passed, which is the maximum length of time he can hang onto the world before he disappears and is reincarnated. (The *Bardo Thödol* states that, should reincarnation take place, the passage between two lives lasts forty-nine days.)

Bardo or Not Bardo

Death does not imply the absence of sensations, however, and Volodine repeatedly plays upon the double meaning of *souffrance* (suffering and deferral), as in the previous epigraph and in the one to *Rituel du mépris*, also from Infernus Johannes: "As a child, you suffered already, so it seems, but chaos fits you like a mask." With such inauspicious incipits the Volodinian cycle inscribes itself within a thanatophilic perspective (not thanatocratic), where death designates not the terminal point of the narrative act, but its modus operandi.[46] The death of the narrator constitutes the narrative's pretext, just like revolutionary entropy justifies its negentropic reencoding. "The investigators did not appreciate the answers

I had given to their questions. There was still some biographical haziness concerning my supposedly heroic death in the cocambo area of Mapiaupi," admits Golpiez in *Naming the Jungle* (35). But death does not induce the narrator's silence; instead it dialogizes the speaking voice separated from the living self, the dispersion of the narrative voice echoing the fragmentation of the character. "What I scream does not correspond to what I whisper," says Golpiez in *Rituel du mépris* (9).

The postmortem dispersion of the self is a classic topos of Eastern philosophy, and notably Buddhism. The *Bardo Thödol* asserts that, after death, the soul of the departed must transmigrate into a new self that is chosen among various orders of life (animal, vegetal, demonic), and various categories within each order, until the individual has become sufficiently enlightened to avoid further reincarnations. But whether they elevate into a higher plane of existence or reincarnate, the dead may wander for up to forty-nine days in limbo (Bardo), where they face hallucinatory re-creations of their past lives (as is made explicit in *Dondog* and *Bardo or not Bardo*). But however much Volodine uses the *Tibetan Book of the Dead*, he only draws on its structural makeup, not its philosophical or religious implications, in order to "dispossess" the unitary (Balzacian) character of his or her authenticity. Here again the intertext fails to give the reader keys to unload the text, even readers familiar with Eastern esoteric traditions.

No longer actors in their own lives, postexotic narrators must elect to branch out to other lives, in hypertextual fashion, and model reality through storytelling. "I must speak," the anonymous narrator of Beckett's *The Unnamable* announces, "even if I have to do it with their [someone else's] language."[47] For their part the wandering dead must speak, and be spoken to, for fear of getting lost, while on the other side the monks keep up a running narrative, in turns talking to, admonishing, encouraging, and manipulating the dead as they attempt to guide them toward enlightenment. But the journey from one life to the next is anything but a pleasing passage for those who must go across. Indeed, physics shows that movement requires energy, and in this case the energy comes from the individual's slow death in the flames, for which Volodine creates a grating neologism: *flambulatory* (*flambulant* = flame + ambulatory) (53). And as the flames wipe out the old world, a new one emerges, where things are "different" (*Dondog* 365), where, as the individual merges into others, a new union may still be sought, no matter how briefly (366), a new dialogue may begin, a new quest for the end: "Each of us is stuck inside his own horrible dream, the clown said. There you are, petrified with pain on the stinking sand, and, as petrified as you may be, you keep on moving and making noise. . . . You wait for some friendly laughter that wakes you in the dark. You wait for some friendly voice to encourage you, to approve you, to get you out of there. . . . And nothing. Nothing happens. . . . The darkness remains silent (*Bardo* 233).

Lisbonne, dernière marge too is the last stop before the end and paints a similar portrait of life as transition, as Kurt Wellenkind (German for "son of the wave") and Ingrid Vogel (German for "bird") gradually "flow" into Konrad Etzelkind ("son of Attila" in Wagner's *Niebelungen*, and thus "scourge of God; destroyer by the fire") and Katalina Raspe, Ingrid's own fictional creations, until their original envelopes are discarded and, in reptilian fashion, new ones have emerged. The names "Wellenkind" and "Etzelkind" remind the reader that the wave and the fire are emblematic topoi of Volodinian mythology. Both symbolize the entropic impermanence of things and their renewal. Likewise Breughel and Kotter (both his creation and his "coauthor") fuse into one new actor-narrator in a traumatic scene of *Le port intérieur*, after Breughel strangles Kotter in a cemetery. Golpiez, in one of his improvised *Bildungsromans*, relates the various reincarnations of Gonçalves: "In my story, Gonçalves wandered for a long time, upriver from the Abacau, before joining insurrectional movements again. . . . Then he was killed, he took upon composing a dictionary of the general language, and was shot in the chest by the Flag police" (*Naming the Jungle* 147). Like the other flambulatory souls of the Volodinian chronotope, this last incarnation of Sisyphus goes through the fiasco of the revolution over and over again, from one shell to the next, passing and rewriting memory with each new life.

For memory is the first to go. Hence the need to reconstitute memory (and the impossibility of doing so) literally "haunts" these wandering phantoms and the ever-present reader-investigator. If the readers of Jorian Murgrave's motley biographies fail to exploit them semantically and politically, this is because, in the words of one school of critics (the Brigade Galdan Ghazan), the sum of documents accumulated on Murgrave constitutes "a sort of troublesome clutter, a memory that's so badly organized that it becomes ineffectual," as subjectivity and objectivity, dreams and reality, self and other become jumbled (*Jorian Murgrave* 37, 77). For another of his biographers Jorian Murgrave "doesn't have a name anymore" (91), the absence dramatizing the unraveling of the self and the erasing of memory, as well as the loss of language (*Rituel du mépris* 20). Caught in the middle of his Bardo, Schlumm, one of the unfortunate travelers of *Bardo or not Bardo*, begins to "splinter off" into several echoes of his former self, none of which is recognizable to him (143). In fact, the further a soul advances in the Bardo, the more he or she forgets about past life: "Even childhood disappears. Memory fades away" (145). Finally, once enough progress has been made or enough ground has been lost, personality becomes "unreadable" (146), and as the self sunders into parthenogenesis, memory shatters as well.

Memory, like weather, this other nonlinear system, experiences turbulence, admits Breughel, the narrator of *Le port intérieur*, especially during moments of high stress, when somebody is pointing a gun at your head (35) and when there is as a consequence a greater need for narrative production. During and in between torture sessions Moldscher relates his own history and that of his people to Otchaptenkho, the military interrogator, but the remembrance of things past is as hazardous as it is trying: "I believe I said it already, during my interrogations: I'll do my best to help the counterespionage. The officers have started the exploration of my inner labyrinths. It's tough going. It wouldn't hurt if we all pitched in" (*Rituel du mépris* 25). To add to the difficulty of autobiographical reconstruction, the speaker (Moldscher in this case) yields, often gladly, to the repeated injunctions of the torturer-listener who wants to take over narrative organization, and the narrator's life story further deviates from its original course. Like Moldscher, Golpiez in *Naming the Jungle*, Breughel in *Le port intérieur*, Dondog, and each of the forty-nine protagonists of *Minor Angels* choose to let their listeners lead them astray in their autobiographical recountings, with the following objective: to lead, and mislead, those who listen. Halfway through his autofiction Moldscher teeters between possible lives: "My uncle, my father, Wolguelam or Golpiez, their first names so close, Volp and Volup: my father, my uncle? Or would it be . . . " (107). At the end of the day the truth about Moldscher remains in suspense. Both his nemesis (Otchaptenkho) and he himself die during a new offensive, but before their passing their eggs, carrying their commingled genetic heritage and troubled memory, lie hidden in the ruins. And the same holds true of the conflictual interactions of *Dondog*, in which revolutionaries and counterrevolutionaries, torturers and victims, swap voices and identities, seemingly willy-nilly, and wind up indistinguishable from one another, pooled into the same fuzziness (79).

For some of Volodine's narrators, if memory is unreliable, it seems logical to infer that one's earliest memory, that is, of childhood, is only an illusion. Some of the writers of the Renaissance in *Lisbonne, dernière marge* flatly deny its existence: "We never crossed the river that separates childhood from adulthood. We never were children," concludes the *compagnie* Inge Albrecht after it fails to explain in satisfactory manner the complete absence of children in the society of the Renaissance (89). In fact, another writing cell, the *commune* Katalina Raspe, asserts that the few samples of children's literature grudgingly published by the state each year are "fabrications, offering insight into nothing but the mind and soul of fabricators, valuable only as they reveal the logic of the society's shadowy ruling class" (89).[48]

In view of how memory fails as individual reconstruction, memory stands here as a collective aggregate, as a collection of individual *lieux de mémoire*, referring to the cultural construction of a mythical past by a social group (in this case the members of the postexotic archive). But the unsaid that characterizes individual memory carries over to its collective counterpart, and reconstructing the mythical past results, within the postexotic archive, in a similar enterprise of falsification. Underlining the question of origins in Volodine's narratives, Briot speaks of "a speech that's more involutive than evolutive."[49] Keeping this in mind, it becomes clear why even a thriller like *Le port intérieur* is less concerned with its hermeneutic code, with the resolution of the enigma—although the novel can be read as a spy story on the first level—than with the decoding of narrative beginnings, and more so the decoding of the narrative's pretext.[50]

What matters in *Le port intérieur* is not so much whether Kotter, the killer on the trail of the two lovers (Breughel and Gloria), will find them and kill them, for the reader understands halfway through the novel that Kotter is Breughel's fictional creation. What is at play is the encoding in Breughel's fractionated narratives of the fractures of history, and notably the decline of ideologies. Here the two heroes, Gloria Vancouver and Breughel, are former fellow travelers who turned their back on the Party and left the old myths behind. But old myths die hard, and the Party soon reappears in their lives under the form of Kotter, sent by the Party (also called "the Paradise") to kill the two "fallen angels."

Lisbonne, dernière marge addresses quite explicitly another of history's traumas: the problem of Germany's Nazi past, and more generally the expunging of national guilt in the mythical reconstruction of the past. Hence the culpability of previous generations, and the amnesia of more recent ones, loom large in the novel. Kurt Wellenkind is the son of Obergefreiter Wellenkind, Ingrid Vogel the daughter of Gefreiter Vogel (80), and the death of billions of butterflies patently evokes the Final Solution (96). Yet as Margaret Scanlan notes, "the text is open-ended," and the Renaissance of

Lisbonne, dernière marge is not so much the amnesiac Germany of today that has forgotten the Nazi episode as "a Foucauldian conception of late capitalist society."[51] In both novels, however, the violence of the collective trauma is reencoded and defalsified in the dissident text, notably through the esoteric *shaggå*: "The *Shaggå* dragged in its wake the concept of human incapacity to measure time, the concept of memory gap, the theme of a generalized falsification of the real world, as well as the mechanisms that kept control of the Renaissance; the *Shaggå* spread the notion of the manipulation of doubles, the notion of all-powerful forgers, who were the only ones to grasp essential truths" (106). In the "Shaggå du Ayarirpu" a man wanders in the chaotic streets of a gutted city, having forgotten the names of things, in search of his past. A critical appendix to the text reveals that the past described here corresponds to "the dark years of the dark war"—an event beyond which the past is unknown, some sort of historical ground zero. The critic concludes: "The humanity of the Renaissance, still uncomfortable in its relationship to the past, finds it painful to name itself. . . . It fears assuming a memory-less identity, it fears now that it is the reflection, and not the original" (116). Paradoxically the text both exhumes the past and erases it, precisely because it reproduces it, confirming that only the narrating of personal and collective disaster—not disaster itself—allows the narrator, and the text, to endure. As Breughel remarks with some cunning and dishonesty: "The mouth quavers. You'd like to stop talking. . . . But unfortunately, you can't shut up" (*Le port intérieur* 9). Like a talking cure, the flow of words carries with it the memories of past traumas, unfulfilled wishes, and parturient culpability. As the words unload the motivations of the narrator's unconscious, the question always remains of whose biographical strands the text is weaving together.

Speaking and dreaming, or daydreaming, partake of the same vital impulse for Volodine's narrators. For Murgrave's adversaries the only way to rid the earth of him is to kill him in his dreams (*Jorian Murgrave* 146). In like manner the main narrator of *Des enfers fabuleux*, Lilith, silences a competing voice, Weyloomaja's, by making him part of "her" dream, thus framing him literally and figuratively. Defining his narrators' propensity to dream, Volodine says: "They daydream about the *Bardo-Thödol* and, by introducing elements in their reference system (the transmigration of souls, journey after death, rebirth, nondualism, the magical approach of a reality that's all an illusion, a unique understanding of time and the infinite, negation of time . . .), they poetically rewrite the world, through both a revolutionary and an egalitarian rumination, and a nostalgia for magic."[52] Acting out the imprisoned narrators' unfulfilled wishes, the counterrevolutionary warlocks of *Un navire de nulle part* attempt throughout the novel to control the physical and oneiric planes and break the vise of Bolshevik rule (34). Like the Red King of Lewis Carroll's *Through the Looking Glass*, who might wipe poor Alice off the map if he stopped dreaming about her, they threaten to turn the universe upside down—at one point they add fourteen floors to a five-story building (14).

The *Bardo-Thödol* predicates the individual's emancipation upon reincarnation. Lama Anagarika Govinda explains that "it, is not a guide of the dead, but a guide for all those who want to go beyond death, by metamorphosing its process into a liberating act."[53] After a number of unsuccessful attempts, and returns to different physical envelopes, the enlightened soul will reach Nirvana and become a Buddha. And this is where Volodine's rhetoric diverges radically from the *Bardo-Thödol*. In the postexotic chronotope, liberation notwithstanding, metempsychosis fails to empower the deferred narrators or provide them with a Joycean epiphany. Eventually each new incarnation must face the same chaos.

Across Volodine's fuzzy landscape the failure of the revolution has ushered in a totalitarian system that controls not only the physical world but also the productions of the unconscious. Locked up in prisons and psychiatric institutions, writers resist—more or less successfully—by narrating, thus creating alternate realities. Twice removed from reality (physically and mentally), they unweave and reweave its fabric in a "conspiracy against reality" (*Jorian Murgrave* 11) and a "generalized subversion of the world" (59). The postexotic narrator "metamorphizes reality's thread" (*Alto solo* 31), becomes entangled in its many strands (*Dondog* 21), or simply ignores it (*Naming the Jungle* 126), and finally ends up unable or unwilling to distinguish truths from nontruths (*Lisbonne* 201).

Discrete Fictions

The more extreme repression becomes, the more radical the fictive terrorism of postexotic narrators, and the more monstrous the narrator becomes for the reader. In a controversial piece on the writings of imprisoned Rote Armee Fraktion members Jean Genet read the monstrosity of the terrorist as the projection of capitalism's sadistic tendencies. Institutionalized sadism, Genet holds, diabolized the revolutionary action of the Red Army Faction: "So that the prisoners would appear monstrous to us, so that their writings would distance us from them, so that their death, slow or brutal, would leave us indifferent; so that we would no longer think it's a question of human beings tortured by others but a monster that has been captured."[54]

The similarities between imprisoned Red Army Faction members and the eponymous hero of *Jorian Murgrave* beckon acknowledgment of the terrorist nature of the postexotic narrator.[55] To the school disciplinarian ("professeur de brègne") Jorian Murgrave and his schoolmates seem nothing less than "crazy, crepitant, adipose and shapeless" (16, 38, 18).[56] In other words, they look grotesque and as such threaten not only aesthetic conventions but also social order. As one would have predicted, Jorian Murgrave does wind up in jail (the Kostychev fortress), after being accused of "oneiric" terrorism (97) and subversive activities against the old order (116), as well as association with a collective of mental patients, "the anthill" (la fourmillière)—a subversive organization that is reminiscent of the German Social Patient Collective (SPK).[57] In Volodine's following opus, *Des enfers fabuleux*, it is the turn of three little girls (Lilith, Leela, and Ulke/Ulrike) to escape from Stammheim (103)—a German high-security prison that became notorious, in the real world, for having held members of the Baader-Meinhof Gang. Having been interned for reasons similar to those given for holding Murgrave, they conduct "armed anti-imperialist resistance in the metropoles" that also seems to have roots in the Red Army Faction's original manifesto. To boot, one of the three girls, Ulke/Ulrike, shares her first name with Meinhof (the original leader of the Red Army Faction), while another girl, Lilith, brings to mind one of the earliest rebel figures of the apocryphal tradition. And the process goes on, as in *Lisbonne, dernière marge*, in which "at least eight characters/communes share their surnames with Red Army Faction members," as Margaret Scanlan states.[58] And even when the links to European anarchist movements are less explicit, the overall reference to the revolution as a crucial component of the novel's backdrop remains constant, as in *Dondog*, where protagonists wonder why the "world revolution did not come to their aid" (89), or in *Bardo or not Bardo*, where revolutionaries, after having failed in their attempt at political revolution, come to the same unfortunate result when the time comes for spiritual revolution (reincarnation in this case).

Isolated at the periphery of official discourse, the narrators' political and discursive resistance—their will-to-knowledge—must be absolute in order to confront an absolutely hostile political system, driving them to estrange themselves from what they experience as totalitarianism. Yet because of its alienated and alienating nature, the postexotic novel risks becoming just as much a totalitarian system as the one that elicited it. Being the most extreme manifestation of the narrator's epistemophilic resistance, it must gauge its own validity as a subversive form, and its ability to empower narrators and readers. Inherent to the strategies of deception at work in postexotic fiction is the prospect that they are self-defeating, because their radicalism confines the narrator to an autarchic system, all the more pernicious because it is self-inflicted. But once again the narrating of disaster allows the narrator to break

through the text's own resistance. By locating narrative space inside the prison or inside the psychiatric institution, the postexotic
author escapes repression and decenters, or rather "excenters,"
regulative discourses.

Both the prison and the psychiatric ward function as coercive
spaces where narrating only occurs under the ominous gaze of others, at their prompting, because and despite of them. "The entire
parapenal institution . . . culminates in the cell," Michel Foucault
tells us, "on the walls of which are written in black letters: God sees
you."[59] For Volodine postexotic fiction represents the by-product
of carceral confinement: "The postexotic authors . . . are linked
through a common revolutionary experience, which is diversified
until the mid-1970s (for the first generation), and becomes uni-
fied while they serve their life imprisonment. They get old, away
from the world, in isolation cells, preoccupied with writing, thinking, and rehashing a revolution they could not carry through."[60]
The cell is the focal point of the carceral structure. As such, and
because postexotic authors remain in that circumscribed space, it
plays a determining role in Volodine's fiction, to the point at which
space itself, even outside the cell, reproduces the concentrationary
structure. Thus the postexotic chronotope is a limbo from which
there is no physical escape, not from the ghost town of Puesto
Libertad (*Naming the Jungle*), the phantasmagorical landscapes
of "Au loin une poutre" (*Jorian Murgrave*), the war-gutted cities
of *Rituel du mépris* and *Dondog*, the frondist-dominated town
of Chamrouche (*Alto solo*), or the crypto-fascist second-century
Renaissance and the village island of "Le montreur de cochons"
(*Lisbonne, dernière marge*).

It is telling that for Genet the Manheim prison resembled "an
enormous ear,"[61] for this is where Volodine's prose turns its most
seductive and haunting, in the sadomasochistic relationship, the
uncertain dialogue between speaker and listener. Although actual
conversations (direct or reported) are few and scattered in Volodine's novels, and mostly add up to textual white noise, dialogization plays a major role. For Bakhtin "a word, discourse, language

or culture undergoes 'dialogization' when it becomes relativized, de-privileged, aware of competing definitions for the same things."[62] Dialogization allows the narrator to elude the listener by disseminating narrative authority among a multiplicity of voices, suggesting that narrative authority is permanently deferred and disputed, as the schizophrenic fragmentation of the self allows the narrator to internalize the violence of external oppression and the threat of monolithic unity.

If most Volodinian characters and narrators display schizophrenic behaviors, this is because schizophrenia problematizes both the exploration of the diversity of the self and the "abnormality" of this exploration—and thus the need for its psychiatric treatment. As the mental deterioration of schizophrenic subjects leads to their linguistic and semantic estrangement, the system moves to "cure" their abnormality through internment. Paradoxically it is in the confined space of the cell that narrators can articulate the need for a poetics of liberation, one that allows them to hedge "a closing psychic confusion" (*Jorian Murgrave* 73). This might explain why Gloria Vancouver (*Le port intérieur*) elects to live as an inmate in a Taiwanese asylum and spends her days jotting down dreams, notably a series of surrealist slogans that Breughel, her lover, later turns into stories.[63] Ingrid Vogel (*Lisbonne, dernière marge*) imagines a series of texts that aim to falsify the real, assembled under the generic title *Quelques détails sur l'âme des faussaires* (A few details on the minds of forgers), which testifies to her mental partition from the totalitarian real. And last but not least, Fabian Golpiez (*Naming the Jungle*) invents an autofictional phantasmagoria, or rather a series of impressionist sketches, each different from the others, during forced therapy with a shaman-psychiatrist, in an attempt to elucidate the past. And so on.

The narrators' social schizophrenia may not present much of a threat to the perenniality of the totalitarian system, but their textual polyphonies have far more deleterious consequences. Indeed, in a universe fallen into ideological and aesthetic uniformity they challenge political and cultural dogmatisms and the "ill-meaning good sense of those who think they hold the keys to reality" (*Des enfers fabuleux* 141). In a programmatic statement Jorian Murgrave describes the combinatorial principle of the schizophrenic postexotic text. For him the self amounts to "a multifaceted carapace, which works by sending back to consciousness distorted images of reality, filtered images, and interpretations that vary according to needs and circumstances" (72). Identity is, first and foremost, a composite object, the fractured bodies playing out like a *mise-en-abyme* of textual fragmentation. For Jorian Murgrave, who in his teenage years was a skin trader, bodies are discrete systems, made up of "sheets" and covered with "carapaces" (*Jorian Murgrave* 30, 193). The Bolsheviks of *Un navire de nulle part* claim their right to "a carapace" to protect them from dissident magic (12, 58), while the protagonists of *Des enfers fabuleux* hope to hide behind their skin (247), although Ingrid Vogel doubts she will find a new life and a new carapace away from Europe (*Lisbonne* 19).

Bodies are fragile shells here, "porous," as one anonymous narrator puts it in *Jorian Murgrave* (17), and minds oscillate within and between envelopes, to the point at which the reader finds it impossible to ascertain the identity of any given character at any point of the narrative. Typically *Alto solo* begins with: "It's the story of a man. Two men. In fact they are three." Like a nest of dolls, one character hides another, who hides another, and each is to some degree the virtual incarnation of all others, a fuzzy subset. Each comes to the fore under the reader's gaze, then disappears and reappears behind someone else's skin. "I am clear, then dim, then gone, then dim again, then clear again, and so on, back and forth, in and out of someone's eye," says Winnie to Willie in Beckett's *Happy Days*.[64] Like her, Volodine's protagonists are fuzzy subsets, oscillating between 0 and 1, between absence and presence, being and nonbeing.[65] Breughel, the narrator of *Le port intérieur*, is another, like all the other narrators, himself yet different, here but elsewhere, dead to the world he fashions in his narrative, and hence his Chinese lodger "attempts to believe he doesn't exist" (40).

Agonizing "on the sideway of the imaginary," Breughel is but the most vocal manifestation of an entropic universe that, in his words, is moving toward zero (38). "Everything was sticky," the narrator warns us, and to keep the system from collapsing, he must continue speaking. "He still wanted words," complains Breughel after Kotter has started interrogating him (17), but Kotter, being Breughel's character and double, only provides the necessary counterpoint, eclipsing Breughel and coming to the fore when needed, as in the fragments entitled "Monologue" (74–82, 174–80, 206–18). Breughel and Gloria flee from Kotter, but Breughel keeps pursuing Breughel as a vector of meaning, a locus of stability: "[Breughel] conceives of subjects for operas, film screenplays, and novels. He puts her [Gloria] on stage. From the inner night, he brings forth a detective who is sworn to kill them. He calls him Kotter. Sometimes John Kotter, sometimes Dimitri. Always Kotter" (212). Chasing each other, these provisional narrators create an uncertain world, "a diluted, ruminated reality called existence" (212). This principle of incertitude informs all of Volodinian poetics.[66] As with the fugue of old, it calls for a polyphonic ensemble, a choir of voices that spells the end of certitudes, but also the need to rebuild and constantly readapt systems of representation founded on the very idea of uncertainty. Oblivious of the self-repeating drone of most contemporary fiction, immured between apoliticism and egocentric autobiographies, the Volodinian choir sings sotto voce the emergence of a new poetics, seeking beyond itself to stake a place for the silent other.

6. François Bon
Grueling Prognostications

Calm block here fallen from obscure disaster,
Let this granite at least mark the boundaries evermore

Stéphane Mallarmé,
"The Tomb of Edgar Poe"

Borderland

François Bon is one of France's most prolific and celebrated contemporary writers. His novels include *Sortie d'usine* (1982), *Limite* (1985), *Le crime de Buzon* (1986), *Décor ciment* (1988), *Calvaire des chiens* (1990), and *Un fait divers* (1994), all published by Minuit; *L'enterrement* (1990), *Temps Machine* (1992), *C'était toute une vie* (1995), *Prison* (1998), *Paysage fer* (2000), and *Mécanique* (2001), published by Verdier; and *Daewoo* (2004), published by Fayard. He has also published a number of other works of fiction, some of them written in collaboration with the participants in his writing workshops. Among these we find *Sang gris: Un atelier d'écriture à La Courneuve* (1992), *Dans la ville invisible* (1995), *Phobos, les mal famés* (1995), *Polir nos arêtes vives* (1995), *30, rue de la Poste* (1996), *Les mots sont des fenêtres* (1996), and *Tous les mots sont adultes* (2000). His output further includes several short stories: "A l'espérance," published in the collection *Café nocturne* in 1985; "Fête dans une ville déserte," which appeared in *Serpent à plumes* in 1993; and "Grève," which can be found online. He has authored several plays: *Parking* (1996), whose original version served as the basis for a Romain Goupil film (*Parking*, 1993); *Quatre avec le mort* (2002); and *Daewoo*, adapted from the novel of the same title, in collaboration with Charles Tordjman (Centre dramatique national de Nancy).

Besides fiction writing, Bon's literary work includes articles and books on François Villon, Baudelaire, Rainer Maria Rilke, Bashö, Nerval, Artaud, Claude Simon, and Bernard-Marie Koltès,[1] with a marked interest in Rabelais (see notably *La folie Rabelais*, 1990). Approaching art in general and writing in particular from an interdisciplinary perspective,[2] Bon also takes a devoted interest in other artistic media, claiming affinities with Vermeer, Carpaccio, Opalka, and Bacon, as well as Beethoven, Indian music, and more contemporary artists like the Rolling Stones. (His biography of the Rolling Stones, published by Fayard, has garnered much critical praise and is currently in its fifth printing.) He has written texts on the art of instrument making (*Arauco ou l'énigme de l'oeuvre*, on Ricardo Perlwitz, 1985),[3] illustration (*François Place, illustrateur*, 1994), and finally copperplate engraving (*Le solitaire*, on Jacques Muron, 1996).

The question of representation, which motivates François Bon's novels—and the rest of his work—may well be fiction's oldest trope and intersects the notion of genre. The early pioneers of the novel as a genre (the realists) advocated verisimilitude; for them knowledge had to be filtered through a receptive process, a determinist view on which the naturalists built. Against the conception of representation as medium quo, the surrealists sought to transgress the boundaries between the real and the surreal, between rationality and irrationality. Articulating what Apollinaire called an "esprit nouveau," they sought out an extension of the realists' world-view through a new freedom of form and the practice of free association.

For Sartre representation was bound up in legibility, and aesthetics had to give precedence to politics and philosophy. Finally, for the New Novelists engagement could only concern language and pass through formal experiments. Yet Robbe-Grillet and other Minuit writers had little if anything in common with the Parnassians' concept of art for art's sake. Instead they attempted to translate the real through new means, notably objectivization (*chosisme*) and metatextual interrogations. Like other literary innovators, they believed that only a reflection on linguistic strategies could challenge readers to read through the reasons and means of representation.

Attempting to conjure the need for literature to investigate both the world and itself, Bon's work stands at the intersection of these different—and sometimes contradictory—praxes. More specifically his texts interrogate the paradoxical position of the fiction writer, caught between the urgency of sociological investigation and the need for a poetics whose sole object resides in itself. If, for Patrick Kéchichian, Bon's fiction aims to recover "all" of the real, this is because "his prose, being more than a craftsmanship that finds satisfaction in the formal perfection of its object, aims for reality, all of reality—multiple and unfathomable in a single gaze, unspeakable in a single word."[4] A book must, to borrow Bon's expression, "faire mémoire"; that is, it must uncover (or recover) society's dramas, explore its fault lines, and question its purpose.

If this is the case, the solution does not reside for Bon in the social realism of Sartre's *Les chemins de la liberté* or Aragon's *Les cloches de Bâle*. Sartre himself recognized that "the error of realism has been to believe that the real reveals itself to contemplation, and that consequently one could draw an impartial picture of it. How could that be possible, since the very perception is partial, since by itself the naming is already a modification of the object?"[5] And yet for François Bon most mainstream fiction regrettably shares with commercial cinema and popular art the predictable and sedative aesthetic of social realism, "easily absorbable, where the illusion of reality would build on the banality it attends to, in a manner that's overdone and without ambition."[6] As a logical consequence of this paradox, the novel must implement strategies of deceit and present itself as the opposite of what it is: "To appear credible (and to be really fiction), fiction must present itself as true, in the same manner than an actor on stage is true. *Le rouge et le noir*, and *Madame Bovary*, were not subtitled 'novels' but 'chronicles,' or 'chronicles of the province'" (*Parking* 59–60).

To fulfill its goal the novel must reinvent—and deconstruct—the trappings of social realism, as well as rediscover the understated subversion of nineteenth-century prose. Yvan Leclerc argues that Bon's realism serves to both capture the real and keep it at length.[7] Reacting to a suggestion I made that literature was like a poisonous weed growing between reality and fiction, François Bon elaborated on this idea: "Literature as a bad weed, that's a beautiful picture. A bad weed for the good health or good conscience of the world. It's another beautiful image to prolong it by saying: trace of the mutual contamination of reality and fiction, foreign to each other."[8] The image of literature as disease (and artist as parasite) is yet another classic trope. Michel Butor once wrote that he would like to be an epidemic,[9] while George Bataille, in *La littérature et le mal*, pleaded for a poetics of corruption, of liberation through excess. Such a poetics of corruption manifests itself in Bon's reconstruction—not pastiche—of old forms, like the *polar*, notably in *Décor ciment* and *Fait divers*.[10]

The *polar* partakes of a "subrealism," says Maurice Dantec, of a "profound *de-rangement* of our relation to reality," a desire to "break our routine of perception."[11] It also translates a "polarisation" of reality, argues Jean-Pierre Deloux, for the "criminal nature" of French culture seems, at least from a media perspective, to be on the increase. Stories of the development of criminal pathologies abound on TV and grace the headlines of newspapers, from racket and embezzlement, to illegal phone tapping, electoral fraud, corruption, teenage prostitution, school violence, and gang rape in disenfranchised neighborhoods. But what emblematizes public insecurity is the much ballyhooed existence in the *banlieues* of "zones franches," that is, zones of complete lawlessness where organized crime and random violence have seemingly sanctioned the demise of social stability and crossed the line into what jurists call the demise of the civil pact (*pacte républicain*).[12]

Even if Bon acknowledges the state of things, he endeavors to go past the demonization of the marginal without falling into a mythologization of victimhood and marginality, exploiting the *polar*—a mostly urban genre that was born during the course of the nineteenth century—by describing the urban milieu as a terra incognita, as fuzzy space void of collective meaning, and, conflating Pierre Nora's grand concept of the *lieu de mémoire* with Augé's notion of *non-lieu*, as a "non-lieu de mémoire," implicitly beckoning the reader's active interpretation in what the author calls "faire mémoire de . . . " (to make memory of . . .).[13] In consequence, in the aptly named *Un fait divers* Bon borrows from the traditional material of the *polar*, from its structure and its psychology, to expose the semantic lack of urban space. *Un fait divers* tells the story of a man, Arne F., who crosses half the country on a small moped simply in order to seek revenge on his estranged wife, then proceeds to hold her hostage with some of her friends before he ends up killing an innocent man. The "ordinary incident" of the title comes straight from a short newspaper article that was published in *Le Courrier de l'Ouest* and seems therefore directly plucked from reality. But although Bon rigorously follows the original account (the newspaper article is quoted in the jacket notes, thus remaining outside the text), he evacuates the bathos of pulp literature and the sensationalism of yellow journalism by refusing to participate in the banalization of abjection. Hence from the outset the story takes its distance from the fabula through a process of fragmentation, both narrative and temporal, as it articulates the existence of a cleft, a crack between the facts and their narration, a fuzzy space that the artist must probe and from which he must "draw a story" (faire un roman [114]). The newspaper article, on the other hand, banalizes the atrocity of the fact, adding to its abjection.

The novel is organized on three levels of enunciation, which

Bruno Blanckeman designates as "announcement, enouncing, and erasure" (l'annonce, l'énonce, et l'efface).[14] The text consists of personal testimonies, which are distributed among three groups of actors, themselves distributed in concentric circles around the body of the victim: Arne F. and his victims; the police and their witnesses; and the film crew that shoots a documentary on the events several months later. Each circle, as it widens, proceeds to a reinterpretation of the facts beyond the tragic banality of the event, becoming "a vocabulary that must be rebuilt" (*Un fait divers* 11). Tellingly, like the novelist, the filmmakers do not want to proselytize, but to create a meaning that exceeds the limits of the initial report, so "that people read what was meaningful in their own stories, and not what these stories were supposed to mean" (115).

As each group—and within each group each individual—testifies, contradictions arise, "making the uncovering of a single truth an impossible task."[15] Rather, the novel chooses to focus on the blurring of boundaries, says Blanckeman, on the dissolution of individual responsibilities and collective answers, that is to say, on the fuzzification and hyperbolic expansion of meaning, under "the zero pressure of civil urbanism."[16] For the violence of Arne F.—the name recalls *hargne*, which means "resentment" in French—manifests as much the hostility of a single individual as the criminalization of society as a whole. (Arne speaks as "the man" [l'homme], and his patronym [F] suggests not only anonymity but ubiquity.) Hence the murder of the innocent man, tragically absurd though it may be, points first and foremost to the destructiveness of the act as a symptom of collective disturbance, while the novel sets the story in a zone of white noise, in "the discrepancy and extremity where we stand" (9), a zone of semioclasis. In such a place the cries of the victims fall on deaf ears, and no one comes to their aid, though several people hear them; the city remains "indifferent, behind high windows and straight doors" (74, 76). In like manner *Décor ciment* weaves around the body of Raymond Crapin a complex network of voices that not only fail to explain why the crime occurred, beyond an improbable combination of circumstances, but point to the need to acknowledge urban fault lines, "like you would explore the virgin spot on a map" (*Un fait divers* 9). Even Bon's latest text (*Daewoo*), a painstakingly documented account of the closing of several Daewoo factories in northern France, elaborates a *polar*-like structure around the body of a dead woman (an employee who kills herself after losing her job). In *Daewoo* narrators and readers collectively seek to uncover some meaning for the woman's death and, through it, to understand the postindustrial society that would allow it.

Tellingly Bon makes use of the *polar* (a genre that W. Somerset Maugham praised for its conciseness) precisely because the *polar* is deeply predicated on narrative rigor and efficacy. Indeed, the fact that the *polar* has a story to tell, and does so in the most economical manner, seems at variance with the vagueness, the unspeakability, of the social and semantic "fracture" that Bon wants to investigate. But it is in this paradox that Bon's fiction is most effectual, in the "corruption" of a structure-bound genre, as Bon's texts exemplify the formal rigor of the *polar* while they deconstruct its horizon of expectation.

Paraxis: Exploring Fuzzy Space

Justifying the choice of the city as main locus and topos, Bon argues that "real phenomena show in the randomness of existence a fantastic quality much more extraordinary than what the most fecund imagination could make of it. That's what the city is offering everywhere" (*Calvaire* 77). "There's no drama here. Well . . . ," hesitates the narrator of *Sortie d'usine* (46), for factory life, no matter how dreary, does have its share of drama—such as the various movements and tropisms of the production line—and accidents—in terms of both narrative peripateia and chaotic configurations. But the choice of what Perec calls the "endotic" (the nonexotic) in subject matter does not necessarily carry through to aesthetics and form. For Bon, Hoffmann's *Fantasiestücke* provides a case in point: "Hoffmann renews narrative illusion by walking through its frame, barely shining upon its skin, leading us away from its effects to seek only what streams out and walks upon the void, giving everything, to the most simple and ordinary, the obsessive and magical sheen of a dream" (*Calvaire* 70).

No wonder then that, after the *polar*, Bon should make use of the fantastic, yet another popular genre predicated on formal rigor and "literalness of meaning" (to quote from Todorov), and that he should endeavor to hollow it out in the same manner. To be sure, the "fantastic effect" of Bon's texts goes beyond the epistemological interrogation brought by the "intrusion" of the supernatural into the real of classical fantastic texts à la Maupassant. Bon, rather, is interested in the interval that the fantastic creates as a genre, through its process of formal and syntactic defamiliarization, or, as in Blanchot's "Aminadab," of textual displacement.[17] In his study of the fantastic Tzvetan Todorov separates representative modes of fiction (the novel, the short story) from allegoric modes (poetry, fairy tales). According to him, the fantastic belongs to the representative mode in its literalness of purpose and meaning. He explains this literalness by arguing that in order to allow for identification between reader and narrator (a fundamental condition for the fantastic to operate), the text must not scramble the narrative signal and must therefore avoid the presence of polysemiotic elements such as allegories. In addition he states that the real and the supernatural are antagonistic and vie for access to legitimacy and representation.

It may be more useful for readers of Bon to think of the fantastic in terms of the conflict and/or cohabitation of two heterogeneous categories (the real and the unreal). Because it is the "virgin spot on the map" that Bon seeks to survey (fuzzy space rather than nonspace), he embraces the second option (fantastic as synthesis, rather than disjunction), the point being in Bon's words "to flesh out to the observer the juncture between the real background and the painted canvas" (*C'était toute une vie* 25–26). Rosemary Jackson explores this notion by invoking the metaphor of the "paraxis," a

term that she borrows from optics: "A paraxial region is an area
in which light rays seem to unite at a point after refraction. In this
area, object and image seem to collide, but in fact neither object
nor reconstituted image genuinely reside there: nothing does. This
paraxial area could be taken to represent the spectral region of the
fantastic, whose imaginary world is neither entirely 'real' (object),
nor entirely 'unreal' (image), but is located somewhere between the
two."[18] For his part the narrator of *C'était toute une vie* speaks of
"a redoubling of the present, of the déjà vu, even when it's not reasonably possible, of the influence of the heavens, when, sometimes,
you feel like you're not walking but floating above the sidewalks"
(16). This wavering, this ontological and semantic hesitation, this
fuzziness, signals the dissolution of strictly realistic expectations,
as it refutes an openly monological imperative for the novel.

In his study of Rabelais Bakhtin describes the fantastic as a process of linguistic estrangement, as "the destruction . . . of habitual
matrices." He adds that Rabelais's "fantastic realism" includes
"the most surprising logical links [allogisms] and linguistic con-
nections," which for Rabelais concern etymology, morphology,
and syntax.[19] Bakhtin remarks that, through his deconstruction
of the text, Rabelais uses fantastic realism only to affirm the provisional status of truth, as the real becomes unreal in seemingly
random manner. Using a metaphor he borrows from engineering,
Bon describes the same moment and space where the real crosses
over to the unreal as a "bascule" (toppling), a term that is not unlike René Thom's concept of "catastrophe."

It follows that, to outplay the semantic impoverishment of the
urban milieu, Bon's novel must be "this painting you dream, where
all the parts must fit into each other" (*Décor ciment* 133), "mix-
tures where disjointed fragments of places come together, as long
as the plot crosses through the slow stream of images, without
slowing, without vagueness" (*Calvaire* 69). The idea of an isotopic relation of surfaces, between real and fiction, can already be
found in Rainer Maria Rilke, who suggests that in the text everything "must be on the same surface, as in a painting, where each

point is in contact with the others" (*Décor ciment* 143). Conti, the draughtsman of *Dans la ville invisible*, describes the modern chaosphere and the birth of the city (and meaning) in the following terms: "A continuation of superimposed infinite planes, of which we only know one intersection, which we call reality or world. Every small fragment of the visible, plus much larger interconnections of each person's individual past and history, from generation to generation, since the random agglomeration and naissance of dust in a single place that came to be" (92).[20] In such an environment the symbolic fusions with the mimetic, isotopically, and "representation topples into a flat, shiny painting where everything exists evenly" (*L'enterrement* 54). All pictures aggregate to create a textual web, so textual space beckons physical space, grounding "the self-reflection of the subject in language itself" (*Parking* 37). In the jacket notes of *La folie Rabelais* Bon confirms that "language remains the most effective path to subversion." Thus in order to understand the crises that fracture society we must understand that a crisis with language anticipates later sociocultural crises, adds Bon.[21] To understand Bon's style, turbulent and cruel (*Calvaire* 70), the reader must perceive that the choice of turbulence does not deploy, in mimetic fashion, a stylistic violence over a violent "reality," but rather opens up the imaginary, allowing the reader to be "completely in a book."[22] Following in Apollinaire's footsteps, Bon ventures to "design the bases of a new realism,"[23] a realism that, for him, must necessarily eschew exoticism and pass through the endotic.

If for Apollinaire "a handkerchief that falls down may be for the poet a lever to lift the world," Bon molds the fabula of *Un fait divers* as if to point to the "gap" (or chaos) between the lines and testify to his desire to go from the banality of the exotic—such as it appears in the pages of *Le Courrier de L'Ouest*—to a fantastic of banality.[24] Georges Perec calls this the "infraordinary"; it is not the calamity of trains that derail or planes that crash, nor the shock of urban violence, nor the scandal of front-page news, but these common things, this gray banality, that holds the keys to understanding our selves, our space, and our lives, says Perec.[25] But far from suggesting that readers seek a social anthropology of the endotic, Bon endeavors to work first and foremost in the aesthetic domain, even if his work clearly offers venues for sociological investigation. The description of a scene with factory workers in their workshop gives Bon the opportunity to flag, as Apollinaire advises, the most semantically minimal site from which a pole of resistance against the collective loss of the *Zeitgeist*, and the reification of the individual, may be elaborated: "As if we wanted to proclaim, through these images, their resistance against the workshop, an insubordination like the elegance of the [metal] turning, spiraling around and falling down at regular intervals . . . in dull gray tracks, where steel shone under the orange or bluish jet of lubricating oils, punctuated by the precise interlocking of tools going to and fro, until it fell, gently, in the vat" (*Sortie d'usine* 55). Describing his job as a welder during a personal interview, Bon mentioned that it was "Giacometti in real life."[26] Thus, despite Bon's early claims of a purely aesthetic engagement for his novels, we are meant to understand that the author must delve into these "recurrent, abrasive elements" that mark the nodal points of his personal history.[27]

In *The Art of Fiction* Henry James advises writers to pick up subject matter with which they are intimately familiar in order to ensure the aesthetic coherence of their texts, a precept that, for Bon, doubles upon the need for the artist to speak from her or his own "mineshaft" (another industrially poignant metaphor to imply the semantic forfeiture of the postindustrial world)—so that a novel like *Décor ciment* "does not look at the banlieue, but comes from it" (*Parking* 104). For Bon, only in the intimate proximity with what's familiar, in the hollowing out of the self, in what Montaigne called being the subject of one's own book, may the text come to be. But as Christian Prigent argues, Bon does not seek to avoid "the disfiguring impact of reality in the sentence."[28] Bon's sentence declines the clash of language and reality, the aggregation of the banal and the fantastic, the real and the fictional, in the same picture. Jean-Claude Lebrun and Claude Prévost remark that "a novel must not remedy the ills of the times, it's enough to show them. Resistance to an odd and disjointed society will come from the readers: the 'uncanny effect' may bring its own change."[29]

From age seventeen to twenty-five Bon attended and then dropped out of the Ecole Nationale des Arts et Métiers, before going on to become a skilled welder in France, Russia, and India for the aerospace and nuclear industries. After he changed careers and became a full-time writer, he spent a year in the Villa Médicis in Rome, followed by another in Berlin, as a recipient of the Deutscher Akademischer Austauschdienst, and a third year in Stuttgart, as a recipient of the Robert Bosch Stiftung Prize. But besides the academic awards that were showered on him—testifying to his growing fame in European countries—Bon kept traveling off the beaten path, while driving trucks across France and other countries. In so doing he gathered a "plastic stockpile of images" (*Temps machine* jacket notes) that make up the various strands of his travelogues.

Bon's "literary landscape painting" (paysagisme littéraire) partakes of a rich tradition, which includes Victor Hugo (*Notre Dame de Paris*), Baudelaire (*Le spleen de Paris*), Apollinaire (*Le passant de Prague*), and George Perec (*Pereclinations*), as well as Blaise Cendrars, Victor Segalen, Henri Michaux, and Henri Kessel.[30] Bon labels this an art with no name, "that of travelers, those who tell us about the presence of the world, its immense presence, with only a wall, a river or a gas station, that of walkers."[31] Popularized by romantic figures like Novalis and Hölderlin, wandering—that is, *errance*, not *flânerie* or *promenade*—soon takes possession of the urban space that is beginning to leave its mark on the worldview, as Walter Benjamin indicates in *Paris capitale du XIXe siècle*. With the birth of modernity the city, emblem of the nascent industrial age, quickly turns into a privileged staple of modern fiction, one that betrays the fascination of modern artists with the rapid growth of urbanization, but also their interest in its mythical potential. In straight fantasies, like Jules Verne's *Paris au XXe siècle*, but also in purportedly realistic narratives, like Maxim Gorki's description of New York in "The City of the Yellow Devil," and Sartre's in *Situations III*, authors affirm their right to "produce" an urban poesis rather than "reproduce." For Jean-Yves Tadié this is true in great part because the urban novel adds meaning (movement, characters, sequentiability, and thus narrativity) to function (social, economic, financial, and religious).[32]

For Bon, however, the postindustrial city stands as a space where meaning and function fail to coincide, thus creating a fuzzy space, not empty but unknown or unread. Throughout his texts Bon is quick to underscore a crucial fault line of contemporary society, if not the pivotal one: the death of the urban utopia exemplified by Ildefonso Cerda, founder of modern progressive urbanism. Alluding to the emblematic fiasco of one of Cerda's most celebrated epigones, Le Corbusier, and his *Cité lumineuse* in Bacalan,[33] Bon condemns "dead-end urbanism" (*Sang gris* 125) and castigates the "immense exclusion" that modern urbanity has generated.[34] For Bon this sense of physical and psychological "deportation" affects all that urban-dwellers see, displacing their categories of representation, and themselves, as a space of production of this representation, as well as their symbolic structures (*Sang gris* 125).

For Konrad, the sculptor of *Décor ciment*, the symbolic and physical weight of urban destructuring forces the artist to engage in a poetics of excess: "You don't force a fable through without being first possessed by its outlandishness and sadness, however, like a tall tale that would be strong enough to change the world, but takes fright when the play goes offstage. . . . Today, before the revolt comes to be, we still miss a white sheet against which we may project the monstrosity of dreams: just an empty space over the opaqueness of things . . . , something as vast as these ghettoes we live in" (175). The point is to "put in a word what resists all words," say the three mourners of *Un fait divers* (63), even in the face of the depraved bestiality of brutes and criminals (the wild beasts ["fauves"] of *Un fait divers* [63]). But life in the urban chaosphere is marred by violence, says a character in *Un fait divers*, by "man's capacity for the worst" (25). "Man's worst was always part of man," confirms Brocq in *Le crime de Buzon* (45). Worse, for Michel Raulx, Buzon's codetainee, "from the dawn of time, the first tool was meant to kill, before thought even could emerge, and it came bloodied into the world" (*Le crime* 49). Finally, Céline's ghost cautions that "life is covered by shadows" (*Le crime* 110). In the face of such tragedy the strength of Bon's novels derives from the fact that they interrogate man's atavistic need for violence, without giving in to moralizing or demagogy. Rather, Bon seeks to go "where man feels confused" and translate contemporary aporias ("a negative, or at least absent notion of destiny").[35]

"Who knows what corrupts men's lives," reads the incipit of *Le crime de Buzon*. A key motive in Bon's fictions, past traumas time and again mark characters' lives. Louise Buzon is beaten by a brutal father as a child, before being sent to "the handicapped school" (18) and, at the time of narration, oscillates between catatonia and hysteria, only finding solace in the company of dogs. Across Bon's social dramas dysfunctional parents molest their children, and single-parent families sag under the weight of economic and moral difficulties, as in *C'était toute une vie*, *Parking*, and *Daewoo*. They may also have to grapple with the trauma of abortion (*Limite*); rape, which Buzon calls "a drop of poison" (*Le crime* 195); and domestic violence (*Le crime de Buzon*, *Un fait divers*). Individuals are the victims of industrial accidents (*Sortie d'usine*, *Limite*) and of the vagaries of the new economic global order (*Daewoo*); they witness racism and exclusion (*Limite*) and murder ("in your hands, like a solid yellow block" [*Un fait divers* 7]). Finally, for many of them suicide remains the only option, as in *Limite*, *L'enterrement*, *C'était toute une vie*, and *Daewoo*. Says the young woman of *C'était toute une vie*, after making the decision to end her life: "I'm from the planet of those who jump into the void" (62).

The violence of the world is "daily, petty and polymorphous," says a character in *Un fait divers* (17), and for old Brocq, who has witnessed many of the horrors of the century, from death camps (Buchenwald) to more ordinary tragedies, it would be madness to

seek harmony in the world ("it's madness to ask men to be in harmony with themselves" [*Le crime* 197]). For there is madness in
Bon's world, an overwhelming pathology of terror, a bestialization
of the self, which goes a long way toward explaining the symbolic
reappearance of dogs throughout his texts, and notably in *Sortie
d'usine*, *Le crime de Buzon*, and *Calvaire des chiens*.[36] *Calvaire des
chiens*, which alludes explicitly to Cervantes's *Coloquio de los per-
ros*, articulates the ignominy of this violence the most forcefully.
Emblematized by the presence of the dogs, folly becomes a recurring topos in Bon's novels—reinforced by the symbolic presence
of Kafka, Hoffmann, Strindberg, and Pirandello in the intertext
(*Calvaire* 47). "We don't know the depth of our own madness,"
warns Isa Waertens, the oracle of *Décor ciment* (28): "Wherever
we step, in our countries that are too old, there's a face standing
next to us, the weight of a gaze like a secret thread harpooned into
the threatening collective madness, that those people, the insane,
standing on a corner or locked up in a hospital, embody for the
rest of us." (32) For madness stands as yet another locus of semioclasis, as a fuzzy space occupied by some (the insane), but one
that comes to signify for all of us ("collective madness"). Through
the trope of madness it is the pain of loss that transpires, loss of
identity, self-respect, and the links that tie the individual to society.
Ultimately it is the loss of meaning that madness epitomizes, but
also its reconstruction.

Portrait of the City as Strange Attractor

Because we live in a predominantly metropolitan environment,
Bon takes to task urban mythologies, in the sense Roland Barthes
gives to the term. But his intention is not to do an ethnographic
study of urban and industrial spaces, like David Lepoutre's *Coeur
de banlieue*, centered around a significant *non-lieu de mémoire*
in the urban wasteland: La Courneuve, which provides both the
topos and the logos of *Sang gris* and *Décor ciment*. The Robert
dictionary defines the *lieu de mémoire* as "a significant constitu-

ent, material or figurative, which, through the will of men or passage of time, has become an element symbolizing whatever community"; this includes events, monuments, emblems, celebrations, museums, institutions, books, and ideas, that is, all the "places that are part and parcel of national memory." Here La Courneuve stands not only as a place but as an idea that should be constitutive of national memory but has turned into an entropic force, a destructuring and desubjectivizing presence for the individuals who interact with it—in much the same way that dystopia constitutes the inverse of utopia, but has as much ontological coherence.

Painted with the garish traits of an "urban disaster" (*Sang gris* 125), the urban project stands for Bon as "the worst, most rotten part of the world" (*Décor ciment* 21), coming across as a series of "disjointed blocks and chimneys, broken by the plowshare of highways" (157). There lives a fuzzy figure, under erasure, "an interchangeable man" (26), "tossed on the shores of a planet of scrap" (27). But beyond *les grands ensembles*, which the French christened "la zone" (the zone), without any qualifier, as if these zones of economic poverty only had one possible semantic corollary, lies unknowability.[37]

And beyond the zone other peripheral spaces, like the small towns on the border of metropolises, fall in the same bag, like Mirambeau in *L'enterrement*, Ribandon in *Calvaire des chiens*, and Lodève in *C'était toute une vie*. Mere satellites of the great ensembles, these small provincial towns find themselves caught in their metastasis, laments Bon, that of "the big city that devoured everything" (*C'était toute une vie* 11). And their misery, moral and economic, is identical to the projects', if only more discreet, notes Bon, for the same pathologies of maladjustment surface everywhere, the same incapacities to adapt to changes brought on by technological evolution, and the same difficulty of transition between archaic behaviors and modern life. Overall Bon depicts a city that destroys sign systems through its excesses, leaving only "a civilization whose foam reaches the top floors, and fills the cubes with grayish matter, then the ocean's vital waters flow elsewhere" (*Décor ciment* 44).

But Bon not only tells the fringes of the city; he portrays the city itself: from Berlin to Paris, through Niort, La Rochelle, Arçais, St-Hilaire La Palud, Bombay, Vitry, and Koenigsberg—that is, the urban everywhere we inhabit today, which Michel Foucault calls "heteropia" (*La folie Rabelais* 242). In so doing he mythifies the city as much as he mystifies the reader bent on a realistic reading of the text. Instead of serving as a the simple projection of our fears and fantasies, the urban everywhere he depicts turns into a dystopia, a "world deprived of positive utopias," "an immense cemetery of things" (*Décor ciment* 98), "a country with no horizon" (46), and thus not only a space of social disaffection but a fuzzy space, with no fixed ontological boundaries, and in the end "a zone of literary criticism."[38] It comes as no surprise then that for Lambert, the blind storyteller, the city is an "abstract space" (47), a ghost city, or what Rabelais names a Médamothi (a non-place, *nul lieu* in French).[39]

"A train station if you must know, which station, who cares, it's early." With these words *Sortie d'usine* opens, as if the exit from the factory were first and foremost an exit from the kind of mimetic fiction the classical realist novel has accustomed readers to. From the outset Bon puts us in the "hors-lieu," outside the grid as it were. Hence the abandoned town of Ribandon—the name itself suggests "abandon"—where the film crew of *Calvaire des chiens* passes a few days, is not only a ghost town but also stands as the mirror image of a Berlin that, after the fall of the wall, is struggling with its past and failing to retain its memory. Deprived of the *Vergangenheitsbewältigung* (knowledge of the past) that would anchor them in the collective unconscious, both towns have now become lost cities, like "two inverted triangles" (8), and Berlin, now just an acronym ("B"), has turned into a postmodern *non-lieu*, "a theatrical town" where one learns "techniques of falsehood" (58). In the end the dyadic formation (Berlin-Ribandon) problematizes what's at the heart of Bon's project, the representation of the city that the city itself imposes on the artist: the "metaphorical city" (32), the "mental idea for a city" (77).

Among the various markers Bon places along the lines, several figures of land surveyors (*arpenteurs*), modern-day travelers, appear, like Barbin, the narrator of *Calvaire des chiens*, who hails from the same village as Copernicus (108), and as Lambert in *Décor ciment*. But like Kafka's K, these land surveyors find out there is more to the world than meets the eye. If, for the inmates of *Le crime de Buzon*, "the walls are your clothes" (16), this is because they are unable to represent themselves—Buzon is illiterate—and go, literally and metaphorically, beyond themselves. For them "prison is a skin" (26), and horizons are barred to those who can't access the imaginary. Tellingly Bon invokes the presence of a number of explorers in his texts: Dumont d'Urville, Cook, and Guillaume de Rubrock (*François Place, illustrateur* 45), but also Scott and Amundsen, the explorers of the South Pole (*C'était toute une vie* 131). However, for him these land surveyors, while filling out the white spaces on the map, show that "the unknown part of the world is much greater than we thought."[40]

For this reason the narrator of *Sortie d'usine* may well claim that, at the plant, "stories stay outside the door" (45). Bon insists that there still are stories in the world of the factory, but the ability to recount them may depend first on the narrator's ability to find the exit door, "the small basement window" from which the individual might escape the cage he or she is in.[41] "With your eyes closed, you have inner visions," closes *C'était toute une vie*, in what is not a redundancy but the affirmation that the mapping of the world begins with the exploration of the uncharted territories of the imagination. In this context the disappearance of the heteropia—which bespeaks the artist's inability to represent the city—proves to be as disquieting an experience as its stifling presence. The narrator of *Calvaire des chiens* thus laments the fall of the wall of Berlin, "a town that no longer exists" (8), "a town that suddenly disappeared" (59, 83), for the fall of the wall destroys more than a piece of masonry.

As a consequence the name "Berlin" appears only in the jacket notes of *Calvaire des chiens*, not in the body of the text, where

only an initial signals its presence; the result of this lack is troubling for Barbin. Perceived as "a pallid dream," "a muted hub-
bub" (8), the city's outline appears blurred, like Ribandon's, which
is emptied of its inhabitants after a cholera epidemic. But despite
the loss of *Vergangenheitsbewältigung*, both cities can hope to revive their memories and their images, Berlin being, like Ribandon,
"an enduring picture of the old world" (85), one of its *lieux de mémoire*. Before the fall "the wall created some very strange figures,"
says Barbin (24); indeed, for him Berlin, archetypal metropolis,
holds the strands of the urban web together: "A town that has
always worked like a strange attractor . . . and pushed to their end
all those she takes in, who came from all over the continent, so
much that she seems, as soon as you live there, to weave you into
an origin that you didn't know for itself; and perhaps, through
that ability, you can begin again, once the upheaval passes, after
the locks are lifted, when we remain standing on the edge" (191).
Here Berlin marks that point in the system's cycle that attracts the
system to it and may still allow us, after the fall of the wall, and
the collapse of the system, to bind meaning and space. As such
Berlin functions as a relay between barren reality and its eventual
reinvention: "Which town today would, like she did, convey for
all the other cities this dreamy nocturnal face, emerging here only
because the wall could preserve the sacrifice of the ancient capital
city that they had destroyed?" (24). With the dismantling of the
Berlin Wall went the ability to delineate ourselves, claims Barbin;
wiping of that fuzziness means recreating B's boundaries around
Ribandon, the mirror city that, like the other Médamothis, "invokes the misery of its fallen houses and dead factories" (*C'était
toute une vie* 88).

For Ribandon alludes to *ripa* (*rive* in French, that is, "shore" or
"bank"), while Sauveterre (yet another ghost city in Bon's long urban litany) means "salva terra," a safe ground, an asylum ("terre
sauve, jouissant du droit d'asile"). In an emblematic and paradoxical passage of *Calvaire des chiens* a flood forces the inhabitants of Sauveterre to leave their homes and seek shelter at the

local madhouse (asylum), along with the inmates. Forced into an undesirable confrontation with madness, the inhabitants become aware—though they may deny it—of the aleatory nature of their own normality, for only through the contraposition of normality and madness does the possibility for truth emerge, says Bon. In a shift both tectonic and semantic Berlin (B) drifts to the banks of Ribandon, then Sauveterre, and finally Babylon, the Ur-city of *Décor ciment*, "not Babylone the city, but the fascination for the excess of the city, even after its destruction, an excess that perdures as if only the pounding of a name mattered (in that place where writing was invented on clay)" (78).

And in the end, to edge out chaos and loss, the city must live in that name, lest meaning, like architecture, become normative and soulless, like Berlin after the wall: "The impression, Barbin said, of a concrete city: that we stood on an evil core, that the enclosure would let it through the cracks with the wind, and now that they had broken the wall, they had made it the best possible configuration, what they wished, the refurbished model of shop windows and perishables" (19). And (new) Berlin turns into a "gigantic supermarket" (19), where Apollinaire would have unmasked "the useful and fearsome sign of money."[42] With the city abandoned to urban revitalization projects, the loss of the stage on which the *teatrum mundi* was played out ultimately results in the failure of Barbin's film project, on the reinvention of Berlin (through Ribandon). It must be said that the project had few chances of succeeding, since GmbH, the film company that sponsored the film, epitomizes the blunt anonymity of (new) Berlin, its postmodern vagueness and anonymity. In German "GmbH" stands for "Gesellschaft mit beschränkter Haftung" (Company with limited liability), which Bon shortens to an even more dismal "beschränkter Haftung" (19), or "limited liability," when the production company finds that the creation of meaning and the reinvention of memory hold little market value.[43] If GmbH does not find itself liable for the creation of meaning, no wonder Isa Waertens, the concierge of *Décor ciment*, rails against the well-known publicity

slogan (and very succinct example of media newspeak) for Conforama, a chain of French supermarkets: "Conforama, the land
where life comes cheap" (Conforama, le pays où la vie est moins
chère). She denounces, like Barbin, the moral and formal impoverishment that the slogan implies, "as if we didn't try on the contrary
to make our life more dear" (69).

But with the loss of the wall we lost the capacity to mark the
limits of the cage we are in, warns Barbin. Berlin then comes open
"like the rest of the world" (11), not in the sense that Roberto
Rossellini spoke of in *Roma città aperta*, but without markers to
plot, picture, and track the fuzziness around. Describing the urban
endotic must thus begin with what Hélène Milliex dubs "seizing
back the erosion of the self through a poetics of erosion."[44] Extrapolating from Rabelaisian poetics, Bon defines his own project
along similar lines: "to conquer the highest levels of language from
nothing, the roughest transcription of the city pavement" (*La folie
Rabelais* 29), a task that he summarizes pithily with "the street,
the night, and shit" (162) and that implies "finding on a square
meter of pavement all the signs that were left there, down to matter itself, asphalt, concrete and gravel" (*C'était toute une vie* 19).

Under the constraints of such a proposal the urban poet finds
him- or herself in an ectopic position, forced into deportation,
like a romantic wanderer drawn toward exile, "a wanderer, away
from home, without country or identity. A heavenly or terrestrial
bum."[45] But if wandering bespeaks the loss of transcendence and
the dissolution of the self that characterized romantic fiction, the
internal exile of Bon's characters inscribes itself more in the wake
of the cryptic and "unmentionable" quest of Beckett's Molloy.
The vagabondage of Bon's characters takes them to the margins,
not only of geographical space—as in the exotic fiction of Pierre
Loti—but also of the inner topographies already explored by the
Proustian quest. In fact, as displacement betrays immobility, Bon
tracks that dispersion on the white page, making this relation between fixity and travel a crucial theme of his fiction (*Parking* 34).

A century earlier Nerval's urban topologies—notably *Les nuits d'octobre*—had already superimposed the exploration of the self on the description of the urban milieu: "corridors, endless corridors, stairs going up, and down, and up again, which dip in dark waters troubled by waterwheels, under the immense arches of bridges, through inextricable frameworks" (*C'était toute une vie* 18). Following Nerval, Etienne Rozier, an oddball known as "the king of dogs," contends in *Calvaire des chiens* that "man is made up of rooms, . . . and you should go through them to know him" (178).[46] "I am that lost rambler, crossing dreams," confirms the young Ophelia of *C'était toute une vie* (22), right before killing herself, in a move that seems as oneiric as it is physical. If Nerval equates "perception" with "vision,"[47] in Bon's fiction too the narrative evolves from the mimetic to the oneiric. "It's a difficult exercise," says Bon of the art of wandering, "which must be constantly renewed, but you must seek to see, seek visions," as if what is most significant in the poetics of urban ambulation is the hallucinatory transfiguration of the city, its liberation from physical bonds and semantic dearth.[48]

In what amounts to a reinvention of Montaigne's ideal, for Bon traveling acquires genuine meaning when one finds oneself confronted with the need or obligation to stay in one place, the same way movement becomes meaningful when considered in relation to immobility. Thus despite an affirmed preference for the nomadic lifestyle of some of his characters (Joël in *Limite*, Konrad in *Décor ciment*), Bon shows profound interest in life in the housing projects, like Bobigny, or what he has called on numerous occasions life in the cage. After he began a career as a full-time writer, first with Editions de Minuit and then with several other publishing houses such as Verdier, Gallimard, and Seuil, Bon set out to give writing workshops for the underprivileged, first in what the Ministère de l'Education prudishly describes as "priority educational zones" (zones d'éducation prioritaires), like La Paillade in Montpellier, and Lodève, but also in schools, like the Lycée Jacques Brel at La Courneuve, and finally in prison, like the juvenile facility of Bordeaux-Gradignan.

Tuned early on to the dysfunctions of postindustrial France, Bon has always insisted on the many marginalities that riddle it, aiming to elaborate new representative strategies for the most trivial, least meaningful segment of the urban nowhere and "turn into literature the most contemporary fringe of the city's image" (*Parking* jacket notes), interrogating in the process the position the artist occupies vis-à-vis marginality. Like Bernard-Marie Koltès and Jacques Séréna—both published by Minuit—Bon sees the artist as condemned to the limits, "always on the fringe" (*Limite* 105), not to be fashionably eccentric but to become irretrievably exogenous and tease meaning out of the world's dead zones. Thus Konrad, the claustrophobic sculptor of *Décor ciment*—a double for the author—opts to squat in an abandoned gas station outside the towers of the city, while Brocq, the antisocial encyclopedist of *Le crime de Buzon*—and a fictional Doppelgänger of the writer—chooses to stay in an old decrepit farm beside Buzon's house, a dwelling that stands, we are told, at the very limits of dry land. What Konrad and Brocq tell us is that, for the poet be able to peer into vagueness and heckle meaning out of lack, he or she must stand on the edge of the world and at the edge of meaning, a lesson that was not lost on the explorers of Rabelais's *Quart livre*, whose influence is felt throughout Bon's fiction.

No wonder then that the disenfranchised should end up exiled to the margins of the urban landscape in Bon's dystopic fictions, whether that exile is self-imposed or forced upon them by others. Aware as he is that he's become an "untouchable," Yves, an unemployed man, knows to stay off-limits (*Limites*), whereas Alain, the suicide of *L'enterrement*, is buried outside the town's cemetery, like the anonymous girl of *C'était toute une vie*, or like the unwanted of old, buried away from the good townsfolk. In much the same way the "crazies' cemetery" (cimetière des fous) exists in an isolated section of the abbey in *Le crime de Buzon* (130), away from everyone's view, nameless, fuzzified, outside language and history, for there one finds "the mad, buried naked, dead just covered by earth, nameless crosses" (130). For the insane, like artists and suicides, remain physically marginalized, symbolically positioned on the fault line between the world and its outer limits, between meaning and absence of meaning. Hence literature can only arise from that "line of fracture,"[49] from the fuzzy zone where the real and the fictional commingle, where language faces the danger of its own undoing, its own destructuring, its own semioclasis. Because it is exogenous, writing must be envisioned as a challenge (*Sortie d'usine* 19) and a transgression. Thus if the emblematic figures of the *poètes maudits* (Rimbaud, Mallarmé, Lautréamont) regularly appear in Bon's texts, this is because their prose defies precisely what Bon names "the opaqueness of a doomed destiny" (*La folie Rabelais* 10), that is, the dead weight of the real. For Bon it is by pushing language to its extremes, exploring its capacity to tell under duress, that the artist becomes a trailblazer, "crossing over perilous trails," as Bon subtitled his study of Rabelais. Following upon the tracks of writers of travel literature, like Joseph Conrad, Bon chooses instead to take readers on an elusive search for a truth that must necessarily be found elsewhere, in a fuzzy space, at the margins of our industrial wasteland and at the margins of language.

Each of Bon's texts offers at least one marginal figure, a protagonist who functions, if not as the author's mouthpiece, at least as a presence—more than a character in the Balzacian sense of the term—a strange attractor that serves to affirm the vitality and need of literature in particular and art in general (the polyanonymous narrator of *Sortie d'usine*, Joël; the guitar player of *Limite*, Louis Lambert; the blind storyteller of *Décor ciment*, a dead ringer for Homer; and Barbin, the scriptwriter in *Calvaire des chiens*, to name but a few).[50] Besides these, other marginal figures—artists, architects, musicians, and storytellers—appear throughout Bon's work. Among them Pozzo, the clownish personage of *Dans la ville invisible*, stands as the most outlandish, dressing in "a gray suit [and] black shoes . . . two sizes too big" (40). Pozzo not only lives at the margins of society; he literally stands at the edge of the real. And although he owns an apartment, like all the other tenants of the building, he prefers to live and "travel" on the elevator at night, an elevator that becomes in his eyes a "machine, the universe's coach" (43), a coach that journeys continuously between infinite space and the chthonian underworld (45).

While Caniche, the young drifter of *30, rue de la Poste*, decides to leave the dreariness of his hometown, Sète, only to find that other Sètes can be found all over the map (he ends up in Quimper, diagonally across the map), Pozzo does not seek to free himself by moving out. Pozzo does not leave the city but travels through it, following its lines of force. While the dominant image of Baudelaire's Paris deploys itself as "a cluster of intersecting trajectories, a fantastic, palimpsest arabesque of crisscrossing paths,"[51] its dominant feature still remains the horizontal. For Bon, however, the city defines itself through its verticality; one must seek "the geometry of pillars, of concrete basements and access ramps" (*Parking* 64), to understand how power and meaning are distributed across the urban landscape. Thus only Pozzo, traveler of the vertical, "is free to leave, no ties, no affection, no hindrance, no constraint nor routine" (*Dans la ville invisible* 44), even though (and precisely because) his liberation happens in the imaginary.

A survey of Bon's urban topography shows that the most recurrent geometrical figure is the square, "closed-up space, in a violent relation with the outside."[52] "We are walled in," the young woman of *C'était toute une vie* records in her notebook (65), locked inside "this closed reality" (*Sortie d'usine* 165).[53] It's no surprise then that the prison should become a recurring motif in Bon's vision, a Kafka-like superstructure, a "blind castle" (*Le crime* 39) within which smaller squares—the cell, the execution pad—mark out the limits of individual lives.[54] Bon explicitly mentions the death camp of Treblinka in *Le crime de Buzon* and the prison of Ploetzensee in *Calvaire des chiens* (173). (Ploetzensee is a Berlin jail where German resistors were executed on 20 July 1944.) In addition the prison becomes replicated in a number of other spaces, like the factory of *Sortie d'usine*, where the guards become screws ("matons" [19]); or the postfactory world of *Daewoo*, locked up in depression, where, says Rabelais in the epigraph, "half the world ignores how the other half lives"; or the football field of *Limite*, which stands as "nothing more than a flat hard sheet, where you're caged up" (57); or again a "gridlike world" (60): the parking lot and the tunnels of *Décor ciment*, the dog pound of *Calvaire des chiens*, which metaphorically doubles as a Nazi death camp, and the asylum of *Calvaire des chiens*, where military authorities have quartered those who were disfigured on the battlefields of World War I so as to avoid the spread of antiwar sentiments among the general population (53, 205). If the prison of *Le crime de Buzon* holds "caged men . . . in airtight cells" (15), the city itself pushes that carceral confinement to a macroscopic extreme, becoming "an all-pervading gridlike world" (*Décor ciment* 94).

Situations of social distress emphasize the feeling of immurement and borrow from the same semantic field. For Yves, whose entire life comes to be defined through his unemployment, entrapment and exclusion are one and the same: "you're in a cage . . . excluded" (*Limite* 72). His only exit is reverie, "the world inside against the gridlike world" (62). Trapped in like situations of social exclusion and economic poverty, the young kids of Lodève see themselves walled in, with no exit: "there's nothing in Lodève. Lodève is walled in" (*C'était toute une vie* 16). Pursuing this feeling of exclusion and immurement, a young rape victim, Buzon's kid sister, finds a cheerless refuge in the (mental) confines of catatonia, and the (physical) enclosure of a dog pound, in order to escape the traumatic memories of her molestation (*Le crime de Buzon*). For some of the younger characters of Bon's fictions, like the young woman fired from her job in *Daewoo*, or the young teenage mother of *C'était toute une vie*, suicide sadly appears like the only way out of the cage, because "in the end, one can't take it any more" (*C'était toute une vie* 28). But death does not release from the cage, and the tomb only closes the lid over it, a move that Paul Claudel compares to a Calvary without resurrection: "man does not exit his self-made Calvary."[55]

As for television, not surprisingly Bon argues that, far from offering a space of emancipation, it reduplicates urban internment in mental space, battering the imaginary into the mediocrity of consumerism. In a key scene at the beginning of *Décor ciment* a grim murder (that of the aptly named Raymond Crapin) is discovered, but while everybody flocks to the crime scene, one man stays put (a war veteran). Traumatized by the war, we learn, he shot himself in order to be discharged from the military. Now he remains chained to his TV set, watching the popular show *Champs Elysées* (Elysian Fields—-both Parisian glitter and pre-Christian Hell), trapped in the inferno of memory and the false glitz of consumerist entertainment (31). But space, whether mental or physical, stays sealed, and the recurring presence of dogs across Bon's fictional landscape reminds readers that in a dog-eat-dog world there is no escape. In the end one of the most emblematic scenes of *Décor ciment* describes how a man actually ends up eaten by his dogs, which are locked with him inside his apartment (154).

In this urban valley of tears the dynamic between possession and dispossession remains highly symbolic, dramatized through cultural and economic alienation: "each mutation of the world burdens the dispossessed so," confirms Rainer Maria Rilke, "[that] what was no longer belongs to them and what will be doesn't belong to them yet" (*Temps machine* epigraph). "The world's greatest madness comes from thinking there are stars for kings, Popes and great men, but not for the poor and suffering, as if new stars had been created since the time of the Flood," reads the incipit of *La folie Rabelais*. Like Rabelais, Bon does not hide his sympathy for the down-and-out, for "people of low stature" ([les] gens de bas estat [10]). In his monograph on Rabelais he eschews the traditional view of the Renaissance as an enlightened age and represents it as a time marred by barbarism, wars, pogroms, and ignorance; for him Rabelais's world, plunged in chaos, had much in common with our postindustrial world, the "ravaged broken-down world of factories" (*Temps Machine* jacket notes), the "failed industrial empire" (14).

But sympathy for the excluded does not connote engagement,

says Bon: "paucity is social, not literature."[56] He adds that "what frightens in the poor suburbs is the destiny they bestow on the world, and for which the world is responsible" (*Sang gris* 136). The task assigned to the artist then is to find a way to take into account the mental squalor occasioned by urban decomposition, as well as the disappearance of the old industrial world, "the end and relegation of the world of iron and steel . . . , a great dead organism of which we were a part" (*Temps machine* 98). Doubling upon the need to find new forms, the need to inscribe the old forms in our cultural patrimony ensues: "One had to answer the threat, and etch in our memory what the making of alternators meant in this age when everything was toppling over and falling apart" (74), a task made all the more difficult since the factory, unlike the *banlieue*, already belongs to the industrial past.

Bon makes it clear that the artist's task is urgent, for the old world is on the brink of collapse: "A falling glass never breaks when it hits the ground first. No matter how high it's falling from, it bounces back, elastic and vibrant, with a deep sound, as if it were happy to still be itself after such a demonstration. It hardly bounces the second time: only the sound remains, already polluted but stronger, saturated. And at last, almost with shame, it falls back down from a finger's height, and shatters. . . . And we would be the generation of the second bounce" (*Limite* 157). The sound is saturated at the second bounce, as if the information provided by the falling glass were too much for the senses, as if meaning were overwhelming or meaningless, as if the listener had entered a zone of white noise, confusion, and loss. And to remedy such a fate the poet must find a language that will be porous to the world at its least accessible, "a language that stands apart from facts, and keeps its stature, when the facts are chosen precisely because they have nothing to say, like an obscure piece of the town's obscurity that only affects those whom we don't usually count" (*Un fait divers* 29–30). Flaubert wanted to write a book on nothingness, because through nothingness "you face each day a world of impoverished signs, of smaller words, and adventure is much more difficult to capture."[57] Heeding Flaubert's example, Bon makes form—not theme—the main vector of meaning.

Verbal Plasticity

As a consequence Bon's prose strives for the lyrical, taking liberties with syntax that few since Rabelais have dared. Speaking of a "deforming syntax," as does Barbin (*Calvaire* 152), is no overstatement, for Bon gives French grammar a plasticity that is both innovative and old-fashioned, reminding readers of the upheaval of Rabelaisian prose (an upheaval that ushered in a linguistic and literary revolution). One must "save his own language by envisioning it through a foreign language," suggests one of the protagonists of *Calvaire des chiens* (151). "How can we go across the foggy looking glass, for self and country, to gain some perspective from differences," Bon adds (*Temps machine* 67), so as to find "under the tongue what the cousin tongue reveals about the chewing inside, the silent heavy wheel of meaning's inertia" (*Calvaire* 154).

To combat the inertia words—verbs notably—must come missing, leaving gaps in their place, while the recurring use of ante-position puts the finishing touches on the disjointing of the sentence. The multiplication of ante-positions, and the rejection of verbs at the end of sentences, may remind readers of German syntax as much as preclassical French, and Barbin confesses his fascination—and Bon's—with "these sentences that begin with a series of nouns, shoveled in, that accumulate until they burst out in the end with the verb" (152). This comment must be read metatextually, for Bon's sentences also keep pressure building, in entropic fashion, only to discharge it at the final stop. For instance, in the following passage Barbin relates his visit to a hospital:

> *At the bottom of the stairs a glass door blocked the way;*
> *the stretcher came in from a yellow corridor, with the*
> *dead man lying down on the frail legs of four rolling*

> *tubes, pushed by an old Turk, wearing a fur hat, who was obstinately staring at the tiled floor. And in that enormous hall, more crowded than a train station above which they suddenly stood, said Barbin, old men in pajamas who seemed separated from their voices, above the sick walking their perfusion along, or dragging on their cigarettes like clandestine passengers, a vague hubbub that white coats crossed more rapidly, other brown coats pushing piles of dirty things, then the quicker gestures of a tiny hairdresser in a shop in the back, a line in front of the telephone, and in front of them the country's mandatory spread of porno magazines on the rack with their distended women, all that a mute world, too slow, he finished.* (Calvaire 8)

Characteristic of Bon's chaotic prose, these two sentences form a lexia, where pressure mounts, accelerating, until its final release, going from "blocked," to "dead," "pushed," "walking," "more rapidly," "quicker," "line," "distended," "too slow," and eventually "he finished." The impression is one of a series of stills, or snapshots ("a glass door," "an old Turk," "old men," "white coats," "porno magazines"), brought together by the sheer force of syntax, despite the absence of verbs of agreement (*to be*, *to have*) and verbs of action (*to see*, *to do*), like memories aggregating along the thread provided by the act of remembrance.

Like the fuzzy world he describes (fuzzy because seemingly atrophied, but still brimming with information), Bon's sentence is syncopated, paroxystic, and, borrowing from the Célinian model, marked by an abundance of punctuation that signals the opening and fragmentation of the text at its most basic level. Sentences stop abruptly or unravel themselves over entire chapters, while blocks of texts seem to be drifting into one another like elements hurled together in a chaotic environment, following a rhythm that mimics the cadence of the narrators' mental uncertainty. Provoking a visceral impact on the reader, the uneven and catastrophic rhythm of

Bon's prose suggests that the text should be read aloud, like poetry, in order to take in the logic of its flow.[58]

Readers will have guessed that Bon's prose does owe much to poetry and pays particular attention to prosody. But it is rhythm that, before anything else, serves to organize the narrative, since, as Joël (a bass player) puts it, "rhythm comes first, the beginning, cadence" (*Limite* 109). "Rhythm's course carries everything," confirms Joël (*Limite* 109), allowing the sentence to deploy itself and meaning to surface "as you endlessly seek to join the unarticulated foundation of language with cadence's percussions, into the orderly partition of meaning" (*Calvaire* 153). Contrasting sharply with the muted fuzziness of the world around, setting the rhythm right becomes all the more significant; from "the hook" of the song (l'accroche [7]) meaning can be pieced together. "Everything depends on the first song; you must be precise, set everything straight," warns Joël (*Limite* 19).

Needless to say, Joël's own "rhythmic send-off" is as straight as a die, as in the following passage, where the initial alexandrine is followed by a transition, a coordinating conjunction that lets the sentence hang in midair, before it cuts down to the two following octosyllabic verses, thus speeding up the rhythm, then moves to two other hexameters—the beat becoming shorter, like the breath of the narrator—down to one final tetrameter, then the concluding dimeter, "bonsoir," which ends the sentence and opens the text: "A détaché le micro du support de fer / et / dans le cône bleu des lumières / grande boucle du cable rouge / un chassé de la jambe / une torsion des hanches / et ça suffit. Bonsoir" (He unhooked the mike from its steel support, and, in the blue cone of light, the red cable hooks around, the leg shifts sideways, the hips swivel, and that's it. Good night) (19). Starting from the initial alexandrine, with a caesura that separates subject from object, the singer-narrator—here metonymically represented by the microphone—stands out from the world of iron that surrounds him—the industrial wasteland where the story is located.

Incipits are always significant in a narrative, but they take on a particular weight in Bon's proesis. Hence the first lines of *Le crime de Buzon* not only set tone and rhythm but constitute a rhythmic *mise-en-abyme* of the entire text, as if rhythm were a pole around which meaning spun itself, against the fuzziness of the dead world: "And it was the first wakening without the clunking of steel on steel, without the formidable rumbling of men in their cages, as they shake themselves awake to the drumming of time, this puppet of steel whose jerky beats swell up against the smooth walls, and advance effortlessly across the metal gates before they spill into the hermetically sealed floors, and echo back against the five hundred identical doors, until, finally, they butt against the fixed Plexiglas of the airtight cells" (15). Here everything begins with a sound, a noise that ripples across the walls of the prison, with ample though constantly interrupted movements, only to end against the wall of the prison, running literally out of breath within the last part of the sentence. The circular movement described by the initial clanking of the door bars, a noise that circulates within the closed space of the jail, illustrates metaphorically the tragic destiny of Boson, who, after his liberation from jail, "winds up" in jail again, as a guard this time, once all the narrative tension and possibilities have been exhausted. All is told there, the personal and collective traumas, and the tragedy of internment, but it is the rhythm, its iterative isochronies, that warps the yarn, as if in that sentence human time were caught in a loop, self-repeating until consumption.

Bon likes to multiply these *mise-en-abymes*, "as if you were to find in certain sentences the architecture and rhythm of a whole book" (*Calvaire* 50). The next sentence shows the film crew of *Calvaire des chiens* discovering the abandoned village of Ribandon. Once again the writing demonstrates the importance of prosody and the attention paid to classic poetic forms, as well as the defamiliarizing torsion that exists between syntax and meter: "Tandis qu'ils descendaient de voitures, les corneilles, folles au couchant, hurlaient en tournant sur les toits, revenant en nuage s'abattre sur la moitié de clocher qui restait, c'est-à-dire une élévation du mur avec en haut ces deux échancrures ouvragées et reprenant en découpe . . . la ligne du fronton." (As they got out of the car, the crows went mad in the setting sun, and screamed as they swirled above the roofs, and flocked back to the remaining half of the church spire, that is to say a wall rising and at the top, two finely worked indentations that mirrored the lines of the front wall.) Once again the rhythm of the sentence is ample, and this time it is marked by the metronomic succession of classic alexandrines (numbering six), with the interposition of one hexasyllabic verse ("revenant en nuage"), which gives even more sweep to the following alexandrine ("s'abattre sur la moitié de clocher qui restait"), as if the sentence, like the crows mentioned in it, were looping down on the church spire. Besides its rhythm, the passage is also significant as it brings together in a sentence all of Bon's fundamental topoi: the mapping of space; the narration of time and memory; but also madness, tragedy, and the need to bring oneself to the zone where meaning and noise coexist—"fronton" alluding homonymically to "frontière."

Paraphrasing Philippe Sollers, Bon speaks of literature as "conquering darkness, . . . an experience of the limits," and of "a push against that border line."[59] However, the search for meaning is a perilous one, and "when he reaches the apex of any word that may be spoken, man does not reach the heart of him, but his own limits: in that region that borders death, and where thought comes to die, where the promise of an origin constantly falls back" (*La folie Rabelais* 211). No doubt his experience as a factory worker led Bon to pay particular attention to the notion of rhythm, notably to the vital need there is to swerve away from preimposed cadences, to go beyond mechanical time, beyond rhythmic sameness, beyond the numbing habitus of everyday life. What is binding in his fiction is physical repetition— notably that of the production line: mental habits, cultural customs, and the identicalness of commercial products (*Limite* 79), all in all a network of forces that confine individuals within recurrent dynamics and reproducible spaces. Thus Bon suggests that each sentence, each line, "swerves from the one that precedes it, and forces us to become aware of ourselves in that swerve" (*Un fait divers* 128).

Mieke Bal shows how the relation between the time of the fabula and the time of the story—that is, the relation between the
time of the various series of events recounted and the time of their
narration (through summaries, ellipses, scenes, slow-downs, and
pauses)—may produce five different "tempi."[60] What renders Bon's
prose unique, and characterizes more particularly his later, more
openly theatrical texts—from *Calvaire des chiens* on—resides precisely in the very systematic changes in tempo, in the "structural
ruptures, and the plasticity of rhythms" (*La folie Rabelais* 19).
Seemingly random changes of rhythm also imply that intervals
(between beats) turn into something more than just absence of
sound, forcing readers to pause and question their rhythmic atavisms, the numbing "natural" rhythms of everyday life. In the first
scene of *Sortie d'usine* the narrator begins to describe the daily
routine of going to the factory by metro, contemplating how social
classes are divided not by space but by time, blue-collar workers
going to work earlier in the morning because of the work-shift
system, white-collar employees able to go to their jobs later during
the day. Each social category, though, tarries in the same "fixity, in
the repetition of things" (13), in "the now customary footsteps"
(15), in the immense succession of days" (34) and "the automatism of movements" (38). As in a linear system life unfolds like
an "automatic procession" (41), channeling energies, subsuming
individuals to "the bromide of obedience" (*Limite* 120). For the
narrator of *Sortie d'usine* "the cycle's inertia sets the week in motion" (41).

But like the skipping of a beat, small events soon throw the
system in unsuspected directions. Because he fails to wake up in
time, the narrator makes a series of mistakes: he takes the train at
the wrong time, or he climbs in the wrong wagon. In any case, the
harmony of the day and of the social body is lost, as cultural con-
ditionings fail to give answers to the newly created situation (13).
Besides being altered, the rhythmic constant—metro-work-home,
métro-boulot-dodo—can also come to a stop, as it does during a
strike at the plant (117). Rather than being the tragic apotheosis

of Zola's *Germinal*, the strike here is perceived as an awkward and unwelcome swerve from normal habits, but one that, gradually, allows the narrator to become conscious of his rhythmic atavisms, offering him an exit from the inertia of mechanical time, from the "frozen, fallen time" (jacket notes) of daily life.

Rhythm being the fundamental element of music—and the projection of poetic meter—it should come as no surprise that Bon harbors an unusual passion for music, from classical music (Bach, Yzaye, Giacinto Scelsi, and Arvo Pärt) to rock (the Rolling Stones). That Bon should like to put his prose through what Flaubert called *l'épreuve du gueuloir* by working on his texts with a composer (Kasper Toeplitz) only goes to show that he works the sentence like Flaubert and Dylan Thomas, by manipulating that "unstable mix of commotion and silence, sometimes exploding into sudden bursts of furor."[61] From rustle ("the noise of what works well . . . noise at the limit of noise, . . . impossible noise, . . . noise of what works perfectly, noiselessly") to stridence (that is, cacophony or auditory semioclasis), Bon's musical prose is a "language of splinters and syncopes," pushing meaning to its limits, to the edge of blankness.[62]

In light of this one understands why moments of cacophony should waymark crucial episodes, syncopated epiphanies, in Bon's novels, remaining the most significant as well as the most problematic moments of the narrative. For Bon the poet must map "the white zone of man at the end of himself,"[63] the same way the musician must confront the "white fire" (*Limite* 7)—white being the sum of all colors—that marks the utmost limit of noise, where the overload of information threatens to overwhelm the minds of players and listeners, destabilizing cognitive structures and falling into utter fuzziness: "Tuning, full blast, straight up: it goes from the gut and slams in the brain, behind you the wall of the amplifier bombards your back with your sound, full on, you can't move back and in front of you there's that blinding white fire, dazzling you, a single beat erecting your own wall against the wall of their collective screams, they push against each other for a while, evenly, but immediately fall apart, split by the same crack" (7). The fear then is that one might be unable to extract meaning from and find predictable patterns in that white zone, but also that the only other alternative would be to fall back into the mind-numbing rhythms of daily reality. In *Sortie d'usine* the narrator relates how each worker who dies at his post is taken through the factory on a pallet carrier, in a mock rendition of a rite of passage (84). As the pallet carrier drives the body of the dead through the workshops, workers start making noise, banging metal on metal, in paroxystic frenzy and confusion, to a point of complete phonoclasty, where "the factory's own structure seems to be bawling" (81). Yet even if the ceremony aims at taking revenge on the factory, attempting to repay "the violence made to matter by the laws of commodity" (59), as the factory workers attempt to violate convention, and as sound must "gush forth in excess" (80), it soon becomes clear that the workers do not have the means to master, let alone understand, the implications of the massive output of noise. Indeed, no one remembers the historical origins of the ceremony nor its ideological implications; they do not even know where the pallet carrier comes from, as if the mechanical object and its mysterious driver were endowed with all the mystery of old myths but escaped interpretation.

The ritual then turns into a simulacrum, "abstruse rites" (93) that only serve to assure the perenniality of tradition and the authority of the upper class, like "a base that doubled tradition, and kept it alive almost in spite of itself" (93). In fact, the clashes and clatters of the factory denote all too well the workers' deep-seated malaise, which amounts to "a saturation that was too shrill to be a grumbling, not the very high pitch of the engines, no. A whiter noise, like a thousand vibrations, all mixed up. Yes a saturation, but with subjective unease on top" (43). Ultimately the plant remains "a temple dedicated to the power of steel, and the blind belief in noise" (84). "WE'RE DEAF. ALL DEAF. ALL OF US," wails the anonymous narrator of *Sortie d'usine* (77), as deafness compounds the inability that the working poor show to mold meaning out of the "screaming paste," out of the aural fuzziness that encases them (*Limite* 7) and that they cannot interpret. It is extremely signifi-cant too that the first section of Bon's liminal text opens with the subtitle "the scream" (le cri), here a reference to the "growling" of a worker (feulant comme [29]) who is wounded in an industrial accident after he is snatched by a lathe, like a sacrificial victim to the machine (31).

After that liminal episode, and through the rest of his texts, Bon's characters attempt to fathom themselves and the world out of that noise, struggling to come out of "that wall with its millions of faces and gigantic crane jibs, its crosspieces and rolling frame-works and its incredible, terrifying percussion noise" (*Temps ma-chine* 49–50). "They live in an excess of noise," says Isa Waertens, speaking of those who have been exiled to the *banlieues* (*Décor ciment* 22), an opinion that is echoed by Etienne Rozier, the mad "king of dogs" of *Calvaire des chiens*, with a sentence oddly remi-niscent of Racine: "of whence comes the noise we hear: if you do not shut your ears, the storm comes inside your head" (160). For the illuminated junkie of *Décor ciment*, during crises the world is all sound and fury: "inside, there were screams" (7). But the junkie's withdrawal also foretells other lacks, other crises that af-fect the entire social body. "And if solitude frightens" are the first words he utters, as well as the incipit of the novel, putting the nar-rative finger from the outset on the fault lines that crisscross con-temporary society, "an avaricious country where we will always be orphaned of long-term friends" (11).

However, Bon posits two forms of turbulence, different in na-ture and purpose. First, there is the turbulence all individuals face in their daily lives, but as information increases in complexity, and the need for new interpretive structures is felt, a second type of turbulence appears, a wake turbulence this time, which translates the capacity of the artist, and the text, to produce meaning from excess.[64] This advice is also heeded by the singer-storyteller of *Limite*—though indirectly—for whom epiphany ensues precisely from excess: "between your hands you hold this earsplitting, plastic paste, you feel like a cat, a tiger, powerful and supple, you walk into the fire, to the edge, the very edge, a chord, and you go deaf from the beginning, as deaf as you are when you end it: deaf drunk" (8).

Monsters

As in fantastic stories, the capacity to exceed bespeaks vagueness and monstrosity, if not the polymorphous monstrosity of gothic monsters—although Bon does speak of "a wall with its millions of faces and gigantic crane jibs"—at least their semantic monstrosity, their irreducibility to common patterns and tropes.[65] Traditional myths tell us that the capacity to "see" a pattern in chaos devolves upon the enlightened and, more often than not, that ontological difference bears the mark of madness and monstrosity. Thus the young addict of *Décor ciment* who prophesies the fall of the modern *cité*, of the new Babylon, with a rage reminiscent of the Old Testament—"woe betide him who builds his city with blood, may decay take him" (9)—is missing a thumb on his left hand, a mark of his distinctiveness.[66]

A metaphoric double for Habakuk, one of the minor prophets who foretold the fall of the Jews at the hands of the Chaldeans, the junkie is nothing but a human dreg, who stammers his imprecations and barely retains the ability to speak.[67] But it is precisely because he evolves at the border of sanity and language that he is in contact with realities untouched and, like Brocq—the simpleton of *Le crime de Buzon*—seeks out "words under a fistful of hate" (*Décor ciment* 78). A more serene—but not less woeful—figure, Lambert, the blind man, builds in his mind a world of imaginary perspectives, a necropolis that he contemplates with "dead eyes, prisoners of a bedazzled world" (*Décor ciment* 45, 92). For him cities come in dreams (44), visions, in fact, that allow him to hear out and map out, through mental space, circumambient white noise, that is, the white zone from which instability threatens and, paradoxically, informs narrative order.[68]

Though deafness means disempowerment, blindness does not, for deafness results here from an overload of information, whereas blindness only denotes the absence of visual input, a condition that does not affect the individual's capacity to build and design and allows Lambert to process and internalize information at a much more manageable level.[69] But all these illuminati face the same fear at the margins, their own and others', as fiction becomes fiction of fuzziness, "a scream thrown back at dread and meaninglessness."[70] They give voice, physically and metaphorically, to the violence done to the individual, the physical violence of chain work, the accidents, the mutilations, and the physical and verbal aggression of the *cité*. But first and foremost they give voice to "the worst mutilation" (la mutilation la plus grave), says Yvan Leclerc, which "affects man through language."[71]

So to reverse the human incapacity to speak, Bon multiplies situations in which individuals relay one another in the communal telling of their collective story. Such is the case of Lambert, the blind man, who pays regular visits to Jean Jeudy, a former sailor who recounts the story of his life, the years he spent traveling around the globe in a world wrecked by wars and human folly. One day Jeudy dies, while the whole story remains unfinished. So Lambert continues the story in place of the original narrator, picking up the thread where Jeudy left it. Like Panurge coming out of Pantagruel's mouth, Lambert comes through death, from the other side, to allow the story to perpetuate itself. Another character, Isa Waertens, describes herself as the guardian (*gardienne*, not *concierge*), or caretaker, of the city and the keeper of its memory (*Décor ciment* 204). Like Lambert, she feels it is her duty to keep memory alive and pursues the story begun by another by weaving narrative strands back together, bridging discourse from others to herself. "They dream; one can't give up completely," she says of the clients who seek the keys to decode their dreams (21), for "if something new should happen, it can only take place inside, within dreams" (*La folie Rabelais* 9).

As the storyteller must unload the memories of others, narrative activity grounds itself in testimony and becomes a regression "to the world of old, a world without exit where dreams were all powerful" (*Limite* 127). Thus the embeddings of *Calvaire des chiens*— "Andreas finished, Barbin said" (48), "Andreas told me, Barbin said" (152)—signal that verbal performance must exceed monody and account for language's fuzzy polyphony. Says Lambert, "There are few gathered words that don't come across a prism, vast as humanity itself, and also end up distorted and divided, before we make them our truth and act accordingly" (*Décor ciment* 164), for the mystery of literature "may only come from the collective elevation of men" (*Décor ciment* 195). Such collective vision doesn't remain wishful thinking on the part of the author, though. Polyphony, when practiced within a writing workshop, articulates a real and actual need for collective vision and discourse, "as if being together gave more strength to face oneself and the world. . . . In the end, it's the linguistic community that matters" (*Les mots sont des fenêtres* 5).

In *C'était toute une vie*, which was written in part as the result of the experience gained during writing workshops he conducted, Bon multiplies the number of voices that intervene during the narrative—even though polyphony had been a traditional staple of his style before. Organized around the death of the anonymous main character, each new microstory draws a compendium of her life, before the various testimonies crystallize to form a composite picture of the figure in the narrative carpet, "center of tension and strength, . . . light of madness, . . . mouth of the abyss" (22, 128). But each mininarrative also forms a new eddy in the narrative flow and throws, each time, a new, different light on the text. For its part *30, rue de la Poste* has a more conventional narrative organization, largely because it was published at Seuil Jeunesse for a younger readership. Yet it still tells the interrelated stories of nine young persons who all spend some time at a center for the homeless run by Ali. The book is divided into twelve chapters, and each youth tells her or his story in a chapter, with the exception of Ali, who has three chapters to himself because he serves to tie all the narrative strands together.

In this regard *C'était toute une vie*, and the other texts produced
with the material gathered in the writing workshops (*30, rue de
la Poste, Polir nos arêtes vives, Les mots sont des fenêtres*, and to
a certain extent *Daewoo*), differ fundamentally from the rest of
Bon's work.[72] For his other novels tend to underline the solitude
of each individual voice rather than underscore crisscrossing patterns. In a sense the major part of Bon's fiction operates like Beckett's *Comédie*, deploying a series of voices that, like parallel lines,
never intersect and only speak for themselves: "no one speaks to
anyone," summarizes one character (*Décor ciment* 51). However,
each text produced by François Bon, whether or not it consists
of material compiled in a writing workshop, endeavors to bring
otherwise disparate voices together. Therefore there might be only
one narrator in *Sortie d'usine*, but it is a multiple narrator, both
external and character-bound—that is, someone who is speaking
both for himself and for others.[73] In this sense there is no inside
monologue in Bon's texts, but an external monologue,[74] and the
speaking "I" necessarily bespeaks another, for here one is always
dispossessed of oneself, desubjectivized. Hence the return to Rabelais allows Bon to problematize a return "before the philosophy of
the subject, which will come later, with the arrival of Montaigne
and Descartes."[75] Because the urban environment deconstructs
the notion of subject, Bon argues, we are "facing a new enigma
on individuality." Thus rereading Rabelais gives us the chance to
perceive the absence of "character" because the Rabelaisian actor
precedes the notion of subject, confirms Bon.

If Rabelais's poesis is characterized by an extensive use of multilayered narratives, so is Bon's. In *Limite* Bon introduces the polyphonic mode that became the hallmark of all his texts. It is in fact
a quadraphonia—a four-character lay-up: Joël, Joly, Alain, and
Yves—in the form of a fugue, with contrapuntal figures that evoke
the characters' inability to communicate. A similar pattern deploys
itself in *Le crime de Buzon*. As usual a prologue lays out the main
elements and sets the tone, while voices speak up in alternating
patterns during the entire novel. Tellingly enough the voices of the

two ex-convicts (Buzon and Raulx) do not open or close the text but remain framed within. The form of *Décor ciment* remains identical, but *Calvaire des chiens* introduces a less geometrical pattern, a fractal structure in which voices open into other voices in a series of embeddings. *Calvaire des chiens* is Bon's most accomplished work in terms of formal complexity; after that novel he returned to a more straightforward polyphonic mode, inspired, he says, by his work in a Centre de Jeunes Détenus: "Many faces, many fragments, appear while I listen, and suddenly, there are ruptures that zoom on a given sentence. What's new is that I manage to keep my own voice more effectively within the choir, as if other voices forced me to find my own."[76] Bon believes that "art allows access to the conscience of things," in a world "that would find again the meaning of History, where adventure would still be possible."[77]

Brocq too believes in the therapeutic power of literature: "a book like *Don Quixote* only comes to humanity every few centuries," says Céline to Brocq during their captivity (37). Reading Cervantes, like Rabelais, implies that one must "seek through language, sentence and story, what's inside our own darkness, and go where you are under duress, think in that danger, write in that danger, in the common obligation of building knowledge and telling stories, and the need to do so with humility, because there we touch the border with what's outside language, where language was born" (*Le crime* 12). Affirming the prevalence of a common house of language over an agonistic conception of intertextuality, Bon speaks of a "relay" (passage de relais),[78] a testimonial transference between one speaker and another, each the witness of her or his predecessor. Filiation (not affiliation) plays an important role here, and Bon's filiation stretches out like an intertextual arborescence that includes the Apollinaire of *Zone*, the Rabelais of the *Quart Livre*, the Thomas Bernard of *La cave*, the Claude Simon of *Les Géorgiques*, as well as the Faulkner of *Wild Palms*. With them he seeks to "share for an instant the old communal night" (*Calvaire* 65), sharing with others like Hoffmann, Nerval, and Kafka "a taste for somber writings" (77).

In 1533, 1535, and 1547 Rabelais made a somber prognosis regarding the chaotic state of things. In those years, comments Belleforest, "a strange storm comes over France."[79] A devastating war breaks out between François I and Charles V; the Société de Jésus and the Holy Inquisition are born; and the party of "the Hydra that hurls perversities into our world" (l'Hydre des perversitez ruées de notre temps), that is, Luther, comes under increasing threat from the Catholics, while those who refuse to abide by papal rule are simply and expeditiously condemned to the stake. Eventually the Sorbonne censors *Pantagruel*, *Gargantua*, and the *Quart livre* for obscenity and condemns Rabelais, while Copernicus, and later Galileo, meet with persecution for saying that the earth revolves around the sun.[80] In the face of such chaos—"for the world is in such chaos" (*Décor ciment* 150)—Rabelais elects to systematically explore "incoherence and madness" (*La folie Rabelais* jacket notes).

Dead Center

Almost five centuries later Bon's prognostications are equally sobering. The world is a building rotten from the inside, on the edge of collapse; "under the concrete sets, the nerve sickens," says the narrator of *Décor ciment* (105), warning that "we live in a rotten tooth: hard around the edges, but eaten away inside" (105).[81] There is in Bon's novels the notion that we have reached the end of a cycle, of a "dying world" (144–45). In an oneiric scene of *Sortie d'usine*, placed between the narrator's departure from the factory and his "return" as a writer, the narrator attempts to look at the space of his death by entering his own grave.[82] This act, far from betraying any sort of self-necrophilic desire, serves to display a liminal presence in Bon's chronotope, that of "death that shadows us all" (*Le solitaire* 12).

All of Bon's novels revolve in fact around the idea—and the very physical body—of death. Often a murder or a suicide serves to set the narrative in motion. "It is through the memory of the young dead that the city unfolds before us," confirms the narrator of *C'était toute une vie*, for "what's at stake here, in the small city, is more than just a fragment of the world, but all of the world's tensions brought together" (jacket notes). Thus the very absence of the young woman allows for a coalescing of various heterotopic elements into the body of one text, while she becomes the strange attractor around which the destinies of all the characters revolve, intersecting in crisscrossing patterns.[83] Likewise the murder of Raymond Crapin constitutes the initial moment in the fabula of *Décor ciment*, whereas the action of *Un fait divers* revolves around the "presence" of the crime victim. For the narrator of *C'était toute une vie* "it's the death of the city and its human bodies that commands the words" (94).

In *Prison* it is the equally immaterial figure of a vagrant called Brulin that gives the text its balance. From the incipit we learn that the man in question has been stabbed, "planté," in the words of the warden who informs François Bon of Brulin's demise: "Did you know Brulin was stabbed?" Brulin has been "planté," that is, "killed," but also, symbolically, planted, inscribed forever in the urban scenery that composes the text. The man without a home, the man who had just left the prison system, has become that anchor, that strange attractor, that physical and semantic place around which the text now begins to deploy.

Around the death of Brulin the texts of the other inmates begin to form a polyphonic whole, which the narrative weaves together like voices in a chorus. The death of Brulin remains a taboo subject within the workshop: the inmates do not write about Brulin's death. Instead they are asked to write about other subjects: facing rejection, traveling, describing a house. All these topics seem at first to be culled from Creative Writing 101, yet they all aim to establish a genealogy of the inmates' *lieux de mémoire* against the loss of that memory. What is being attempted here is nothing less than the reconstruction of a social and semantic tapestry from its thinnest thread and least significant marker.

In the shadow of the city a listener, sometimes several, gath-

ers and modestly inherits stories, confronting "the world through
its obscure part,"[84] for the place of gathering remains under "the
constant threat of the flagstone that would crumble away, and as
you stand on it, topple into the abyss" (*Limite* 104). Heirs to Rimbaud, poets become fire thieves ("des voleurs de feu"),[85] handling
language like "a burning mass that you shape" (24), chipping
away "the block of basalt, . . . the dark world" (103), sharpening
the fuzzy and "obscure part of language" (*La folie Rabelais* 42).

7. Vague Becomings

Strategies of Fuzziness in
Twenty-first-Century Fiction (Conclusion)

> Not belonging to any place, any time, any love. A lost
> origin, the impossibility to take roots, a rummaging
> memory, the present in abeyance. The space of the for-
> eigner is a moving train, a plane in flight, and the very
> transition that precludes stopping. As to landmarks,
> there are none. His time? The time of a resurrection that
> remembers death and what happened before, but misses
> the glory of being beyond: merely the feeling of a re-
> prieve, of having gotten away.
>
> Julia Kristeva, *Strangers to Ourselves*

On 2 November 2004 President George W. Bush won his bid for
presidential reelection after a campaign that catered to reactionary notions of fear, paranoia, and xenophobia, sprinkled with a
hefty dose of French bashing. In a world beset with ever more
changing or vanishing borders, at a loss for moral and ideological
certainties, Bush offered a return to a golden age (circa the 1950s)
fueled by nostalgia for simpler moral values, for a Christian utopia where social and sexual hierarchies would be set, inflexible,

nonthreatening to the conservative base. A few months earlier the French far-right Front National had made a shocking appearance of its own in the second round of France's presidential elections; if the political platform of the National Front catered less directly to conventional evangelical beliefs than did the Bush platform, its almost panicked fear of (ethnic and religious) hexogeneity was no less pronounced, appealing to the same social anxieties before an uncertain future. In short, the National Front and the neoconservative wing of the Republican Party shared the same broad refusal of variability and change; for that reason they offered the same unmitigated support for traditionalist values.

Undoubtedly much of this reactionary reflux resulted from insecurity brought about by recent and far-reaching sociopolitical developments, such as the emergence of the European Union, the war in Iraq, and the conflict in the Middle East, but also, and perhaps more deeply, by previous fractures that heralded the end of the modern period (Indochina, Algeria, Vietnam). Indeed, three decades before the fall of the Berlin Wall, and the beginning of the War (or crusade) on Terror, a political commentator on the Vietnam War had this to say about the disquieting fuzziness of America's future political landscape: "Now America finds itself entangled in a conflict that does look suspiciously like an open-ended war for *vague* or shifting strategic aims on behalf of an ungrateful, if not incomprehensible people."[1] In light of such disquieting "vagueness," the moral clarity of World Wars I and II may have looked to the commentator like a lost Shangri-La, or, for today's neoconservatives, like a Jerusalem occupied by left-leaning infidels.

If for traditionalists (but also liberals) political discourse aims primarily to counter such vagueness, introduce order in a chaotic environment, and therefore forego the sort of quagmire mentality that has haunted much of American and French politics since the 1960s, the task of literature, especially literature with a strong formal bent, appears decidedly different. Rather than subsuming the multiple, the unknown, into a totalizing discourse, fiction (and most notably the novel—that most gargantuan of genres, according to Bakhtin) aims to incorporate vagueness into a larger aesthetic project, making it the very force that drives the narrative onward, replacing the orthogenetic drive best embodied by the Balzacian novel with the fuzzy interlacing that today's novel inherited from John Dos Passos's *Manhattan Transfer*.

This has put many contemporary fiction writers at loggerheads with their political counterparts and should reassure all those who have prognosticated, a little early perhaps, the end of the avant-garde and the final decline of French fiction. To wit, Luc Lang's complex and modulated reading of the tragedy of September 11 in *11 septembre mon amour* casts itself as the opposite of the to-talizing and totalitarian efficiency of the political response to the same event. While Lang, on September 12, started attempting to account for the symbolic impact of the terrorist acts of the previous day, linking the heartrending massacre of the Twin Towers to the catastrophes of Hiroshima and Nagasaki, the U.S. media (soon followed by the world press) did not hesitate to mention "Pearl Harbor." In doing so the Bush government conveniently eschewed the moral ambiguity of the nuclear attacks on Japan (and their grave social consequences), replacing it with a historical precedent that laid the groundwork for the "just wars" the United States was about to embark upon in Afghanistan and Iraq. (It is no surprise that the word *crusade* began popping up in official speeches early in the Afghan campaign, before Arab American organiza-tions started complaining about the ideological implications of the term.) From one media spin to the next, and in spite of its varied reincarnations (from "weapons of mass destruction" to the old standard "let freedom ring"), the government's doctrine on the War on Terror displayed an amazing and absolute narrative con-sistency.

Standing at the other end of the narrative spectrum, a writer like Patrick Deville, in his novel *Longue vue*, aims to drive home the point that fiction ought to privilege vagueness (not certainty) as a formal imperative, going on to construct a narrative in which

knowledge and observation, knowing and seeing, find themselves
contested at each turn. In doing so Deville invokes some of the
most iconic figures of the post-Newtonian world, none of whom
is likely to make an appearance in today's political speeches.
Among these founding fathers of uncertainty one finds Bohr and
Schrödinger and, last but not least, Heisenberg, who developed
the now famous "uncertainty principle," which states that it is
impossible to measure the position and momentum of a particle
with more than limited precision, insofar as the observer will always affect the conditions (and results) of the observation. Even
though the uncertainty principle only concerns the infinitely small,
and has little bearing on phenomena that can be observed with the
naked eye, the notion that there can be (at the microscopic level)
no absolute difference between the observer and the observed, that
the world does not exist independent of the observer's gaze, has
significant consequences.

What we observe, found Heisenberg, can never be totally "true,"
nor can it exist separately from us. Our knowledge of reality is not
infinite, for there always is uncertainty, an inherent randomness,
in nature. Zola claimed he could write the truth (or its abstraction,
drawn from social archetypes); Robbe-Grillet countered that no
one could write the truth, that we were all separated from others,
"disjecta membra" or disconnected entities.[2] So, in what is perhaps
the most significant development of the past twenty to thirty years,
contemporary writers have made peace with the fact that there
can only be some degree of truth, that truth is inherently fuzzy,
and that comprehensiveness (total knowledge) and nihilism (the
absence of knowledge) necessarily mark the two opposite ends of
the poet's world-view.

The presence of Heisenberg in Deville's text signals a shift that
not only affects narrative certainty in the field of the novel but,
more largely, emphasizes the loss of determinism as the basis for
the certainties that make up our collective cultural dogmas, our
Zeitgeist. Unlike President Bush, Skoltz, the protagonist of *Longue-*
vue, does not assume that he can, or ever will, see the whole pic-

ture and base his actions or opinions on absolute epistemological certainty. For him no mission is ever fully accomplished, no goal ever entirely fulfilled, no paradise reached. Rather, Skoltz's inability to take the whole world in, his shortsightedness and constant hesitations—"I don't know," he blandly admits—only emphasize the needlessness of determinism as social praxis and modus operandus. In Deville's fuzzy world no one ever has the "full picture"; no one is ever entirely objective; but, most significantly, no one ever feels the need to be.

For the main three characters of Deville's novel—Skoltz, Jill (the woman he loves), and her father (Körberg)—observing, like narrating, remains at best a dubious proposition, both frustrating and inadequate. As a consequence in *Longue-vue* characters live on, partially unaware of each other's origins and intentions, but—and this is a key point that Deville makes over and over again—this unawareness (to some degree) does not preclude the story from unfolding. Indeed, quite the opposite is true. Skoltz may not know who Jill's parents are, while Jill may have no prior knowledge of her own father, Körberg, who in turn comes into the story perfectly unaware of his daughter's existence; Körberg and Skoltz (the father and the potential son-in-law) are indeed supremely oblivious of each other's roles in this comedy of errors. And yet the world still goes on, and so does the story. For the characters, as well as the readers, the action in *Longue-vue* may well be driven by ignorance, misconception, and misapprehension, but narratologically speaking *Longue-vue* still functions as a novel, and a story still is told, one that has a beginning, a middle, and an end, no matter how fuzzy or undecidable.

A cursory glance at contemporary fiction will suffice to demonstrate that, like Patrick Deville, many contemporary writers have chosen the long view in this matter: that it is only "through" the use of uncertainty and fuzziness as narrative devices that today's writers may come to terms with the challenges of an uncertain world. For his part, in *Les ombres errantes* Pascal Quignard assures us that "*irresolution* is a more profound possibility than freedom, and hazard is a more ingenious disposition than tactics."[3] Of course Quignard may be quite disingenuous here in opposing ir-resolution and freedom, for it is irresolution that provides the very basis for the freedom that he claims, and it is the use of fuzziness as a narrative device that allows him to take account of imprecision. Like many of his peers, Quignard has come around to underscor-ing the crucial need the author has to present life as an ongoing and only partially comprehensible process, as an inherently vague environment, the uncertainty compounded by the ambiguity of language and perception: "Lying, metamorphosis, fight endlessly against the real, against the state of things, against the trading of men, animals, objects, against the commandments of language and the tyranny of set roles in the performance of groups."[4] For some this may sound like a simple reshuffling of some of the categories that entered into elaboration of the term *postmodernism*. For me, however, *postmodernism* has become increasingly irrelevant, in part because its attachment to *modernism* makes it a lame-duck concept, and because the question of whether fiction after Robbe-Grillet should fall into a late modernist phase or exist as a *sui generis* category ultimately yields little insight into contemporary works. No present-day reader would overlook the influence that the literature of the modern era has had on today's literary pro-duction, but it might be more fruitful to focus on what distin-guishes today's literary works from yesterday's—namely the need for today's fiction to engage uncertainty as the dominant cultural paradigm and replace the closed ontological rigidity of the Cold War with the open-ended deterministic plausibility of the postin-dustrial age.

In her work on contemporary Francophone fiction Lydie Moudileno argues that a new identity has emerged for the post-colonial subject, that of the "sans-papier" (literally the "undocu-mented worker"—a concept that appeared in France after 1986 and the Pasqua anti-immigration laws).[5] The *sans-papier* does not have the benefit of any nationality, Moudileno says, nor can he freely cross borders. His status is undecidable, since he not only finds himself excluded from his country of origin but can only remain in his host country as long as he does not reveal what his land of origin is. (This is different from the situation of the "Creole," whose hybrid status gives him the ability to exist in more than one environment.) The *sans-papier*'s identity is therefore transitory, as he finds himself physically as well as psychologically in transit. But one may argue that the transient nature of being, for a subject who is permanently in transit and undefined, is a staple of contemporary French fiction as well, and, beyond French fiction, seems to be a dominant paradigm of identity in contemporary Western art.

The protagonist of today's novels is, by and large, a fuzzy subject, caught between presence and absence, never fully realized but always already there, and, for all we can see, he or she seems pretty content with being so. In this fuzzy world names and identities may be freely exchanged, and traded, for undefined periods of time, as characters hopscotch among incarnations, allowing the story to jump from one nodal point to another, in a manner that is reminiscent of baroque narrativity. In the following extract from Christian Oster's *Les rendez-vous* the narrator goes to pick up his mail. As he arrives at the mailbox, he notices that he hasn't replaced the name of the previous tenant yet: "I noted in passing that I had not put my name down on the small, apportioned slot, and that my name still read Truong, even though I live there now. In truth, it didn't bother me that much to have somebody else's name, and if I had wanted to smile, I would have said I found it amusing, but let's not exaggerate, I didn't find it amusing, let's say I didn't mind."[6] The narrator's impassivity with regards to selfhood and identity should not be mistaken for indifference. And the seemingly offhand manner in which he adopts, for the time being, some stranger's name should not be assumed mere intellectual laziness (even though that may have something to do with it). For what the narrator offers us here is nothing less than a quirky yet strangely relevant example of a "vague predicate." A vague predicate, says Richard Rorty, is something like the paradox of the heap: "If one has something that is not a heap of sand, and one adds a single grain to it, the result is still not a heap of sand."⁷ What then is in a heap of sand, or in a name, or in a rose, for that matter? How many grains? How many semes? How many petals? In the case of Christian Oster's protagonist, the narrator is and is not Truong, just as he may well be Paul, Pierre or Jacques, Smith or Brown, without deciding to ever settle on a definite identity, always in transit, never fully realized.

What may matter more then is not so much what's in a character's name, or what's in the heap of sand, but rather only that an ecology of vagueness will allow us to exist within vague borders. In her novel *Anchise* (winner of the 1999 Prix Fémina) Maryline Desbiolles makes an analogous point, soberly reassessing some of our most basic environmental beliefs through the sieve of ambiguity: "On the radio, you hear that 80 percent of people live in the cities. Where do the remaining 20 percent live? In the country, you think straight away. But where does the country begin? A lot of grass with trees? Gardens? Cultivated fields?"⁸ For a French writer to wonder where the country begins, or what it actually is, may seem like something of a revolution four centuries after Sully established, once and forever, that France is an agricultural country. (Sully's maxim is well known: "Tilling the soil and pasturage are the two breasts of France" [Le labourage et le pâturage sont les deux mamelles de la France].) Yet if one is to believe Rorty's quip, nowadays "vagueness is huge," and one hundred years after communism, a new specter has begun haunting Europe (and the world). This new specter has effectively crept into most fields of knowledge, from mathematics to logic, from philosophy to economy, from literature to robotics, and interchangeably goes by the name of "fuzziness" or "vagueness." For Desbiolles, we may not know where we live any longer, in the city or in the country, or somewhere in between; we may not know who we are, or are not, or whom we've loved, or not. But such uncertainty should not be endured as a loss. Instead being, like remembering, should be experienced as "the triumph of unlimited variance on the finite horizon of theme," to quote from Yann Apperry, who, like Desbiolles, aims to show how our sense of self, and memory, is affected by the fuzziness of our lives, and how vagueness, in turn, affects memory (and quiddity):

> *I tried to recall Adriana's face, but my memory kept on conjuring the image of her breast, which she had let me see the day before I left. As for her face, it became Anna Lisa's, like the profile of a saint in one of the church's stained-glass windows. I consoled myself with the thought that a memory is only ever a set of variations on a lost melody, and that the* Art of the Fugue *may have only been, for Bach, the occasion to recall the traits of a woman he loved, and I wondered if his impending blindness . . . was not the ultimate scoring through, the triumph of unlimited variance on the finite horizon of the theme.*[9]

Alina Reyes makes much the same point in *Nus devant les fantômes*, a novel that recounts the epistolary exchange between Franz Kafka and his Czech translator (Milena Jesenská). As the dark narrative unfolds, weaving the conflicted love story of Kafka and Milena into the larger tapestry of World War II and the Final Solution, Kafka's initialized protagonist (K), the poster child of modernity, becomes the anchor, or strange attractor, around which the madness and devastation of the war come to revolve:

> *People's names infinitely reflect themselves in a series of mirrors, and each reflection is susceptible to variation, and deformation. . . . Your grandfather Jakob was a poor Czech butcher; your father was a crooked businessman, also speaking Czech. . . . And you inherited a German first name, to facilitate your inclusion in Prague's good society. . . . A first name to honor the Emperor Franz-Joseph, to finish things off nicely. . . . Of course, behind it your Hebrew name was hiding, Amschel (which is also Adam), like a tongue hiding another, an identity hiding*

another. . . . There's always a name behind a name, and
surely another still. . . . An army of ghost names hiding
in the roots of self. . . . And when none are left, there
still is the initial . . . K. . . . Or even nothing at all, just a
vermin hiding under the old man's bed.[10]

What Alina Reyes builds in this broken-down, fragmented sentence is nothing less than a sorites paradox: if you take a name
off an individual's genealogy, is genealogy still the measure of that
individual's life? What about two names? And how many names
may you take off before that individual's life becomes undone? Ultimately, Reyes assures us, there is always already something at the
core, even when nothing is left, like an initial, K in this case, and
a pregnant one at that, from which the modern novel will emerge
and spin out. In the end what makes a difference is the infinite
plausibility that a name exists, its constant variability and enduring hope for existence, even in the shadow of the Final Solution.

   In this sense the embrace of fuzziness as a loose structuring force
by contemporary writers lays to rest, for the time being, Adorno's
claim that literature has become impossible, along with the West's
legacy of positivity. In Reyes's novel what K has become is not so
much an echo of Robert Musil's everyman, a man without qualities, but instead a man of potentially all qualities, who may always be someone else, a vague paradigm of humanity. Seen in this
dim light, humanity, much ballyhooed and put under the threat
of erasure during the horrors of the past century, makes a striking comeback. In order to bring the point home let's take a last
look at one of today's most nihilistic prose writers, Hélène Lenoir.
Her 2001 family tragedy, *Le magot de Momm*, tells of the chal-
lenging life of what looks like a dysfunctional family, a Beckettian
gynocracy composed of a mother (Momm), her daughter (Nann),
and her three granddaughters (Lilli and the twins), as the middle
woman, Nann, tries and fails to meet her mother's and her children's expectations. Pulled between opposing forces, torn between
the needs of diverse generations and her own needs, Nann fails to

settle into one particular role, becoming, in Momm's words, an in-between: "You are neither flesh nor fish, neither mother nor daughter, in-between, twisting in lukewarm water, responsible for everything and nothing, missing, elsewhere, eternally elsewhere, you float, you glide, you are the last person I can depend on . . . !"[11] At this point readers may rightfully assume that Nann's life is that of a desperate housewife, albeit slightly less romanticized than the hit TV show of the same name, and that Nann has ultimately little hope of escaping being pilloried for her failures as a mother and daughter. And yet applying a fuzzy paradigm to the situation might radically reverse its terms. For Nann is, in the words of her own mother, neither mother nor daughter, that is, neither the full incarnation of one or the other, but she is something in between, the potential subset of all motherly and daughterly qualities she was blamed for missing in the first place. As such she never settles down, is always in motion. In the end Nann is the epitome of a fuzzy subject, floating, gliding between identities; she "is" the last person one may count on, for she is always true to herself, since her truth can assume a continuum of values between 0 and 1. In this era of uncertainty one should be so lucky.

Notes

1. Etat des lieux

1. Lebrun, "Une unité romanesque" 129.
2. Domenach.
3. Nadeau, "L'état des lieux" 3 (unless otherwise noted, all translations are mine).
4. Michon, "D'abord" 18.
5. François Rosset 9.
6. Bourdieu, *Sur la télévision* 67, 72.
7. Toussaint, *La télévision* 14, 10–11.
8. Bourgeade 9.
9. Heise 67.
10. Otchakovsky-Laurens 36.
11. For an overview of late movements and schools in French literature see Magazine Littéraire's special issue on "La relève des avant-gardes," *Magazine Littéraire* 392.
12. Gracq, "La littérature à l'estomac," in *Préférences*. The expression *littérature dégagée* was first coined in the preface to *Le phénomène*, by Robert Mathy, published by Minuit in 1948.
13. Brunel 206.
14. Porush 300–301. Commenting on the state of French literature after the avant-garde, Mark Alizart argues that "literature is no longer imagined as a prophetic 'elsewhere' but as a sensitive surface, as the world's skin, or a panoply of discourses that the avant-garde had kept away from literature, because it wanted no dealings with the language of the commonplace or with the "fascist" tongue of power" (23).

15. Barth, *Further Fridays* 120.
16. See James; Barthes, "L'effet de réel," in Barthes et al., *Littérature* 81–90.
17. Brooks, *Reading* 4.
18. Blanckeman, *Les récits* 15, 17.
19. Fauconnier 64.
20. Roudiez 315.
21. See Safir 3.
22. See Hayles, *Chaos Bound* 265–85.
23. See Knee 312; Ollier 99.
24. Kosko, "Innerview" 2.
25. Kosko, *Fuzzy Thinking* 292.
26. Tye 215.
27. See Chambers, "Etcetera Principle" 3.
28. Blanckeman, *Les récits* 13.
29. Milliex 77.
30. Salvayre 173.
31. Pinget 17.
32. Volodine, *Le port* 38.
33. Bon, *Décor ciment* 144–45.
34. See Miraux 11.
35. Kacem 8.
36. Chevillard, *Palafox* (back cover).
37. Bon, *Sortie d'usine* 19.
38. The impassive protagonists of Toussaint have spawned many avatars in today's literary production, especially the works of Jean-Claude Chanod, Hélène Lenoir, Jean Echenoz, Emmanuel Adely, and Marie NDiaye.
39. Balzac, *Unknown Masterpiece* 22; *Le chef d'oeuvre* 55.
40. See Vullierme 91; Morin and Kern 69.
41. Butor, qtd. in Brunel 69.
42. Bon, *C'était toute une vie* 16; *Décor ciment* 157.
43. Bon, *Décor ciment* 26; "Ecriture" 2.
44. Laurrent, *Liquider* 31, 188.
45. Vonnegut, *Timequake* xi.
46. Rushdie 264; Joyce 45.
47. Chevillard, *Crab Nebula* 1.
48. Joyce 47.
49. Kuberski 5.
50. See Baudrillard, *L'échange*.

2. Jean-Philippe Toussaint

1. See the new works of Jean-Claude Chanod, Hélène Lenoir, and Emmanuel Adely—all published by Minuit—who seem to espouse a significant part of the literary techniques and the impassive tone of Toussaint and Echenoz.

2. The novel that sold the most was Jean Rouaud's *Les champs d'honneur*, which sold six hundred thousand copies and won a Prix Goncourt.

3. Bon, "Un livre" 6.

4. Rosemary Jackson defines *paraxis* in the following terms: "Paraxis is a telling notion in relation to the place, or space, of the fantastic, for it implies an inextricable link to the main body of the 'real' which it shades and threatens. The term paraxis is also a technical one employed in optics. A paraxial region in which light rays *seem* to unite at a point after refraction. In this area, object and image seem to collide, but in fact neither object nor reconstituted image genuinely reside there: nothing does." See Jackson 19.

5. Toussaint, *Making Love* 5. Subsequent references to Coverdale's translation will appear in the text. Subsequent references to the following Toussaint works will also appear in the text: *L'appareil-photo*; *The Bathroom* (Amphoux and De Angelis's translation); *Monsieur* (Lambert's translation); *La réticence*; and *La télévision*.

6. See Meyer Spacks 256.

7. Meyer Spacks 250.

8. See Lipovetsky 9, 13.

9. See Motte, "Clinamen Redux."

10. Baudrillard, *L'echange* 187.

11. Note the switch from *passé composé* to *imparfait*, as the initial action becomes its iterative reduplication.

12. This is in English in the text.

13. Centrale is France's top engineering school, a member of the French Ivy League ("Grandes Ecoles"). The pun plays on the fact that Monsieur is both knowledgeable and poised.

14. Patrick Roegiers's first novel, *Beau regard*, formulates a similar interrogation of the arbitrariness of the gaze and of the imperative need to look. In *Beau regard* narrating is almost exclusively construed as gazing (gazing as the recording and frame-freezing of events in space and in time).

15. Various neologisms have been created to come to terms with this dissolution of univocality in fiction and other types of discourse. British

New Wave practitioner Michael Moorcock speaks of "multiverse," and Stanislaw Lem of "chaosmos" or "chaosphere."

16. Bal 80.

17. Both are characters in Balzac's *Père Goriot*, Rastignac the young, impoverished, up-and-coming aristocrat who will eventually overcome his naiveté and candor to win over a corrupt Parisian milieu, Vautrin a nefarious father figure and escaped convict who will teach Rastignac how to make his way in the world.

18. Bertho, "Jean-Phillipe Toussaint" 18.

19. Brooks, *Reading* 4, 314, 316.

20. Pascal, *Pensées* 66; *Les pensées* 93.

21. In *La réticence* the aleatory does not so much operate at the level of the story, which follows the traditional pattern of the thriller (enigma, search for a solution, discovery of the solution), although Toussaint does give us a parody of this model. Rather, the aleatory resides in that initial moment of reticence (why does the narrator hesitate to go and visit Biaggi?) that triggers in turn a series of reticences, which constitute the whole of the text.

22. Brooks, *Reading* 316.

23. Hayles, *Chaos Bound* 11.

24. Gleick 55.

25. Eric White, "Negentropy" 263.

26. For Toussaint the concept of clinamen is necessarily a critical one. The unpredictability that the clinamen presupposes allows the related concept of entropy to subvert the dominant paradigms of determinist thought. Whether chaos is seen as anarchy (in the traditional Western philosophical perspective) or as stochastic self-organization (in Chaotics), chaos allows chance to become a central figure, although a decentered one, and to invalidate the main orientations of traditional linear and realist narratives. Already, with the invention of pataphysics, Alfred Jarry was trying to articulate a science of chance by drawing up the laws governing exceptions. The presence of clinamen in a system (physical or fictional) goes beyond simply positing the presence of the aleatory along with the necessary; it not only modifies determinist thinking but in fact completely rejects its premises.

27. Motte, "Clinamen Redux" 263.

28. According to narratologists (Gerald Prince, Mieke Bal), time is the primary modus operandi of narratives. It is the representation of real or fictive events in a time sequence. However, in *The Bathroom* the time sequence never reaches its logical—and eschatological—conclusion: expenditure of energy, and textuality.

29. The fact that the figures do not add up in *The Bathroom*—that is to say that the second part multiplied by itself is not equal in length to the sum of the square of the other two parts—is not paradoxical or contradictory. One must not read Pythagoras's theorem literally, but symbolically. The overall narrative structure is a geometrical figure that is equal to itself and geminates upon itself. It points to the necessity for the narrative to retrace its own tracks to avoid finitude and narrative death.

30. See Leclerc, "Autour."

3. Eric Chevillard

The epigraph to this chapter is also quoted by Balzac as an epigraph to *Physiologie du marriage*. The English translation is from the University of Essex: <http://courses.essex.ac.uk/cs/cs101/boug.htm>.

1. Isidore of Seville, author of *Originum seu etymologiarum libri* (seventh century)—one of the earliest known encyclopedias—chastises comedy as "liber acephalus de stupris virginum et meretricum amoribus" (the demented book of the ignominious loves of virgins and whores) (Eco, *Der Name* 378).

2. See Bakhtin, *Dialogic Imagination* 44–45.

3. Bergson, *Laughter* 3. In *Nus devant les fantômes* Alina Reyes makes a similar point: "Laughter often results from a moment of acute awareness of the real, a moment of extreme sensibility and lucidity. It breaks all the glass walls among which we usually move without noticing them" (125).

4. *Humor* and *ludism* are cognates, but they are not synonyms. *Humor* refers to comedy, to the art of making one laugh. *Ludism* refers to the game, and Huizinga and Caillois have shown that games can be played in deadly earnest.

5. Among the most notable new humorists one can identify Minuit novelists Jean-Philippe Toussaint, Eric Laurrent, Philippe Raulet, Patrick Deville, Jean Echenoz, Jean Rouaud, and Christian Oster, and non-Minuit writers like the very "Pataphysician" Jacques Jouet, David McNeil, Marie Darrieussecq, Daniel Pennac, and Didier Daeninckx.

6. In Jameson's Marxist perspective, postmodern fiction, which has seen a substantial development of pastiche and nostalgia, both pertaining to the generic category of humor, commits the deadly sin of allowing indecisiveness and a lack of engagement. I believe, however, that such a critique misses the subversive nature of humor's indecisiveness. See Jameson, *Postmodernism* 16–19, 133–34.

7. I follow Eugenio d'Ors's definition of the baroque as an aesthetic category, "a sort of creative pulsing that comes back, cyclically, throughout history, across artistic manifestations." See Alejo Carpentier 27–31.

8. Chevillard, *Mourir m'enrhume* 7. Subsequent references will appear in the text. Subsequent references to the following Chevillard works will also appear in the text: *Les absences du Capitaine Cook*; *Le caoutchouc décidément*; *The Crab Nebula* (Stump and Hardin's translation); *Le démarcheur*; *Du hérisson*; *Un fantôme*; *L'oeuvre posthume de Thomas Pilaster*; *On the Ceiling* (Stump's translation); *Palafox* (Mason's translation); *Préhistoire*; and "Trois tentatives pour réintroduire le tigre mangeur d'homme en Lot-Et-Garonne."

9. See Rousset 68.

10. Stendhal 57.

11. These writers include Toussaint, Deville, Oster, Echenoz, Laurrent, and Gailly.

12. Bergson, *Laughter* 4.

13. Alain Minc speaks of the postcommunist world as "the era of vagueness" (l'ère du flou) (13). He analyzes contemporary society in these terms: "erasure of legitimate order, apparition of vague and aleatory structures, triumph of the spontaneous, there are multiple assonances" (10). Likewise Edgar Morin argues that in today's postmodern world "to know or to think doesn't consist in building systems with undoubted bases; it's a dialogue with uncertainty" ("Edgar Morin, philosophe de l'incertain" 18).

14. Jean-Marie Gleize sums up the task of today's poets in these terms: "All must disappear. All, from A to Z. The noise of fire burning continuously. The torching of the great dictionary. The exhausting work of poetry (history, philosophy, everything should die)" (back page). Probing the *Zeitgeist*, another intellectual anarchist, Abel, the protagonist of Raphaël Confiant's *Bassin des ouragans*, elects to create the Association Internationale pour l'Euthanasie Intellectuelle (International Association for Intellectual Euthanasia), which would ruthlessly eradicate such bestsellers as the Bible, the Torah, and the Koran for crimes against humanity (12).

15. See Serres, *Hermes* 100.

16. Michaux develops a similar argument to elucidate history: "I saw the times, the bad tumultuous times agitated by the hormones of hatred and the yearning for domination, the times that were destined for fame, for History, which would paint itself with our misery; and it was still him (man), still banging on the same nail." See "Ecce homo" (1945), in *L'espace* 280.

17. On "orthogenesis" see Lesourne 29.

18. See Brooks, *Reading* 6–7.

19. On Flaubert's realism see Watt 39.

20. See Diderot and d'Alembert xii.

21. On "epistemophilia" see Brooks, *Body Work* 212.

22. See Aristotle.

23. By counting the number of internal tissue layers within a tree, one can discern its age. Common sense tells us that the conclusion of any intricate problem always leads to *l'âge du capitaine*.

24. See Braque 34.

25. Chevillard, *45° Nord* 80.

26. Paulson 41.

27. We find Mr. Théo in *Mourir m'enrhume*, Monge in *Le démarcheur*, Palafox in *Palafox*, Furne in *Le caoutchouc décidément*, Thomas Pilaster in *L'oeuvre posthume de Thomas Pilaster*, and Crab in *The Crab Nebula* and *Un fantôme*. The narrators of *Préhistoire*, *On the Ceiling*, and *Du hérisson* are homodiegetic and nameless.

28. "Trois tentatives pour réintroduire le tigre mangeur d'homme en Lot-et-Garonne" was later republished in *L'oeuvre posthume de Thomas Pilaster*.

29. Diderot, *Lettre* 407.

30. See Hayles, *Chaos and Order*.

31. The maxim "mens agitat molem" comes from Virgil's *Aeneid*, VI.727.

32. See Copens esp. 125.

33. The Sanskrit word for *war* means in fact "desire for more cows."

34. See Bakhtin, *Rabelais* 32.

35. See Bakhtin, *Dialogic Imagination* 111–12.

36. See Diderot, *Le neveu de Rameau*.

37. In *Galapagos* Kurt Vonnegut explores the same theme, relating the evolution of a group of tourists stranded in the Galapagos after a virus has annihilated the entire human race. In order to survive the remaining humans learn to devolve into a hybrid species, half human, half seal.

38. On "uchronia" see Emmanuel Carrère. Uchronia is the historical counterpart to utopia. French philosopher Charles Renouvier coined the term in 1876, three centuries after the invention of "utopia" by Sir Thomas More. If utopia is "a place that does not exist," uchronia is "a time that never occurred."

39. See Eric White, "Negentropy" 267.

40. Brooks, *Body Work* 218.

41. Blake 64.

42. See Kristeva, *Powers*.

43. Shakespeare drew upon the concept of the "teatrum mundi," one of the bases of humanist and religious thought at the end of the Renaissance, of which Calderón's *El gran teatro del mundo* is a good example. The line I quote appears in *As You Like It* (II.vii.139, 143–46): "All the world's a stage, / And all the men and women merely players. / They have their exits and their entrances, / And one man in his time plays many parts."

44. A remarkably similar sentiment is echoed in *Macbeth* (V.v.26, 22–31): "To-morrow, and to-morrow, and to-morrow, / Creeps in this petty pace from day to day, / To the last syllable of recorded time; / And all our yesterdays have lighted fools / The way to dusky death. Out, out, brief candle! / Life's but a walking shadow, a poor player, / That struts and frets his hour upon the stage, / And then is heard no more. It is a tale / Told by and idiot, full of sound and fury / Signifying nothing."

45. Morin and Kern 69.

46. Likewise Crab's animal heteronym, Palafox, remains "out of reach" (*Palafox* 46) (hors de portée [61]).

47. On "fuzziness" see Kosko, *Fuzzy Thinking*.

48. While sitting by the fireplace, Descartes is holding a beeswax plug, which in time melts down and dissolves. Probing the plug, Descartes wonders what makes it what it is and where the border lies between the thing and the nonthing (Kosko, *Fuzzy Thinking* 4).

49. Chevillard has stated in several interviews that the character of Crab is central to his oeuvre and that he comes back to it the most frequently.

50. See Kosko's subscthood theory (*Fuzzy Thinking* 55–64).

51. Fauconnier 64.

52. See Brooks, *Reading* 313.

53. William Gibson's electronic poem *Agrippa* was the first to tackle the issue of the impermanence of the work of art. A real page burner, *Agrippa* comes on a disk, each page self-destructing after it has been read.

54. I believe that Chevillard's seventh novel, *Un fantôme*, was written before *Préhistoire*—his sixth—as it is much closer in style and thematics to *The Crab Nebula*, his fifth. *Préhistoire* presents significant changes in tone, narrative structure, and stylistic choices, even though its development clearly germinated in the previous novels.

55. On sequential combinations see Ducrot and Todorov 379.

56. In *Du hérisson* Chevillard cuts up the text into lexias nine to eleven lines long, a physical reminder of the hedgehog's constant interruptions of the author's narrative flow.

57. On the concept of "clinamen" see Serres, *La naissance*; Motte, "Clinamen Redux"; and Bloom.

58. On "inferential walks" see Eco, *Role* 215.

59. Brooks, *Reading* xi.

60. In German *Rückbildung* signifies "decline/decrease" in a medical context, for a tumor or an abscess, for instance.

4. Marie Redonnet

1. See Kuhn 43–51.

2. French novels that have taken to task personal and collective mythologies include Patrick Roegiers's *L'artiste, la servante et le savant*, Annie Ernaux's *Je ne suis pas sortie de ma nuit*, Pierre Michon's *Mythologies d'hiver*, and Jean Rouaud's *Les champs d'honneur*.

3. Leiris 9–24, 30–34.

4. See Stump, "Separation" 106.

5. Redonnet, *Mobie-Diq* 72. Subsequent references will appear in the text. Subsequent references to the following Redonnet works will also appear in the text: *L'accord de paix*; *Candy Story* (Quinn's translation); *Le cirque Pandor*; *Dead Man & Company* (Alter-Gilbert's translation); *Doublures*; *Forever Valley* (Stump's translation); *Hôtel Splendid* (Stump's translation); *Nevermore*; *Seaside*; *Rose Mellie Rose* (Stump's translation); *Silsie*; *Tir & Lir*; and *Villa Rosa*.

6. Blanchot, *Space* 91.

7. I will concentrate on Redonnet's novels, these being her most successful achievements in my view, although I will also refer to the rest of her oeuvre.

8. Beckett, *Fin de partie* 49. An English version is available at <http://www.samuel-beckett.net/endgame.html>.

9. Stump, "Separation" 105–19.

10. Redonnet, letter to the author, 16 May 1994.

11. See Prévost and Lebrun, "Marie Redonnet," in Lebrun and Prévost 193; Barthes, "A Few Words" 1.

12. Redonnet, "Redonne" 160.

13. Motte, "Redonnet's Symmetries" 215.

14. I am referring to Barthes's concept of "lexia"; see *s/z* 20.

15. Redonnet, "Redonne" 161.

16. Redonnet, letter, 16 May 1994.

17. Picard, "Dans le paysage" 235.

18. Redonnet, "Redonne."

19. Redonnet, "Redonne" 162.

20. Went-Daoust 387.

21. See Redonnet, "Redonnet, Marie" 339.

22. Redonnet, personal interview with the author, 27 Jan. 1996; Fallaize 320.

23. See Redonnet, "Redonne."

24. Her last novel, *L'accord de paix*, should be read like a palimpsestic remapping of former geographic and narrative topographies, from the high valley of *Forever Valley*, to the coastal city of *Rose Mellie Rose*, to the departure to the New World in *Silsie*.

25. Went-Daoust 388.

26. Redonnet, letter, 16 May 1994. In her seminar on Jean Genet (Paris III, Institut d'Etudes Théâtrales, 1996–97) Redonnet speaks of "la butée" (the abutment) as a symbolic presence that blocks language and the unconscious.

27. According to Chevalier and Gheerbrant, "the swamp is undifferentiated matter, passive and feminine according to mythology," but also, according to psychoanalysis, "one of the symbols of the unconscious and the mother, the locus of invisible germinations" (611).

28. On the passage from the semiotic to the symbolic see Kristeva, *La révolution*.

29. Redonnet, Redonne" 161.

30. After meeting with his father's ghost and hearing his plea for remembrance, Hamlet replies: "Remember thee? Aye, thou poor ghost, whilst memory holds a seat / In this distracted globe. Remember thee? / Yea, from the table of my memory / I'll wipe away all trivial fond records, / ... And thy commandment all alone shall live / Copied there; within the book and volume of my brain" (*Hamlet* I.5, 100–109).

31. Redonnet, letter, 16 May 1994.

32. "I am not a feminist writer," says Redonnet. "My writing is that of a woman who seeks, beyond the figure of the dead, how to invent a woman's voice" (Redonnet, interview, 27 Jan. 1996).

33. Brémond, "Le mécano" 13; also see "Les bons récompensés."

34. Went-Daoust 392.

35. "With *Candy Story*, Marie Redonnet sought in a way to go from the myth to the novel," Raymond Bellour writes, adding that with *Nevermore* she might be attempting to find "the myth of the novel" (le mythe du roman). See "Le mythe" 89.

36. On "paraxis" see Jackson 19–20.

37. Gusdorf, *Auto-bio-graphie* 480.

38. Miraux 11.

39. On the "subjectivity" of the homodiegetic-autodiegetic narrator see Genette, *Figures III* 36. Also see Zeltner, "Wörter" 212. For all translations from German, I am indebted to Judith Zollinger.

40. Jean-Philippe Miraux explains that autobiographies are autotelic insofar as the object of the narration is the narrator him- or herself (6).

41. Forest et al.

42. Redonnet, letter, 16 May 1994.

43. On the concept of "autofiction," or "writing on the self" (l'écriture sur soi), see Doubrovsky. Also see Marie Redonnet's seminar on Jean Genet (1996–97). Philippe Lejeune argues that autobiographies are rigorously organized around a didactic and dialectic structure that determines the logic of the text. See Lejeune 197–243.

44. Redonnet, letter, 16 May 1994.

45. Redonnet and Françon 121.

46. Redonnet, "Seulement" 54.

47. Redonnet, "Seulement" 48.

48. Motte, "Redonnet's Symmetries" 222.

49. I am alluding to Freud's description of wish fulfillment (*Wunscherfüllung*).

50. Redonnet, interview, 27 Jan. 1996.

51. Koltès, *Koltès*.

52. See Blanchot, "Ecce liber," in "Où va la littérature" 310. The English translation is from *Book* 229.

53. Redonnet, "Seulement" 48. The quote comes from Genet, *Notre-Dame-des-Fleurs*, and refers to the ontological void the young Cullafroi must confront after he throws some consecrated hosts on the ground and the Host fails to materialize and chastise his transgression.

54. Etymologically *chaos* means "abyss, cleft."

55. Redonnet, "Le théâtre."

56. Blanchot, *Book* 238; *Le livre* 324.

57. Corvin 111.

58. Picard, "Dans le paysage" 236.

59. Redonnet, interview, 27 Jan. 1996.

60. On the linearity of tragedy versus the nonlinearity of comedy see Brady, "From Transactional Analysis" 185.

61. Went-Daoust 394.

62. Redonnet, interview, 27 Jan. 1996.

63. Alter-Gilbert 13.

64. Bellour, "Le mythe" 88.

65. A similar episode takes place in *Villa Rosa*, where all the "boarders" of a whorehouse (Chez Lola) share the same name (Lola) and the same anonymity (25).

66. Gobbs and Dora Atter organize the various traffics—prostitution, the trading of favors—around which the economies of San Rosa and Santa Flor revolve.

67. See Picard's concept of matrilinear empowerment ("Dans le paysage" 238) and Fallaize's description of the maternal cave as Edenic (322).

68. Redonnet, letter, 16 May 1994.

69. I will distinguish between my own concept of "thanatophilic" and Michel Serres's concept of "thanatocratic." *Thanatophilia* refers to the use of death as a regenerating force, in aesthetic or metaphysical terms, whereas *thanatocratia* amounts to the totalitarian regimentation of the imaginary. On Serres's concept see Eric White, "Negentropy" 266.

70. See Baudrillard, *L'échange*.

71. Mallarmé, qtd. in Blanchot, *Le livre* 306. Also see *Book* 226.

72. Redonnet, "Seulement" 48.

73. Stump, "Separation" 106.

74. Zeltner, "Wörter" 218.

75. Redonnet, letter, 16 May 1994.

76. Brooks, *Reading* 52.

77. Redonnet, letter, 16 May 1994.

5. Antoine Volodine

1. Volodine, "Image." Henri Michaux described a *champ de bataille* analogous to Volodine's in "Le grand combat" ("The Great Fight"): "He embowerates and enbacks him on the ground. / He rags him and rumpets him up to his drale; / He praggles him and libucks him and berifles his testeries; / He tricards him and morones him, / He grobels him rasp by rip and risp by rap. / Finally he enscorchorizes him" (*Selected Writings* 6). Throughout his texts Volodine makes ample use of neologisms. I will attempt to conserve both his semantic and poetic intentions and effects as I translate them.

2. Briot 7.

3. Volodine, "Justice est fête."

4. See Eco, *Role* 4–5.

5. Volodine, *Le port* 11. Subsequent references will appear in the text.

Subsequent references to the following Volodine works will also appear in the text: *Bardo or not Bardo*; *Biographie comparée de Jorian Murgrave*; *Des enfers fabuleux*; *Dondog*; *Lisbonne, dernière marge*; *Minor Angels* (Stump's translation); *Un navire de nulle part*; *Naming the Jungle* (Coverdale's translation); and *Rituel du mépris*.

6. On the concept of "referential walk" see Eco, *Role* 215–16.

7. Bal 85.

8. Lucien Dällenbach defines *mise-en-abyme* in the following terms: "The term *mise-en-abyme* includes distinct realities, which boil down to three essential figures, which are: simple reduplication (where the fragment is similar to the work that includes it); infinite reduplication (where the fragment is similar to the work that includes it, but also contains another fragment which . . . , and so on); and aporistic reduplication (where a fragment is supposed to include the work that includes it). See *Le récit spéculaire* 51.

9. Jérôme Lindon seemingly objected to the title, and Volodine had to settle for a different one.

10. I chose the term *transmutation* rather than *transformation* because the emblematic figure of the mutant (a being of indeterminate and emergent identity) plays a primary role in some of Volodine's novels, especially *Des enfers fabuleux*.

11. The term *Uber-marionette* was coined by Edward Gordon Craig. See *On the Art of the Theatre*.

12. On Pessoa see Bréchon.

13. See Merwin.

14. Volodine does not always give the authors' full names. Sometimes only the first name or the surname appears. Sometimes the author remains unknown.

15. Margaret Scanlan notes that for Adrian Tahourdin *Lisbonne, dernière marge* seemed "impossibly oblique" (28) and that Pascale Casanova advised that his audience read the book "for the pleasure of getting lost and become a willing victim" (13). See Scanlan 69.

16. On the concept of "grayness" see Kosko, *Fuzzy Thinking*.

17. See Blanchot, *Le livre*. The expression *en porte-à-faux* (in an awkward position, or slanted toward) was suggested to me by Volodine and alludes both to the denormalizing function of subversive fiction and to the *mise à mort* (murder)—as Michel Leiris puts it—of mainstream literature (a reference to the topos of *la grande faucheuse*, the Grim Reaper).

18. Volodine, letter to the author, 12 Sept. 1994.

19. See Péret 9.

20. Hardt and Negri, *Multitude* xii.

21. Briot 210. Coined by Verlaine in 1884, the concept of *poète maudit* was appropriated by Péret in "La parole est à Péret," in *Le déshonneur des poètes* 48.

22. I am alluding here to Zamyatin's concept of "heretical literature." See "On Literature, Revolution, Entropy and Other Matters."

23. Scanlan 79.

24. Volodine, letter to the author, 3 Nov. 1996.

25. According to S. Kemmer, "a *shibboleth* is a kind of linguistic password: A way of speaking (a pronunciation, or the use of a particular expression) that identifies one as a member of an 'in' group. The purpose of a shibboleth is exclusionary as much as inclusive: A person whose way of speaking violates a shibboleth is identified as an outsider and thereby excluded by the group. (This phenomenon is part of the 'Judge a book by its cover' tendency apparently embedded in human cognition, and the use of language to distinguish social groups)." See <http://www.ruf.rice.edu/~kemmer/Words/shibboleth.html>. The story behind the word is recorded in the biblical book of Judges.

26. Char 88.

27. Char 175.

28. On Zamyatin's concept of perpetual revolution see "On Literature, Revolution and Entropy" 12–19.

29. Servier 297.

30. The Cheka (Chresvychainaya Kommissiya) was the special commission founded by Lenin and Dzerjinski, charged with repressing counterrevolutionary activities in the Soviet Union from 1917 through 1922.

31. The Winter Palace, where the Russian government was barricaded, was seized by the Bolsheviks on 25 Oct. 1917, a date that marked their final victory over internal opposition (Anarchists, Socialists, and Mencheviks).

32. Gide, in Breton, *Position* 72.

33. Breton, *Position* 72–73.

34. On the concept of "minor literature" see Deleuze.

35. See Volodine, *Une recette* 24.

36. I will translate *post-exotisme* as *postexoticism* for convenience's sake, but I will retain the dash in French.

37. The dates 1977 and 2012 correspond respectively to the death of the last "urban guerilleros of the Western world" in 1977 (that is, the deaths of Red Army Faction members Gudrun Ensslin, Jan-Carl Raspe, Andreas Baader, and Ingrid Schubert) and the prognosticated end

of Volodine's literary experiment, and of postexotic literature, in 2012 (Volodine, letter to the author, 2 Dec. 1996).

38. Volodine, letter to the author, 6 Nov. 1996.

39. See Jameson, *Postmodernism* 49.

40. Volodine, letter to the author, 12 Dec. 1996. In a previous letter I had suggested to Volodine that his works might be described as *xenoliterary "xénolittéraires,"* thus emphasizing the idiosyncrasy of his novelistic project.

41. Scanlan 75.

42. See Kristeva, *Sèméiotîkè*.

43. On the concept of "hypotext" see Genette, *Palimpsestes* 13.

44. The word *frondisme* evidently brings to mind France's far-right Front National.

45. Volodine says that, in his novels, "one finds a narrated text written by a dead person, or like dead," and, again, that "most major narrators are dead" (Volodine, personal interview with the author, 28 Nov. 1995; letter, 6 Nov. 1996).

46. For Eric White, Serres distinguishes between Venus's "science of caresses," which valorizes "stochastic processes," and Mars's "science of death" (thanatocratic), which reduces reality to "deterministic trajectories." See "Negentropy" 266.

47. *Three Novels by Samuel Beckett* 324; *L'innommable* 46.

48. See Scanlan 72.

49. Briot 210.

50. On the concept of the "hermeneutic code" see Barthes, *s/z* 26.

51. Scanlan 70.

52. Volodine, letter to the author, 26 Nov. 1996.

53. Dargyay 19.

54. Genet, *Declared Enemy* 175; "Violence et brutalité," in *L'ennemi déclaré* 203.

55. The Red Army Faction, also known as the Baader-Meinhof Gang, was an anarchist group that became active in 1970, beginning a series of "armed actions" (assassinations of political figures, bombings) against German and American interests. Though Andreas Baader was arrested in 1970 and Ulrike Meinhof in 1972, the group's second generation remained active until 1992. See Becker.

56. The "professeur de brègne" is literally the "professeur de beignes" (punching professor) in that school of hard knocks.

57. The SPK, an anarchist organization close to the Red Army Faction, was constituted of former psychiatric patients and, under the name

the "Second of June Movement," conducted kidnappings of political figures.

58. See Scanlan 69.

59. Foucault, *Foucault Reader* 235.

60. Volodine, letter, 26 Nov. 1996.

61. Genet, *L'ennemi déclaré* 70.

62. On "dialogization" see Bakhtin, *Dialogic Imagination* 427.

63. Given the physical decay and archaic therapeutic methods of the aforementioned establishment, I have used "asylum" here instead of the more literal "psychotherapeutic center."

64. Beckett, *Happy Days* 40.

65. See Kosko, *Fuzzy Thinking*.

66. See Volodine, *Une recette* 27.

6. François Bon

Epigraph: Stéphane Mallarmé, "The Tomb of Edgar Poe," in *Mallarmé's Collected Poems* 71.

1. See, for instance, Bon, "Claude Simon," *Voleurs*, "Frontières," and *Pour Koltès*.

2. "How would literature become visible to us without the global support of other disciplines?" asks Bon. For him "music and architecture (to mention but these) are metaphors at work" (Bon, personal interview with the author, 9 May 1997).

3. The text was written in collaboration with Paul Badin and Ricardo Perlwitz.

4. Kéchichian, "Grandir."

5. Sartre, *What Is Literature?* 66.

6. Bon, *Calvaire* 30. Subsequent references will appear in the text. Subsequent references to the following Bon works will also appear in the text: *C'était toute une vie*; *Le crime de Buzon*; *Dans la ville invisible*; *Décor ciment*; *L'enterrement*; *Un fait divers*; *La folie Rabelais*; *François Place, illustrateur*; *Limite*; *Les mots sont des fenêtres*; *Parking*; *Sang gris*; *Le solitaire*; *Sortie d'usine*; and *Temps machine*.

7. Leclerc, "Voir le vrai" 257.

8. Bon, interview, 9 May 1997.

9. The quote is from a poem entitled "Blues des projets," in *Travaux d'approche* 135.

10. The term *polar* is frequently translated as "whodunit" or "thriller," but I will retain the French, as these various expressions do not quite

cover the same connotational fields. The word *polar* comes from *police*, which etymologically means a "group of citizens; constitution," a semantic volte-face since the *polar* deals almost exclusively with situations in which the social pact has been violated.

11. Dantec 19.

12. Deloux 23.

13. Among the contemporary writers who have revisited the *polar*, one can point to Jean Echenoz (*Cherokee*), Jean-Philippe Toussaint (*La réticence*), Hervé Guibert (*Les gangsters*), Marie Redonnet (*Candy Story*), Antoine Volodine (*Le port intérieur*), Emmanuel Carrère (*La classe de neige*), and Eric Faye (*Parij*). Alain Robbe-Grillet had already opened the way with *Les gommes*, but today's neo-*polar*, says Jean-Jacques Reboux, has contaminated all of avant-garde literature (*la littérature blanche*). See Reboux 58.

14. Blanckeman, "Les marges" 39.

15. Blanckeman, "Les marges" 39.

16. Blanckeman, "Les marges" 39.

17. Sartre, "Aminadab ou du fantastique considéré comme un langage," in *Situations, I* 113–32. On the "fantastic effect" see Todorov, *Introduction* 29–30.

18. See Jackson 19. Beckett argued: "Such the confusion between them once so twain. And such the farrago from eye to mind. For it to make what sad sense of it may. No matter now. Such equal liars both. Real and—how ill say its contrary? The counter-poison." See *Ill Seen* 40.

19. Bakhtin, *Rabelais* 29.

20. N. Katherine Hayles describes Istvan Csicsery-Ronay's concept of "chaosphere" in the following terms: "A space where no representation can be certain to do more than reflect its creator's face, and where the carousel closes into a solipsistic circle. The only way out is through communication with the Other (the Other being in this case the alien presence in Stanislaw Lem's *Solaris*)." See "Complex Dynamics in Literature and Science," in *Chaos and Order* 28. Also see Csicsery-Ronay.

21. Bon, "Ecrire en prison" 2. Manuscript sent to the author.

22. Bon, letter to the author, 12 Sept. 1994.

23. Apollinaire 18.

24. Apollinaire 23.

25. Perec, "Approches de quoi?" in *L'infra-ordinaire* 9–13.

26. Bon, interview, 9 May 1997.

27. Perec, "Approches de quoi?"; Bon, interview, 9 May 1997.

28. Prigent, *Ceux qui* 267.

29. Lebrun and Prévost 24.

30. For Segalen the traveler must be an *exote* and, to avoid assimilation into the other culture—as well as fathom it—must maintain a gap in between. To sense diversity the subject must necessarily distance him- or herself from his or her object. See Rossi 56. The expression "literary landscape painting" is Gérard de Nerval's (29).

31. Bon, interview, 9 May 1997.

32. Tadié 29.

33. Bon, "Ecrire en prison" 8.

34. Bon, "Ecriture" 2.

35. Bon, interview, 9 May 1997.

36. "For dogs, madness runs in the family," says Buzon; "it comes back and they don't recover" (*Le crime* 62).

37. *Les grands ensembles* designates the urban projects on the periphery of major cities.

38. "World" and "country": Bon, interview, 9 May 1997.

39. The name "Médamothi" appears in *Quart livre* (586). Already in *Pantagruel* we find "Medem," "Uti," and "Udem," which are transcriptions of Greek words meaning "nothing." See Rabelais 311.

40. Bon, interview, 9 May 1997.

41. Bon, interview, 9 May 1997.

42. Apollinaire 25.

43. Bon speaks of "these jobs where you do lunch" (*Calvaire* 24).

44. Milliex 77.

45. Leclerc, "Le XIXe siècle" 32.

46. Nerval, "Capharnaüm," in *Les nuits d'octobro*.

47. Tailleux 22.

48. Bon, interview, 9 May 1997.

49. Bon, interview, 9 May 1997.

50. By "polyanonymous" I mean that several anonymous characters share the same narrative voice.

51. Evans 12.

52. Leclerc, "Voir le vrai" 247.

53. Michaux speaks of "constricted, closed horizons where human life must pass in order to be." See *L'espace* 335.

54. The presence of Kafka is a significant one in Bon's fiction, and the factory of *Sortie d'usine* has much in common with K's castle (165). Like K, Bon's characters map out their environment, but aspire to leave the castle instead of attempting to stay ("leaving the factory" [*Sortie d'usine* 165]).

55. Claudel 28.

56. Bon, interview, 9 May 1997.

57. Bon, interview, 9 May 1997.

58. I am using the term *catastrophic* with the meaning René Thom gives it, as "a series of discontinuities in a system." See Thom 60.

59. Bon, "Claude Simon" 985–86; "Ecrire en prison" 10. For Philippe Sollers see *L'écriture.*

60. Bal 70.

61. Lebrun and Prévost 171.

62. Barthes, *Le bruissement* 100.

63. Bon, "Frontières" 4.

64. See Hayles, "Complex Dynamics in Literature and Science," in *Chaos and Order* 1–33. See also Eric White, "Negentropy."

65. Bon, letter to the author, 29 Feb. 1996.

66. There is a bar named "Le Babylone" in the middle of the city of *Décor ciment.*

67. The story of Habakuk is the story of a man against a city, but a man who is ill like the city, posing the problem of evil and its punishment by one who is more evil than oneself, here Judah by the Chaldeans.

68. Other storytellers appear in the pages of Bon's novels, like Isa Waertens, the fortune-teller of *Décor ciment,* and the tragicomic Desdémone Bertrand of *Dans la ville invisible,* who, like Rossini's Desdemona, could be singing "mura infelici" (unhappy walls), trapped as she feels in the city's disenchantment.

69. The fact that Bon has very poor eyesight—he suffers from myopia—might play a less than anecdotal role in this hierarchization of the senses.

70. Bon, "Frontières" 3.

71. Leclerc, "Voir le vrai" 255.

72. Some of these works are in fact compilations of short texts written by workshop participants—"Ecrire en prison" includes a series of short pieces written by prisoners—while other pieces have been reincorporated by Bon within his own fiction.

73. On "external" versus "character-bound" narrators see Bal 122.

74. Leclerc, "Voir le vrai" 249.

75. Bon, "Rabelais" 124.

76. Bon, interview, 9 May 1997. In *Un fait divers* Bon describes his polyphonic poetics as "choral variations, display of the series of voices" (29).

77. Lebrun and Prévost 179.

78. Bon, "Claude Simon" 992.

79. Rabelais 28.

80. The judgment against Rabelais was passed by Gabriel de Puy-Herbaut, moine de Fontevrault, in his *Theotimus*. See Rabelais 30.

81. Baudelaire says: "I forever live in a crumbling building, in a building that is eaten away by a secret disease." This line is quoted in the epigraph to *L'enterrement*.

82. Bon remarks that this scene was a recurrent dream that preceded the writing of his first novel (interview, 9 May 1997).

83. The same pattern is followed in *Sortie d'usine*, *Limite*, *L'enterrement*, and *Parking*.

84. Bon, "Ecriture."

85. See Bon, *Voleurs* 9.

7. Vague Becomings

1. MSNBC, "The Vietnam Question," <http://msnbc.msn.com/id/4711903/> (italics mine).

2. Kosko, *Fuzzy Thinking* 138.

3. Quignard, *Les ombres* 41.

4. Quignard, *Les ombres* 50.

5. I am grateful to Lydie Moudileno for her insights on the *sans-papiers* and for our conversations on this subject.

6. Oster 47.

7. Rorty 7.

8. Desbiolles 9.

9. Apperry 216.

10. Reyes 25.

11. Lenoir 185.

Bibliography

Adler, Franklin Hugh. "La xenologica: Incontro critico con l'altro." *Ponte* 4 (1995): 54–55.

Albert, Claudia. "L'extrême contemporain: Neue französische Romanciers" [New French novelists]. *Cahier d'Histoire des Littératures Romanes* 14 (1990): 241–44.

Alféri, Pierre, and Olivier Cadiot, eds. *95/2 Digest*. Revue de Littérature Générale. Paris: POL, 1995.

Alizart, Mark. "Paysage après la bataille." *Magazine Littéraire* 392 (2000): 20–23.

Allaire, Suzanne. "Roman et nouveau roman en France." *Français dans le Monde* 212 (1987): 48–53.

Allemand, Roger-Michel. *Le nouveau roman*. Paris: Ellipses, 1995.

Alter-Gilbert, Gilbert. "Translator's Preface." *Dead Man & Company*. Trans. Gilbert Alter-Gilbert. San Jose: Leaping Dog Press, 2004. 12–13.

Althusser, Louis. *Lenin and Philosophy and Other Essays*. Trans. Ben Brewster. London: New Left, 1971.

Amette, Jean-Pierre. "La jeune garde: Littérature." *Point* 972 (1991): 100–101.

Ammouche-Kremers, Michèle, and Henk Hillenaar. "Entretien avec Jean-Philippe Toussaint." *Jeunes auteurs* 27–35.

———. "Entretien avec Jérôme Lindon, Directeur des Editions de Minuit." *Jeunes auteurs* 1–14.

———, eds. *Jeunes auteurs de Minuit*. Amsterdam: Rodopi, 1994.

Anex, Georges. "*Forever Valley, Rose Mélie Rose*." *Le lecteur complice:*

Cinquante chroniques de littérature française 1955–1991. Carouge: Zoé, 1991. 202–5.

———. "Jean-Philippe Toussaint: *La salle de bain.*" *Le lecteur complice: Cinquante chroniques de littérature française 1955–1991.* Carouge: Zoé, 1991. 258–51.

Angenot, Marc. "L'intertextualité: Enquête sur l'émergence et la diffusion d'un champ notionnel." *Revue des Sciences Humaines* 189 (1983): 121–35.

Apollinaire, Guillaume. *L'esprit nouveau et les poètes.* Paris: Altamira, 1994.

Apperry, Yann. *Diabolus in musica.* Paris: Grasset, 2000.

Arbib, Michael, and Mary Hesse. *The Construction of Reality.* Cambridge: Cambridge UP, 1983.

Arent Safir, Margery, ed. *Melancholies of Knowledge: Literature in the Age of Science.* New York: SUNY P, 1999.

Argand, Catherine, Christine Ferniot, and Pascale Frey. "Les filles à l'assaut du polar." *Lire* 253 (1997): 38–47.

Argyros, Alex. "Narrative and Chaos." *New Literary History* 23.3 (1992): 559–75.

Aristotle. *Ars Rhetorica.* Ed. W. D. Ross. Oxford: Oxford UP, 1959.

Armel, Aliette. Rev. of *Le temps-machine*, by François Bon. *Magazine Littéraire* 310 (1993): 100–101.

Arnold, Matthew. *Culture and Anarchy: An Essay in Political and Social Criticism.* London: Smith, 1859.

Arvon, Henri. *L'anarchisme.* Paris: PUF, 1995.

Asholt, Wolfgang. "Trauerarbeit der Moderne in Romanen von François Bon, Jean Echenoz und Marie Redonnet" [Mourning modernity in the novels of François Bon, Jean Echenoz and Marie Redonnet]. *Intertextualität und Subversivität: Studien zur Romanliteratur der achtziger Jahre in Franreich* [Intertextuality and subversiveness: Studies in the French novel of the 1980s]. Heidelberg: Carl Winter U, 1994. 303–14.

Asholt, Wolfgang, and Fieke Schoots. "Une littérature de contrebande: Tendances du roman français des années 80." *Rapports* 55 (1995): 123–30.

Astier, Pierre. *La crise du roman français et le nouveau réalisme.* Paris: Debresse, 1958.

Auerbach, Erich. *Mimesis: The Representation of Reality in Western Literature.* Trans. Willard R. Trask. Princeton: Princeton UP, 1953.

Augé, Marc. *Non-lieux: Introduction à une anthropologie de la surmo-dernité*. Paris: Seuil, 1992.

Bablet, Denis. *Le masque: Du rite au théâtre*. Paris: CNRS, 1985.

Badcock, Christopher. *The Essential Freud*. Oxford: Blackwell, 1988.

Baert, Frank, and Dominique Viart, eds. *La littérature française con-temporaine: Questions et perspectives*. Louvain: PU de Louvain, 1993.

Baker, Charles A. Rev. of *La réticence*, by Jean-Philippe Tousaint. *French Review* 57 (1993): 392–93.

Bakhtin, M. M. *The Bakhtin Reader*. Ed. Pam Morris. London: Arnold, 1994.

———. *The Dialogic Imagination*. Trans. Caryl Emerson and Michael Holquist. Austin: U of Texas P, 1981.

———. *La poétique de Dostoïevsky*. Trans. Isabelle Kolitcheff. Paris: Seuil, 1970.

———. *Rabelais and His World*. Trans. Hélène Iswolsky. Bloomington: Indiana UP, 1984.

Bakounine, Michel. *Dieu et l'Etat*. Ed. Joël Gayraud. Paris: Mille et Une Nuits, 1995.

Bal, Mieke. *Narratology: Introduction to the Theory of Narrative*. To-ronto: U of Toronto P, 1985.

Balzac, Honoré de. *Le chef d'oeuvre inconnu*. Paris: Garnier Flammar-ion, 1981.

———. *The Unknown Masterpiece*. Trans. Richard Howard. New York: New York Review Books, 2001.

Baqué, Françoise. *Le nouveau roman*. Paris: Bordas, 1972.

Barchillon, Jacques. *Le conte merveilleux français*. Paris: Champion, 1975.

Barrois, Claude. "La psychologie du guerrier." *Sciences Humaines* 41 (1994): 27–30.

Barth, John. "A Few Words about Minimalism." *New York Times Book Review* 28 Dec. 1985: 1.

———. *Further Fridays*. Boston: Back Bay Books, 1995.

Barthelme, Donald. *The Dead Father*. New York: Penguin, 1975.

Barthes, Roland. *Le bruissement de la langue: Essais critiques IV*. Paris: Seuil, 1984.

———. *Le degré zéro de l'écriture*. Paris: Seuil, 1953.

———. "Le discours de l'histoire." *Poétique* 49 (1982): 13–21.

———. *Essais critiques*. Paris: Seuil, 1954.

———. *Le plaisir du texte*. Paris: Seuil, 1973.

———. *S/Z*. Paris: Seuil, 1970.

Barthes, Roland, Leo Bersani, Philippe Hamon, Michael Riffaterre, and Ian Watt. *Littérature et réalité*. Paris: Seuil, 1982.

Bataille, Georges. *La littérature et le mal*. Paris: Gallimard, 1957.

———. *La part maudite*. Paris: Minuit, 1957.

Baucquart, Marie-Claire. *Littérature française du XXe siècle*. Paris: PUF, 1992.

Baudrillard, Jean. *L'échange symbolique et la mort*. Paris: Gallimard, 1975.

———. *Simulations*. Trans. P. Beitchman. New York: Semiotexte, 1983.

Bayle, Thierry. "Nouveau roman, romans nouveaux?" *Page des Libraires* 44 (1997): 22–24.

Becker, Jillian. *Hitler's Children: The Story of the Baader-Meinhof Terrorist Gang*. Philadelphia: Lippincott, 1977.

Beckett, Samuel. *Fin de partie*. Paris: Minuit, 1957.

———. *Happy Days*. New York: Grove Weidenfeld, 1951.

———. *Ill Seen Ill Said*. New York: Grove, 1981.

———. *L'innommable*. Paris: Minuit, 1953.

———. *Malone meurt*. Paris: Minuit, 1951.

———. *Mal vu mal dit*. Paris: Minuit, 1981.

———. *Molloy*. Paris: Minuit, 1951.

———. *Three Novels by Samuel Beckett (Molloy, Malone Dies, The Unnamable)*. New York: Grove P, 1991.

Beehler, Michael. "Yevgeny Zamyatin: The Essential, the Superfluous and Textual Noise." *SubStance* 50 (1985): 48–50.

Béhar, Henri. *Littéruptures*. Paris: L'Age d'Homme, 1988.

Bell, Richard. *Circumstances: Chance in the Literary Text*. Lincoln: U of Nebraska P, 1993.

Bellour, Raymond. "La baleine blanche." Rev. of *Tir et Lir* and *Mobie-Diq*, by Marie Redonnet. *Magazine Littéraire* 252 (1989): 55.

———. "Le centre de la mer." Rev. of *Silsie*, by Marie Redonnet. *Magazine Littéraire* 281 (1990): 142–43.

———. "Du mythe au roman." Rev. of *Candy Story*, by Marie Redonnet. *Magazine Littéraire* 302 (1992): 75–77.

———. "Le mythe du roman." Rev. of *Nevermore*, by Marie Redonnet. *Magazine Littéraire* 324 (1994): 88–89.

———. "Une mythologie blanche." Rev. of *Rose Mélie Rose*, by Marie Redonnet. *Magazine Littéraire* 245 (1987): 55.

———. "La pensée—photo." Rev. of *L'appareil-photo*, by Jean-Philippe Toussaint. *Magazine Littéraire* 252 (1989): 50–51.

Benhamou, Anne-Françoise, Samra Bonvoisin, Michel Fournier, and
Jean-Claude Lallias. *Koltès: Combats avec la scène*. Théâtre
aujourd'hui 5. Paris: CNDP, 1995.

Bénichou, Paul. *L'école du désenchantement*. Paris: Gallimard, 1992.

Bergounioux, Pierre. *La ligne*. Paris: Verdier, 1997.

———. "Le tremblement authentique: Entretien avec François Bon." *Le
fait littéraire*. Paris: Quai Voltaire, 1991. 15–21.

Bergson. *Laughter: An Essay on the Meaning of the Comic*. Trans.
Cloudesley Brereton and Fred Rothwell. New York: MacMillan,
1937.

———. *Le rire: Essai sur la signification du comique*. Paris: PUF, 1958.

Bernardi, Bruno. "François Bon: Le lieu des écarts." *Esprit* 182 (1992):
102–10.

Bersani, Leo. *Balzac to Beckett: Center and Circumference in French Fiction*. New York: Oxford UP, 1970.

———. *The Freudian Body: Psychoanalysis and Art*. New York: Columbia UP, 1985.

Bersani, Leo, and Ulysse Dutoit. *Arts of Impoverishment: Beckett,
Rothko, Resnais*. Cambridge: Harvard UP, 1993.

Bersani, Leo, Jacques Lecarme, and Bruno Vercier. *La littérature en
France depuis 1958*. Paris: Bordas, 1982.

Bernstein, Michèle. "Jean-Philippe Toussaint, Françoise Bouillot: Qu'est-
il arrivé?" *Libération* 3 Oct. 1991: 25.

———. "Marie Redonnet: A l'Est, rien de nouveau." Rev. of *Silsie*, by
Marie Redonnet. *Libération* 27 Sept. 1990: 29.

Bertho, Sophie. "L'attente postmoderne: A propos de la littérature contemporaine en France." *Revue d'Histoire Littéraire de la France*
91 (1991): 735–43.

———. "Jean-Philippe Toussaint et la métaphysique." Ammouche-Kremers and Hillenaar, *Jeunes auteurs* 15–25.

Berthomé, J-P. Rev. of *Monsieur*, by Jean-Philippe Toussaint. *Positif* 347
(1990): 75.

Bessard-Banquy, Olivier. "Chevillard, écrivain." *Critique* 559 (1993):
893–905.

———. "Une littérature du trou noir." *Critique* 50 (1994): 975–81.

Bessière, Jean. "Dire la 'mimesis' aujourd'hui." *Neohelicon* 13.2 (1985):
51–79.

———. *L'énigmaticité de la littérature: Pour une anatomie de la fiction
au XXe siècle*. Paris: PUF, 1993.

Biezunski, Michel. *Histoire de la physique moderne*. Paris: La Décou-
verte, 1993.

Biron, Michel. "Fatiguer la réalité." Rev. of *L'appareil-photo*, by Jean-Philippe Toussaint. *Spirale* 87 (1989): 12.

Blake, William. *The Marriage of Heaven and Hell*. London: Heinemann, 1985.

Blanchot, Maurice. *The Book to Come*. Trans. Charlotte Mandel. Stanford: Stanford UP, 2003.

———. *L'écriture du désastre*. Paris: Minuit, 1980.

———. *L'espace littéraire*. Paris: Gallimard, 1955.

———. *Le livre à venir*. Paris: Gallimard, 1959.

———. *La part du feu*. Paris: Gallimard, 1949.

———. *The Space of Literature*. Trans. Ann Smock. Lincoln: U of Nebraska P, 1982.

Blanckeman, Bruno. "Les marges du polar." *Prétexte* 12 (1997): 38–42.

———. *Les récits indécidables*. Paris: Septentrion, 2000.

Bloom, Harold. *The Anxiety of Influence*. Oxford: Oxford UP, 1973.

Boie, Bernhild, and Daniel Ferrer, eds. *Genèses du roman contemporain: Incipit et entrées en écriture*. Paris: CNRS, 1993.

Boisdeffre, Pierre de. *Les écrivains français d'aujourd'hui: 1940–1985*. 7th ed. Paris: PUF, 1985.

Bologne, Jean-Claude. Rev. of *Calvaire des chiens* and *La folie Rabelais*, by François Bon. *Magazine Littéraire* 283 (1990): 73.

Bon, François. Introduction. *Arauco ou l'énigme de l'oeuvre: Entretien avec Ricardo Perlwitz*. Interview with Paul Badin. Bouchemaine: Badin, 1987.

———. "Bâtisseur d'énigme." Introduction. *Le tiers livre*. By Rabelais. Paris: POL, 1993. i–xx.

———. *Calvaire des chiens*. Paris: Minuit, 1990.

———. *C'était toute une vie*. Paris: Verdier, 1995.

———. "Claude Simon: Fantastique et tragédie." *Critique* 511 (1989): 980–95.

———. *Comment Pantagruel monta sur la mer*. Paris: Hatier, 1994.

———. "Côté cuisines." *Infini* 19 (1987): 55–52.

———. *Le crime de Buzon*. Paris: Minuit, 1985.

———. *Daewoo*. Paris: Fayard, 2004.

———. *Dans la ville invisible*. Paris: Gallimard Jeunesse, 1995.

———. *Décor ciment*. Paris: Minuit, 1988.

———. "Ecrire en prison: Réflexions sur un atelier d'écriture au Centre de Jeunes Détenus de Bordeaux-Gradignan." Unpublished ms., Jan. 1997.

———. "Ecriture, monde, valeurs: Intervention aux Etats Généraux de la Culture." Unpublished ms., 1 Feb. 1997.

———. *L'enterrement*. Paris: Verdier, 1990.

———. "Et les abysmes eriger au dessus des nues." Introduction. *Gargantua*. By Rabelais. Paris: POL, 1992. i–xix.

———. *Un fait divers*. Paris: Minuit, 1994.

———. "Fête dans une ville déserte." *Serpent à Plumes* 5 (1993): 153–83.

———. *La folie Rabelais*. Paris: Minuit, 1990.

———. "François Bon ou la folie d'écrire." Interview with Christian Perrot. *Autre Journal* 4 (1990): 180–83.

———. *François Place, illustrateur*. Paris: Casterman, 1994.

———. "Frontières d'écriture." Colloque Salon du Livre de Jeunesse de Montreuil. Dec. 1995.

———. *Grand traverseur des voies périlleuses: Quatre préfaces aux livres de François Rabelais*. http://un2sg1.unige.ch/athena/bon/bon_pref.html.

———. "Grandir." Interview with Olivier Schmitt. *Monde des Livres* 28 Jan. 1994: 1.

———. "Grève." http://www.tiersliver.net/arch/Greve_fr.pdf.

———. Interview with Bernard Rapp. *Caractères*. France 3. 31 Jan. 1992.

———. Letter to the author. 27 Mar. 1994.

———. Letter to the author. 12 Sept. 1994.

———. Letter to the author. 29 Feb. 1995.

———. *Limite*. Paris: Minuit, 1985.

———. "Un livre, comme un miracle." *Quinzaine Littéraire* 532 (1989): 5.

———. *Mécanique*. Paris: Verdier, 2001.

———. *Les mots sont des fenêtres*. Lodève: Bibliothèque municipale de Lodève, 1995.

———. *La pantagruéline prognostication*. Paris: Dé Bleu, 1995.

———. *Parking*. Paris: Minuit, 1995.

———. *Paysage fer*. Paris Verdier, 2000.

———. Personal interview. 9 May 1997.

———. *Phobos, les mal famés*. Paris: Seuil Jeunesse, 1995.

———. *Polir nos arêtes vives*. Lodève: Bibliothèque Municipale de Lodève, 1995.

———. *Pour Koltès*. Paris: Les Solitaires Intepestifs, 2000.

———. *Prison*. Paris: Verdier, 1998.

———. Afterword. *Quartier du Globe*. By Didier Daeninckx. Montreuil: Folies d'encre, 1989.

————. *Le quart-livre de Rabelais*. Paris: Hatier, 1994.

————. *Quatre avec le mort*. Paris: Verdier, 2002.

————. "Rabelais d'aplomb." Introduction. *Pantagruel*. By Rabelais. Paris: POL, 1992. i–xx.

————. "Rabelais en mouvement." *Europe* 757 (1992): 120–28.

————. *Sang gris: Un atelier d'écriture à La Courneuve*. Paris: Verdier, 1992.

————. "Sans retour." Introduction. *Le quart livre*. By Rabelais. Paris: POL, 1993. i–xix.

————. *Le solitaire*. Montolieu: Deyrolle, 1995.

————. *Sortie d'usine*. Paris: Minuit, 1982.

————. *Temps machine*. Paris: Verdier, 1992.

————. *Tous les mots de la langue: Un voyage dans la bibliothèque municipale de Bobigny*. Bobigny: Bibliothèque Elsa-Triolet, 1995.

————. *Tout ce que j'ai dans mon coeur: Ecrire avec Rabelais*. N.p.: Salon du Livre de Jeunesse, 1995.

————. *30, rue de la Poste*. Paris: Seuil Jeunesse, 1995.

————. *Voleurs de feu: Les vies singulières des poètes*. Paris: Hatier, 1995.

Bon, François, Jean-Louis Froment, and Pep Subirós. *Même si c'est la nuit: Absalon, Richard Baquié, Bernd et Hilda Becher*. Bordeaux: CAPC—Musée d'Art Contemporain de Bordeaux, 1995.

Bon, François, and Michel Maffesoli. *Les péchés capitaux: La colère*. Paris: Centre Pompidou, 1995.

Bon, François, Pierre Marcelle, Didier Daeninckx, and Hervé Prudon. *Café nocturne*. Paris: Harpo, 1985.

Bonnefoy, Claude. *Panorama critique de la littérature moderne*. Paris: Belfond, 1981.

Borges, Jorge Luis. *Labyrinths*. Ed. Donald Yates and James Irby. New York: New Directions, 1954.

Bouise, Jean. "*Tir et Lir* au Théâtre National de la Colline: Jean Bouise ou les passions d'un artisan." Interview with Olivier Schmitt. *Monde* 10 Dec. 1988: 20.

Bourdieu, Pierre. "L'emprise du journalisme." *Actes de la Recherche en Sciences Sociales* 101–2 (1994): 3–9.

————. *Les règles de l'art*. Paris: Seuil, 1992.

————. *Sur la télévision*. Paris: Liber, 1995.

Bourgeade, Pierre. "Idées sur le roman en 1989." *Infini* 27 (1989): 5–10.

Brady, Patrick. "Chaos Theory, Control Theory and Literary Theory." *Modern Language Studies* 20 (1990): 55–79.

————. "From Transactional Analysis to Chaos Theory: New Critical Perspectives." *Australian Journal of French Studies* 25 (1989): 175–93.

Brandeau, Michel. "Les lois de la pesanteur." Rev. of *Le caoutchouc décidément*, by Eric Chevillard, and *Tout doit disparaître*, by Benoît Duteurtre. *Monde des Livres* 2 May 1992: 22.

Braque, Georges. *Le jour et la nuit: Cahiers 1917–1952.* Paris: Gallimard, 1988.

Brami, Joseph, Madeleine Cottenet-Hage, and Pierre Verdaguer, eds. *Regards sur la France des années 80: Le roman.* Saratoga: ANMA Libri, 1994.

Bréchon, Robert. *Étrange étranger: Une biographie de Fernando Pessoa.* Paris: Christian Bourgois, 1995.

Brée, Germaine. *Du surréalisme à l'empire de la critique.* Paris: Arthaud, 1990.

Brée, Germaine, and Margaret Guiton. *The French Novel: From Gide to Camus.* New York: Harbinger, 1952.

Brémond, Claude. "Les bons récompensés et les méchants punis." *Sémiotique Narrative et Textuelle.* Paris: Larousse, 1973. 95–121.

————. "Le mécano du conte." *Magazine Littéraire* 150 (1979): 13–15.

————. "Le message narratif." *Communications* 4 (1954): 4–32.

Brenner, Jacques. *Histoire de la littérature française de 1940 à nos jours.* Paris: Fayard, 1978.

Breton, André. *Manifestes du surréalisme.* Paris: Gallimard, 1992.

————. *Position politique du surréalisme.* Paris: Pauvert, 1971.

————. *Les vases communicants.* Paris: Gallimard, 1955.

Briot, Frédéric. "Les chimères d'Antoine Volodine." *Roman 20–50* (1995): 205–14.

Britton, Celia. "The Nouveau Roman and Tel Quel Marxism." *Paragraph* 12 (1989): 55–95.

Broekstra, G. "On the Foundations of GIT (General Information Theory)." *General Systems Methodology: Mathematical Systems Theory: Fuzzy Sets.* Ed. Robert Trapple, George Klir, and Franz R. Pichler. Washington DC: Hemisphere, 1982. 23–30.

Brooks, Peter. *Body Work: Objects of Desire in Modern Narrative.* Cambridge: Harvard UP, 1993.

————. "Fiction and Its Referents: A Reappraisal." *Poetics Today* 4.1 (1983): 73–75.

————. *Reading for the Plot: Design and Intention in Narrative.* Cambridge: Harvard UP, 1984.

Brulotte, Gaétan. "L'homme indifférent de Jean-Philippe Toussaint." *Liberté* 187 (1990): 125–30.

Brunel, Pierre. *La littérature française aujourd'hui: Essai sur la littérature française dans la seconde moitié du XXe siècle*. Paris: Vuibert, 1997.

Burke, Sean. *The Death and Return of the Author: Criticism and Subjectivity in Barthes, Foucault and Derrida*. Edinburgh: Edinburgh UP, 1992.

Burton-Page, Piers. "Dangerous Delusions." Rev. of *Monsieur* and *La réticence*, by Jean-Philippe Toussaint. *Times Literary Supplement* 1 Nov. 1991: 20.

Butor, Michel. *Essais sur le roman*. 2nd ed. Paris: Gallimard, 1977.

Caillois, Roger. *Les Jeux et les hommes*. Paris: Gallimard, 1987.

———. *Travaux d'approche*. Paris: Gallimard, 1972.

Caldwell, Roy C. "Jean-Philippe Toussaint." *The Contemporary Novel in France*. Ed. William Thomson. Gainesville: U of Florida P, 1995. 359–82.

Calvino, Italo. *The Uses of Literature*. Trans. Patrick Creagh. New York: Harcourt, 1985.

Caminade, Pierre. Rev. of *La salle de bain*, by Jean-Philippe Toussaint. *Sud* 54–55 (1985): 253–54.

Camus, Albert. *Carnets II: Janvier 1942–mars 1951*. Paris: Gallimard, 1954.

———. *The Myth of Sisyphus and Other Essays*. Trans. Justin O'Brien. New York: Vintage, 1991.

Carlson, Marvin. *Theories of the Theatre: A Historical and Critical Survey, from the Greeks to the Present*. 2nd ed. Ithaca: Cornell UP, 1993.

Carpentier, Alejo. "L'éternel retour du baroquisme." *Magazine Littéraire* 300 (1992): 27–31.

Carpentier, Pierre. "Marie Redonnet: L'éclat feutré d'une soixante-huitarde assagie." *Nuit blanche* 55 (1994): 10–15.

Carrère, Emmanuel. *Le détroit de Behring: Introduction à l'uchronie*. Paris: POL, 1985.

Carroll, David. "History as Writing." *Clio* 7.3 (1978): 443–51.

Carroll, Lewis. *Alice's Adventures in Wonderland* and *Through the Looking-Glass*. London: Penguin, 1970.

Casanova, Pascale. "Pour le plaisir de se perdre." *Quinzaine Littéraire* 553 (1990): 13.

Cccatty, René de. "La folie Bon." Rev. of *Calvaire des chiens*, by François Bon. *Monde des Livres* 28 Sept. 1990: 24.

———. "La mort en ce marais." Rev. of *L'enterrement*, by François Bon. *Monde des Livres* 31 Jan. 1992: 25.

Certeau, Michel de. *L'écriture de l'histoire*. Paris: Gallimard, 1975.

Chaillou, Michel. *La petite vertu*. Paris: Seuil, 1990.

Chambers, Ross. "The Etcetera Principle: Narrative and the Paradigmatic." Henry 1–24.

———. *Story and Situation: Narrative Seduction and the Power of Fiction*. Minneapolis: U of Minnesota P, 1984.

Champagne, Patrick. "La construction médiatique des 'malaises sociaux.'" *Actes de la Recherche en Sciences Sociales* 90 (1991): 54–75.

Char, René. *Le nu perdu*. Paris: Gallimard, 1978.

Chassay, Jean-François. "Les nouveaux itinéraires du roman." *Europe* 731 (1990): 24–30.

Chenétier, Marc. *Au-delà du soupçon*. Paris: Seuil, 1989.

Chevalier, Jean, and Alain Gheerbrant. *Dictionnaire des symboles*. 2nd ed. Paris: Robert Laffont, 1982.

Chevillard, Eric. *Les absences du capitaine Cook*. Paris: Minuit, 2001.

———. *Au plafond*. Paris: Minuit, 1997.

———. *Le caoutchouc décidément*. Paris: Minuit, 1992.

———. *The Crab Nebula*. Trans. Jordan Stump and Eleanor Hardin. Lincoln: U of Nebraska P, 1997.

———. *Le démarcheur*. Paris: Minuit, 1988.

———. *Du hérisson*. Paris: Minuit, 2002.

———. *Un fantôme*. Paris: Minuit, 1995.

———. *45° Nord & Longitude 0*. Bordeaux: Mollat, 1995.

———. *Mourir m'enrhume*. Paris: Minuit, 1987.

———. *La nébuleuse du crabe*. Paris: Minuit, 1993.

———. *L'oeuvre posthume de Thomas Pilaster*. Paris: Minuit, 1999.

———. *On the Ceiling*. Trans. Jordan Stump. Lincoln: U of Nebraska P, 2000.

———. *Palafox*. Paris: Minuit, 1990.

———. *Palafox*. Trans. Wyatt Mason. New York: Archipelago Books, 2004.

———. Personal interview. 12 Nov. 1995.

———. *Préhistoire*. Paris: Minuit, 1994.

———. "Trente autoportraits sur mon lit de mort." *Serpent à Plumes* 17 (1995): 43–55.

———. "Trois tentatives pour réintroduire le tigre mangeur d'homme en Lot-Et-Garonne." *45° Nord & Longitude 0*. Bordeaux: Mollat, 1995.

———. *Le vaillant petit tailleur*. Paris: Minuit, 2003.

———. "La vie future du professeur Leroi-Gourhan." Alferi and Cadiot n.p.

Chevillot, Frédérique. *La réouverture du texte*. Stanford: ANMA Libri, 1993.

Chevrier, Marc. Rev. of *La salle de bain*, by John Lvoff. *Cahiers du cinéma* 417 (1989): 51.

Cioran. *All Gall Is Divided*. Trans. Richard Howard. New York: Arcade, 1952.

———. *Syllogismes de l'amertume*. Paris: Gallimard, 1952.

Claudel, Paul. *La ville*. Paris: Mercure de France, 1957.

Clavel, André. "Alice au pays de Beckett." Rev. of *Silsie*, by Marie Redonnet. *Evènement du Jeudi* 308: 124.

Cloonan, William, and Jean-Philippe Postel. "The Business of Literature: The Novel in 1992." *French Review* 55 (1992): 851–58.

———. "New Voices: The French Novel in 1991." *French Review* 55 (1991): 955–52.

———. "Prizes and Surprises: L'année romanesque en 1990." *French Review* 54.5 (1991): 915–20.

Combes, Francis. Rev. of *Sortie d'usine*, by François Bon. *Europe* 545–45 (1983): 211–14.

Confiant, Rafael. *Bassin des ouragans*. Paris: Mille et Une Nuits, 1994.

Copens, Yves. *La plus belle histoire du monde*. Paris: Seuil, 1995.

Cortanze, Gérard de. "La relève romanesque ou la trace de la savonnette." *Page des Libraires* 44 (1997): 34–35.

Corvin, Michel. "Le théâtre de Genet: Une apparence qui montre le vide." *Europe* 808–9 (1995): 110–23.

Coulet, Corinne. *Le théâtre grec*. Paris: Nathan, 1995.

Craig, Edward Gordon. *On the Art of the Theatre*. London: Heinemann, 1914.

Criso, Rachael Anne. "The Verbosity of Minimalism: Sarraute, Duras and Redonnet." *Women in French Studies* 1 (1993): 38–42.

Criton, Michel. *Les jeux mathématiques*. Paris: PUF, 1997.

Csicsery-Ronay, Istvan. "Modeling the Chaosphere: Stanislaw Lem's Alien Communications." Hayles 244–52.

Culler, Jonathan. *On Deconstruction*. London: Routledge, 1983.

———. *The Pursuit of Signs: Semiotics, Literature, Deconstruction*. Ithaca: Cornell UP, 1981.

Curval, Philippe. "A travers les enfers intérieurs." Rev. of *Des enfers fabuleux*, by Antoine Volodine. *Magazine Littéraire* 250 (1988): 84.

————. Rev. of *Lisbonne, dernière marge*, by Antoine Volodine. *Magazine Littéraire* 282 (1990): 85.

————. "Rituels du rêve." Rev. of *Rituel du mépris*, by Antoine Volodine. *Magazine Littéraire* 237 (1987): 92.

D., F. Rev. of *La salle de bain*, by Jean-Philippe Toussaint. *Elle* 2079 (1985): 48.

Dällenbach, Lucien. *Le récit spéculaire: Essai sur la mise en abyme*. Paris: Seuil, 1977.

Dantec, Maurice. "Trips." *Magazine Littéraire* 344 (1995): 18–20.

Darcos, Xavier. *Histoire de la littérature française*. Paris: Hachette, 1992.

Dargyay, Eva K., ed. *Bardo-Thödol: Le livre tibétain des morts*. Paris: Albin Michel, 1981.

Defays, Jean-Marc. *Le comique*. Paris: Seuil, 1995.

Deleuze, Gilles. *Critique et clinique*. Paris: Minuit, 1993.

Deleuze, Gilles, and Félix Guattari. *Kafka: Pour une littérature mineure*. Paris: Minuit, 1975.

Delon, Michel. "Les Lumières entre l'euphorie et l'angoisse." *Magazine Littéraire* 312 (1993): 52–54.

Deloux, Jean-Pierre. "Polar à la française: Treize ans de bonheur." *Magazine Littéraire* 344 (1995): 22–25.

Delvaille, Bernard. "Une quête métaphysique." *Magazine Littéraire* 353 (1997): 18–21.

De Man, Paul. *Allegories of Reading*. New Haven: Yale UP, 1979.

Derrida, Jacques. *La dissémination*. Paris: Seuil, 1972.

————. *L'écriture et la différence*. Paris: Seuil, 1957.

————. "Une mythologie blanche." *Poétique* 2.5 (1971): 1–52.

————. "The Supplement of Copula: Philosophy *before* Linguistics." *Textual Strategies: Perspectives in Post-Structuralist Criticism*. Ed. Josué Harari. London: Methuen, 1979. 28–120.

Derrida, Jacques, and Roger Chartier. "Le livre à venir." Address. Conference cycle, "Les fins du livre." BNF Tolbiac. Paris, 20 Mar. 1997.

Desbiolles, Maryline. *Anchise*. Paris: Seuil, 1999.

Deshoulières, Christophe. *Le théâtre au XXe siècle en toutes lettres*. Paris: Bordas, 1989.

Desportes, Corinne. Rev. of *La salle de bain*, by Jean-Philippe Toussaint. *Magazine Littéraire* 225 (1985): 50.

Deville, Patrick. "Je travaille avec méthode et tâtonnements." *Quinzaine Littéraire* 532 (1989): 12.

———. *Longue-vue.* Paris: Minuit, 1988.

Di Bernardi, Domenico. Rev. of *L'appareil-photo,* by Jean-Philippe Toussaint. *Review of Contemporary Fiction* 5.1 (1990): 298–301.

Dictionnaire des personnages de tous les temps et de tous les pays. Paris: Laffont, 1950.

Diderot, Denis. *Lettre sur les aveugles à l'usage de ceux qui voient.* Paris: Gallimard, 1955.

———. *Le neveu de Rameau* suivi de *Six textes philosophiques.* Paris: Gallimard, 1955.

———. *Supplément au voyage de Bougainville.* Paris: Gallimard, 1955.

Diderot, Denis, and Jean d'Alembert. *L'encyclopédie, ou dictionnaire raisonné des sciences, des arts et des métiers.* Paris: Bordas, 1985.

Dion, Marie-Pierre. "La révolution du codex." *Quinzaine Littéraire* 598 (1995): 14–15.

Dion, Robert. "Les romanciers de Minuit." *Nuit blanche* 47 (1992): 50–52.

Domenach, Jean-Marie. *Le crépuscule de la culture française?* Paris: Plon, 1995.

Doubrovsky, Serge. "Sartre: Autobiographie/autofiction." *Revue des Sciences Humaines* 98.4 (1991): 17–25.

Dubois, Jacques. *Le roman policier ou la modernité.* Paris: Nathan, 1992.

Duby, Jean-Jacques. "Sciences: La fin du déterminisme." *Magazine Littéraire* 312 (1993): 31–34.

Ducrot, Oswald, and Tzvetan Todorov. *Dictionnaire encyclopédique des sciences du langage.* Paris: Seuil, 1972.

Dulot, Stéphanie. *Le roman policier.* Toulouse: Milan, 1995.

Dupin, Jean-Patrice. "Riche, profond, drôle." Rev. of *Préhistoire,* by Eric Chevillard. *Quinzaine Littéraire* 1 Nov. 1994: 10.

Eco, Umberto. *Ecritures d'aujourd'hui: Anthologie littéraire des années 80/90.* Berlin: Cornelsen, 1995.

———. "Les Editions de Minuit." *Acta Litteraria Academiae Scientiarum Hungaricae* 1–2 (1983): 157–74.

———. *Der Name der Rose.* Munich: Deutscher Taschenbuch Verlag, 1985.

———. *Le nom de la rose.* Trans. Jean-Nöel Schifano. Paris: Grasset, 1980.

———. *L'oeuvre ouverte.* Paris: Seuil, 1955.

———. *Postcript to* The Name of the Rose. Trans. William Weaver. New York: Harcourt, 1984.

————. *The Role of the Reader: Exploration in the Semiotics of Texts.* Ed. Thomas A. Sebeok. Bloomington: Indiana UP, 1984.

Ekeland, Ivar. *Le chaos.* Paris: Flammarion, 1995.

Ellison, David R. *Of Words and the World: Referential Anxiety in Contemporary French Fiction.* Princeton: Princeton UP, 1993.

Emelina, Jean. *Le comique: Essai d'interprétation générale.* Paris: Sedes, 1991.

Erasme. *Eloge de la folie.* Trans. Thibault de Laveaux. Paris: Mille et Une Nuits, 1997.

Ernaux, Annie. *Je ne suis pas sortie de ma nuit.* Paris: Gallimard, 1997.

Evans, Margery A. *Baudelaire and Intertextuality: Poetry at the Crossroads.* Cambridge: Cambridge UP, 1993.

Evanson, Brian. Rev. of *Le caoutchouc décidément,* by Eric Chevillard. *World Literature Today* 57.2 (1993): 322.

Evrard, Franck. *L'humour.* Paris: Hachette, 1995.

Ezine, Jean-Louis. "Châteaux en Berry." Rev. of *La nébuleuse du crabe,* by Eric Chevillard. *Nouvel Observateur* 11 Feb. 1993: 322.

————. "François Bon: Français, 35 ans, romancier." *Nouvel Observateur* 14 Dec. 1989: 9.

————. Rev. of *Le nom des singes,* by Antoine Volodine. *Nouvel Observateur* 27 Oct. 1994: 50–51.

————. Rev. of *La réticence,* by Jean-Philippe Toussaint. *Nouvel Observateur* 19 Sept. 1991: 54.

Fallaize, Elizabeth. "Filling in the Blank Canvas: Memory, Inheritance and Identity in Marie Redonnet's 'Rose Mélie Rose.'" *Forum for Modern Language Studies* 28 (1992): 320–33.

Fauconnier, Bernard. "Des avatars du sujet romanesque." *Magazine Littéraire* 312 (1993): 54–55.

Fauvel, Maryse. "Jean-Philippe Toussaint et la photographie: Exposer le roman." *Romance Languages Annual* 5 (1994): 38–42.

Federman, Raymond, ed. *Surfiction: Fiction Now . . . and Tomorrow.* Chicago: Swallow, 1981.

Ferrara, Lina. Rev. of *La salle de bain,* by Jean-Philippe Toussaint. *French Review* 50.5 (1987): 732.

Ferruci, Roberto. Rev. of *La salle de bain,* by John Lvoff. *Contemporanea* 3.4 (1990): 84–85.

Ferry, Luc, and Claudine Germé. *Des animaux et des hommes.* Paris: Librairie Générale Française, 1994.

Finkielkraut, Alain. *La défaite de la pensée.* Paris: Gallimard, 1987.

Fix, René. "Botho Strauss: Les singulières considérations d'un poète." *Cahiers Comédie-Française* 17 (1995): 93–100.

Fletcher, John, and John Calder, eds. *The Nouveau Roman Reader*. London: Calder, 1985.

Flügge, Manfred. "Fatiguer la réalité: Jean-Philippe Toussaint." *Die Wiederkehr der Spieler: Tendenzen des französischen Romans nach Sartre* [The return of the ludic: Tendencies in the French novel after Sartre]. Marburg: Hitzeroth, 1993. 54–74.

———. "Fruchtloser Zorn: Die Romanwelt von François Bon" [Useless wrath: The novelistic world of François Bon]. *Die Wiederkehr* 75–78.

———. "Neue Sterne bei Minuit" [New stars at Minuit]. *Lendemains* 14.54 (1989): 11–15.

———. "Wie man die Wirlichkeit Weismacht: Der Romancier Jean-Philippe Toussaint" [How to simulate reality: The novelist Jean-Philippe Toussaint]. *Merkur* 43 (1989): 111–15.

Forest, Philippe. *Histoire de Tel Quel: 1950–1982*. Paris: Seuil, 1994.

Forest, Phillipe, Alexandre Fillon, Nadine Trintignant, Michel Crepu, and Jean Malaquais. "La vogue de l'autobiographie." Round table. Salon du Livre. Paris, 10 Mar. 1997.

Formentelli, Eliane. "Les langues sont des êtres de fuite." *Littérature* 77 (1990): 72–74.

Foucault, Michel. *The Foucault Reader*. Ed. Paul Rabinow. New York: Pantheon, 1984.

———. *The History of Sexuality: An Introduction*. Trans. Robert Hurley. New York: Vintage, 1990.

———. *Language, Counter-Memory, Practice: Selected Essays and Interviews*. Trans. Donald F. Bouchard and Sherry Simon. Ithaca: Cornell UP, 1977.

Fournel, Paul. "Premiers romans." *Magazine Littéraire* 210 (1984): 52–54.

Fragonard, Michel. *La culture du 20e siècle: Dictionnaire d'histoire culturelle*. Paris: Bordas, 1995.

Frank, Bernard. *Grognards et hussards*. Paris: Le Dillettante, 1989.

Frankel, E. R. *Revolution in Russia: Reassessments of 1917*. Cambridge: Cambridge UP, 1992.

Freud, Sigmund. *Le mot d'esprit et ses rapports avec l'inconscient*. Trans. Marie Bonaparte. Paris: Gallimard, 1974.

Garcin, Jérôme, Corinne Scemama, and Jean-Charles Lajouanie. "Les romanciers d'aujourd'hui payent leur dette au XXe siècle." *Nouvelles Littéraires* 14 Apr. 1983: 38–42.

Gaudet, Jeannette. "L'aventure de la littérature féminine contemporaine." Diss., Dalhousie University, 1994.

Gavronsky, Serge. *Toward a New Poetics: Contemporary Writing in France*. Berkeley: U of California P, 1994.

Genet, Jean. *The Declared Enemy: Texts and Interviews*. Trans. Jeff Fort. Stanford: Stanford UP, 2004.

———. *L'ennemi déclaré*. Paris: Gallimard, 1991.

———. *Notre-Dame-des-Fleurs*. Paris: Gallimard, 1975.

———. *Les paravents*. Lyon: L'Arbalète, 1951.

Genette, Gérard. *Figures II*. Paris: Seuil, 1959.

———. *Figures III*. Paris: Seuil, 1972.

———. *Palimpsestes: La littérature au second degré*. Paris: Seuil, 1989.

Giavarini, Laurence. "Un monsieur gris et précis." Rev. of *Monsieur*, by Jean-Philippe Toussaint. *Cahiers du Cinéma* 454 (1992): 52–54.

Gibson, William. *Agrippa*. New York: Kevin Begos Publishing, 1992.

Gingrass-Conley, Katharine. "Check-Out Time at the Splendid Hotel: Marie Redonnet's New Mythological Space." *Neophilologus* 77 (1993): 51–59.

Girard, René. *Mensonge romantique et vérité romanesque*. Paris: Grasset, 1951.

Gleick, James. *Chaos: Making a New Science*. New York: Penguin, 1987.

Gleize, Jean-Marie. *Le principe de nudité intégrale: Manifestes*. Paris: Seuil, 1995.

Glissant, Edouard. *Introduction à une poétique du divers*. Paris: Gallimard, 1995.

———. "Le relatif et le chaos." *Poétique de la relation*. Paris: Gallimard, 1990. 147–54.

Goertzel, Ben. *Chaotic Logic: Language, Thought, and Reality from the Perspective of Complex Systems Science*. New York: Plenum P, 1994.

Goldmann, Lucien. *Pour une sociologie du roman*. Paris: Gallimard, 1954.

Gorki, Maxim. *Articles and Pamphlets*. Moscow: Foreign Languages Publishing House, 1950.

Gracq, Julien. *Préférences*. Paris: Corti, 1951.

Grainville, Patrick. "Promenade somnambulique." Rev. of *L'appareil—photo*, by Jean-Philippe Toussaint. *Figaro Littéraire* 9 Jan. 1989: 22.

Green, André. *Narcissisme de vie, narcissisme de mort*. Paris: Minuit, 1984.

Guattari, Félix. *Chaosmosis: An Ethico-Aesthetic Paradigm*. Trans. Paul Bains and Julian Pefanis. Bloomington: Indiana UP, 1995.

Guiou, Dominique. "Fête barbare." Rev. of *Alto solo*, by Antoine Volo-
    dine. *Figaro Littéraire* 18 Nov. 1991: 4.
Gunn, Dan. "Catching it on the Wing." Rev. of *The Bathroom* and
    L'appareil-photo, by Jean-Philippe Toussaint. *Times Literary
    Supplement* 28 Apr. 1989: 452.
Gusdorf, Georges. *Auto-bio-graphie*. Paris: Odile Jacob, 1991.
Hamon, Philippe. "Clausules." *Poétique* 24 (1975): 495–525.
———. "Texte et architecture." *Poétique* 73 (1988): 3–25.
———. "Texte et idéologie: Pour une poétique de la norme." *Poétique*
    49 (1982): 105–25.
Hardt, Michael, and Antonio Negri. *Multitude: War and Democracy in
    the Age of Empire*. London: Penguin, 2004.
Harvey, David. *The Condition of Postmodernity*. Oxford: Blackwell,
    1992.
———. "The Cuisine of Post-Modern Simulacra." *Casabella* 50 (1995):
    101–5.
Hayles, N. Katherine. *Chaos Bound: Orderly Disorder in Contemporary
    Literature and Science*. Ithaca: Cornell UP, 1994.
———, ed. *Chaos and Order: Complex Dynamics in Literature and Sci-
    ence*. Chicago: U of Chicago P, 1991.
Heim, Michael. *The Metaphysics of Virtual Reality*. Oxford: Oxford UP,
    1993.
Heise, Ursula. *Chronoschisms*. Cambridge: Cambridge UP, 1997.
Henry, Freeman G., ed. *Discontinuity and Fragmentation in French Lit-
    erature*. French Literature Series 21. Amsterdam: Rodopi, 1994.
Hermosilla Alvarez, Concepción. "*L'appareil-photo* est-il un roman post-
    moderne?" *Cuadernos de Filología Francesa* 5 (1992): 51–81.
Hippolyte, Jean-Louis. "Chevillard's Aleatory World: Toward a French
    Postexotic Literature." *Cincinnati Romance Review* 15 (1995):
    27–34.
———. Rev. of *Un fantôme*, by Eric Chevillard. *French Review* 70.5
    (1997): 748–49.
———. Rev. of *Le port intérieur*, by Antoine Volodine. *French Review*
    70.5 (1997): 950–51.
———. *Xenofiction: Fictional Alterities in Contemporary French Fic-
    tion*. Ann Arbor: UMI, 1998.
Hollier, Denis, and R. Howard Bloch, eds. *A New History of French Lit-
    erature*. Cambridge: Harvard UP, 1989.
Holzberg-Namad, Ruth. Rev. of *Limite*, by François Bon. *French Review*
    50.3 (1987): 424–25.

Houppermans, Sjef. "Mille pertuis." *Recherches sur l'oeuvre de Claude Ollier.* Cahiers de Recherches Interuniversitaires Néerlandais 12. Ed. Sjef Houppermans. Groningen: Institut de Langues Romanes, 1985. 120–47.

Huizinga, Johan. *Homo Ludens: A Study of the Play-Element in Culture.* Boston: Beacon, 1952.

Hutcheon, Linda. *A Poetics of Postmodernism.* New York: Routledge, 1988.

Huyghe, Jean-Bernard, and Pierre Barbès. *La soft-idéologie.* Paris: Robert Laffont, 1987.

Ireland, Susan Elizabeth. "Reflexivity in the Contemporary French Novel." Diss., University of Colorado at Boulder, 1990.

Irigaray, Luce. *Ce sexe qui n'en est pas un.* Paris: Minuit, 1977.

Issacharoff, Michael. *Le spectacle du discours.* Paris: José Corti, 1985.

Jackson, Rosemary. *Fantasy: The Literature of Subversion.* London: Routledge, 1981.

James, Henry. *The Art of Fiction.* New York: Oxford UP, 1948.

Jameson, Fredric. *The Political Unconscious: Narrative as a Socially Symbolic Act.* Ithaca: Cornell UP, 1981.

———. *Postmodernism: The Cultural Logic of Late Capitalism.* Durham: Duke UP, 1992.

Janvier, L. *Une parole exigeante, le Nouveau Roman.* Paris: Minuit, 1954.

Jardon, Denise. *Du comique dans le texte littéraire.* Bruxelles: De Boeck-Duculot, 1988.

Jarry, Alfred. *Gestes et opinions du docteur Faustroll pataphysicien.* Paris: Stock, 1923.

Jencks, Charles. *What Is Post-Modernism?* New York: Saint Martin's, 1989.

Jones, Gregory V. "Stacks Not Fuzzy Sets: An Ordinal Basis for Prototype Theory of Concepts." *Cognition* 12.3 (1982): 281–90.

Josselin, Jean-François. "Toussaint à la fête." Rev. of *L'appareil-photo,* by Jean-Philippe Toussaint. *Nouvel Observateur* 19 Jan. 1989: 59.

Jourde, Pierre. "Les petits mondes à l'envers d'Eric Chevillard." *Nouvelle Revue Française* 485–87 (1993): 204–17.

Jouve, Vincent. *L'effet personnage dans le roman.* Paris: PUF, 1992.

Joyce, James. *Ulysses.* New York: Vintage, 1951.

Kacem, Belhaj. "L'impératif d'un affrontement." *Quinzaine Littéraire* 712 (1995): 8.

Kaeppelin, Olivier. "L'avant-garde va mal. Pourquoi?" *Quinzaine Littéraire* 339 (1981): 5–7.

Kafalenos, Emma. "From the Comic to the Ludic: Postmodern Fiction." *International Fiction Review* 12 (1985): 28–31.

———. "Toward a Typology of Indeterminacy in Postmodern Narratives." *Comparative Literature* 44 (1992): 380–408.

Kafka, Franz. *The Castle*. Trans. Edwin Muir and Willa Muir. New York: Knopf, 1948.

———. *Le château*. Trans. Alexandre Vialatte. Paris: Gallimard, 1994.

———. *The Metamorphosis*. Trans. Stanley Corngold. New York: Bantam, 1988.

———. *The Trial*. Trans. Edwin Muir and Willa Muir. New York: Random House, 1988.

Kéchichian, Patrick. "Grandir avec François Bon." Rev. of *Un fait divers*, by François Bon. *Monde des Livres* 3 Feb. 1994: 14.

———. "La loi du désordre." Rev. of *Nevermore*, by Marie Redonnet. *Monde des Livres* 25 Aug. 1994: 11.

———. "Les mots pour le fer." Rev. of *Temps-Machine*, by François Bon. *Monde des Livres* 21 May 1993: 19.

Keller, Luzius. "Der abweichende Blick: Gerda Zeltners Essays zur französischen Literatur" [The deviant gaze: Gerda Zeltner's essays on French literature]. Rev. of *Aesthetik der Abweichung: Aufsätze zum alternativen Erzählen in Frankreich* [Aesthetics of deviation: Essays on alternative fiction in France], by Gerda Zeltner. *Neue Zürcher Zeitung* 20–21 Jan. 1995: 47.

Kibédi, Varga. "Les années 80." *Rapports* 50 (1990): 157–59.

———. "Le récit post-moderne." *Littérature* 77 (1990): 3–22.

Kingcaid, Renée A. "After the Nouveau Roman: Some New Names in French Fiction." *Review of Contemporary Fiction* 8 (1988): 300–312.

Knapp, Bettina L. Rev. of *Monsieur*, by Jean-Philippe Toussaint. *French Review* 51.3 (1988): 527–28.

Knee, Robin. "Unmuddling Claude Ollier's Fuzzy Sets: An Intra/Intertextual Essay." *Symposium* 38.4 (1984–85): 311–20.

Kokos, Yannis. "Pour moi la scénographie c'est Mobie Dick." Interview with Olivier Kaeppelin. *Opus International* 84 (1982): 30–33.

Kolbert, Jack. "L'année littéraire 1985." *French Review* 50.5 (1987): 752–71.

Kolbert, Jack, and Nancy Lee Cairns. "L'année littéraire 1987." *French Review* 51.5 (1988): 845–58.

———. "L'année littéraire 1988." *French Review* 53.1 (1989): 1–15.

———. "L'année littéraire 1989." *French Review* 53.5 (1990): 927–58.

Koltès, Bernard-Marie. *Dans la solitude des champs de coton*. Paris: Minuit, 1985.

———. *Koltès, combats avec la scène*. Interview with Jacques Lemire. *Théâtre aujourd'hui* 5. Audio recording. Paris: CNDP, 1995.

Kosko, Bart. *Fuzzy Thinking: The New Science of Fuzzy Logic*. New York: Hyperion, 1993.

———. "Innerview." *Networker* 8:3 (1998): 2.

Kristeva, Julia. *Desire in Language: A Semiotic Approach to Literature and Art*. Trans. Léon Roudiez. New York: Columbia UP, 1980.

———. *Powers of Horror: An Essay on Abjection*. Trans. Léon Roudiez. New York: Columbia UP, 1982.

———. *La révolution du langage poétique*. Paris: Seuil, 1974.

———. *Sèméiotîkè: Recherches pour une sémanalyse*. Paris: Seuil, 1959.

———. *Strangers to Ourselves*. Trans. Léon Roudiez. New York: Columbia UP, 1994.

———. "Le temps des femmes." 3444 5 (1979): 5–19.

Kuberski, Philip. *Chaosmos: Literature, Science, and Theory*. Albany: SUNY P, 1994.

Kuhn, Thomas S. *The Structure of Scientific Revolutions*. Chicago: U of Chicago P, 1970.

Kundera, Milan. *L'art du roman*. Paris: Gallimard, 1985.

———. *Les testaments trahis*. Paris: Gallimard, 1993.

Labat, Joseph. Rev. of *Le caoutchouc décidément*, by Eric Chevillard. *French Review* 57 (1993): 900–901.

Lacan, Jacques. *Ecrits I*. Paris: Seuil, 1955.

Lachman, Renate. "Bakhtin and Carnival: Culture as Counter-Culture." *Cultural Critique* (1988–89): 115–52.

Landel, Vincent. "L'enfant naturel de Monsieur Teste." Rev. of *Monsieur*, by Jean-Philippe Toussaint. *Magazine Littéraire* 235 (1985): 58–59.

Lang, Luc. *11 septembre mon amour*. Paris: Stock, 2003.

La Palma, Marina. "The Human Figure as Simulacrum." *Artweek* 20 (1989): 3.

Lapouge, Gilles. "La naissance du palimpseste." *Quinzaine Littéraire* 598 (1995): 11–12.

Larroux, Guy. *Le mot de la fin: La clôture romanesque en question*. Paris: Nathan, 1995.

———. *Le réalisme: Eléments de critique, d'histoire et de poétique*. Paris: Nathan, 1995.

Laumonier, Alexandre. "L'errance ou la pensée du milieu." *Magazine Littéraire* 353 (1997): 20–25.

Laurrent, Eric. *Coup de foudre*. Paris: Minuit, 1995.

———. *Liquider*. Paris: Minuit, 1997.

Le Bris, Michel. "Ecrivain-voyageur?" *Magazine Littéraire* 353 (1997): 24–28.

Lebrun, Jean-Claude. *François Bon: Un écrivain en Seine-Saint-Denis*. N.p: Conseil Général de la Seine-Saint-Denis, 1987.

———. *Jean Echenoz*. Paris: Editions du Rocher, 1992.

———. "Une unité romanesque dans la diversité." *Pensée* 302 (1995): 129–38.

Lebrun, Jean-Claude, and Claude Prévost. *Nouveaux territoires romanesques*. Paris: Messidor, 1992.

Leclair, Bertrand. "Pourquoi y a-t-il de la littérature plutôt que rien?" *Quinzaine Littéraire* 712 (1997): 11–12.

———, ed. "Où va la littérature française (1)?" *Quinzaine Littéraire* 711 (1997): 4–10.

———, ed. "Où va la littérature française (2)?" *Quinzaine Littéraire* 712 (1997): 5–12.

Leclerc, Yvan. "Abstraction faite." *Critique* 510 (1989): 889–902.

———. "Autour de minuit." *Dalhousie French Studies* 17 (1989): 53–74.

———. "Le XIXe siècle deçà, delà." *Magazine Littéraire* 353 (1997): 32–35.

———. "Voir le vrai tomber juste." *Critique* 503 (1989): 247–58.

Lecomte, Jacques. "Regards multiples sur l'être humain." *Sciences Humaines* 54 (1995): 18–23.

Leféburc du Bus, Olivier. Rev. of *Monsieur*, by Jean-Philippe Toussaint. *Séquences* 155 (1991): 75–77.

Leiris, Michel. *L'âge d'homme* précédé de *De la littérature considérée comme une tauromachie*. Paris: Gallimard, 1939.

Lejeune, Philippe. *Le pacte autobiographique*. Paris: Seuil, 1975.

Lemaire, Gérard-Georges. "Les années 70: L'ère des revues." *Page des Libraires* 44 (1997): 25–27.

Lenoir, Hélène. *Le magot de Momm*. Paris: Minuit, 2000.

Lepape, Pierre. "Jean-Philippe Toussaint ou l'art du minimum vital." Rev. of *L'appareil—photo*, by Jean-Philippe Toussaint. *Monde des Livres* 5 Jan. 1989: 13.

———. "Le pari manqué de Toussaint." Rev. of *La réticence*, by Jean-Philippe Toussaint. *Monde des Livres* 15 Nov. 1991: 12.

———. "Pascal qui rit." Rev. of *La télévision*, by Jean-Philippe Toussaint. *Monde des Livres* 17 Jan. 1997: 11.

Lepape, Pierre, and Michèle Gazier. *Romanciers du XXe siècle.* Alleur: Marabout, 1990.

Lepoutre, David. *Coeur de banlieue: Codes, rites et langages.* Paris: Odile Jacob, 1997.

Lesourne, Jacques. "Les scénarios du futur." *Magazine Littéraire* 312 (1993): 29.

Le Touze, Philippe. "Aspects de l'esthétique du temps chez quelques romanciers de Minuit." *Passage du temps, ordre de la transition.* Ed. Jean Bessière. Paris: PUF, 1985. 187–200.

Le Sidaner, Jean-Marie. Rev. of *Doublures*, by Marie Redonnet. *Magazine Littéraire* 228 (1985): 72.

Lewin, Roger. *Complexity: Life at the Edge of Chaos.* London: Dent, 1993.

Lièvre-Crosson, Elisabeth. *Du cubisme au surréalisme.* Toulouse: Milan, 1995.

Lindemann, Uwe. "Toussaint." *Kritisches Lexikon Zur fremd Sprachigen Gegenswartliteratur* 35 (1995): A1+.

Lindon, Jérôme. Interview with Bernard Pivot. *Apostrophes.* France 2. 18 Oct. 1985.

———. "On ne se baigne pas deux fois dans le même fleuve." *Quinzaine Littéraire* 532 (1989): 34–35.

———. Personal interview. 28 June 1995.

———. Personal interview. 10 June 1997.

Linze, Jacques-Gérard. "Eloge du désordre." *Bulletin de l'Académie Royale de Langue et de Littérature Française* 57 (1990): 202–17.

Lipovetsky, Gilles. *L'ère du vide: Essais sur l'individualisme contemporain.* Paris: Gallimard, 1983.

Lotman, Iouri. *La structure du texte artistique.* Paris: Gallimard, 1973.

Luckhurst, Roger. "Border Policing: Postmodernism and Science Fiction." *Science-Fiction Studies* 18 (1991): 358–55.

Lucrèce. *De la Nature.* Trans. Henri Clouard. Paris: Garnier, 1954.

Lukács, Georg. *The Historical Novel.* Trans. Hannah and Stanley Mitchell. London: Merlin, 1952.

Lvoff, John. "Le carré de l'hypothénuse est égal à la somme des carrés des deux autres côtés: A propos de *La salle de bain.*" *Licorne* 25 (1993): 5–5.

———. "The Director." Interview. *Contemporanea* 3.4 (1990): 87.

Lyotard, Jean-François. *The Postmodern Condition: A Report on Knowledge*. Trans. Geoff Bennington and Brian Massumi. Minneapolis: U of Minnesota P, 1984.

———. *Le postmoderne expliqué aux enfants*. Paris: Galilée, 1988.

Macé, Marie-Anne. *Le roman français des années 70*. Rennes: Presses Universitaires de Rennes, 1995.

Macherey, Pierre. *A quoi pense la littérature? Exercices de philosophie littéraire*. Paris: PUF, 1990.

Mahony Greening, Marcella. "The Sense of Chaos: A Dynamical Theory of Narrative." Diss., University of California, Santa Barbara, 1993.

Mallarmé, Stéphane. *Collected Poems*. Trans. Henry Weinfeld. Berkeley: U of California P, 1994.

———. *Poésies*. Paris: Gallimard, 1945.

———. *Poésies*. Paris: Gallimard, 1948.

Malraux, André. *Man's Fate*. Trans. Haakon M. Chevalier. New York: Vintage, 1990.

———. "L'utopie terroriste." *Monde: Dossiers et Documents Littéraires* (Oct. 1995): 2.

Manchette, Jean-Patrick. *Chroniques*. Paris: Rivages, 1995.

Margolin, François, and Patrick Théveron. "La salle de bain: Une caméra dans le lavabo." *Globe* 35 (1989): 111–15.

Martindale, Colin. "Chaos Theory, Strange Attractors, and the Laws of Literary History." *Empirical Studies of Literature: Proceedings of the Second IGEL Conference*. Ed. Elrud Ibsch and Dick Schram. Amsterdam: Rodopi, 1991. 381–85.

Mary, François. Rev. of *L'enterrement*, by François Bon. *Plein Chant* 59 (1995): 120.

Mauriac, Claude. *L'alittérature contemporaine*. Paris: Albin Michel, 1959.

Maury, Pierre. Rev. of *Monsieur*, by Jean-Philippe Toussaint. *Revue Générale* 11 (1985): 95–97.

Mathy, Jean-Philippe. "The End of Philosophy and the Pragmatisation of French Thought, Culture, and Society." *History of European Ideas* 20 (1995): 545–51.

McGarry, Pascale. "La dame blanche et le coeur à la crème." *Estudios de Lengua y Literatura Francesas* 8–9 (1994): 101–14.

Mercier, Christophe. "La fin des grands romans?" *Commentaire* 18 (1995): 455–57.

Meriwether, James. "Chaos and Beckett's 'Core of Murmurs': Toward a

Contemporary Theoretical Structure." *SubStance* 23.1 (1994): 95–108.

Merwin, W. S. "Footprints of a Shadow." *New York Review of Books* 3 Dec. 1998: 41.

Meyer Spacks, Patricia. *Boredom: The Literary History of a State of Mind.* Chicago: U of Chicago P, 1995.

Michaux, Henri. *L'espace du dedans.* Paris: Gallimard, 1955.

———. "Le grand combat." *Anthologie de la poésie française au XXe siècle.* Paris: Gallimard, 1983. 372.

———. *Selected Writings: The Space Within.* Trans. Richard Ellman. New York: New Directions, 1958.

Michon, Pierre. "Un auteur majuscule." Interview with Thierry Bayle. *Magazine Littéraire* 353 (1997): 97–103.

———. "D'abord, contemporain." *Quinzaine Littéraire* 532 (1989): 17–18.

———. *Mythologies d'hiver.* Paris: Verdier, 1997.

Miguet, Marie. "Critique, autocritique, autofiction." *Lettres Romanes* 43.3 (1989): 195–208.

Miller, D. A. *Narrative and Its Discontents: Problems of Closure in the Traditional Novel.* Princeton: Princeton UP, 1989.

Millet, Catherine. *L'art contemporain.* Paris: Flammarion, 1997.

Milliex, Hélène. "Ecrire comme on tue." Rev. of *Un fait divers*, by François Bon. *Magazine Littéraire* 319 (1994): 77.

Minc, Alain. *Le nouveau Moyen Age.* Paris: Gallimard, 1993.

Miraux, Jean-Philippe. *L'autobiographie: Ecriture de soi et sincérité.* Paris: Nathan, 1995.

Mitterand, Henri. *La littérature française du XXe siècle.* Paris: Nathan, 1995.

———. "1950–1997: Un demi-siècle de romans." *Page des Libraires* 44 (1997): 18–21.

Mongin, Olivier. "Le goût du réel en littérature." *Esprit* 192 (1993): 115–25.

Monsieur. Dir. Jean-Philippe Toussaint. With Dominic Gould and Wojciech Pszoniak. Films des Tournelles, 1990.

Moraly, Jean-Bernard Yehuda. "Le livre impossible." *Europe* 808–9 (1995): 134–43.

Moreau, Jean-Luc. *La nouvelle fiction.* Paris: Critérion, 1992.

Morin, Edgard. "Le besoin d'une pensée complexe." *Magazine Littéraire* Hors-Série (1995): 120–23.

———. "Edgar Morin, philosophe de l'incertain." Interview with François Ewald. *Magazine Littéraire* 312 (1993): 18–22.

———. *L'homme et la mort*. Paris: Seuil, 1970.

Morin, Edgard, and Anne Brigitte Kern. *Terre-Patrie*. Paris: Seuil, 1993.

Mortimer, Armine Kotin. *La clôture narrative*. Paris: José Corti, 1985.

Motte, Warren F., Jr. "Clinamen Redux." *Comparative Literature Studies* 23.4 (1985): 253–81.

———. "Literary Ludics." *Esprit Créateur* 31.4 (1991): 3–5.

———. *Playtexts: Ludics in Contemporary Literature*. Lincoln: U of Nebraska P, 1995.

———. "Redonnet's Symmetries." *French Forum* 19.2 (1994): 215–28.

———. "Toussaint's Small World." *Neophilologus* 78.4 (1994): 549–59.

Mournier, Pierre-François. "Littérature et engagement." *Esprit* 211 (1995): 195–201.

Musil, Robert. *L'homme sans qualités*. 2 vols. Trans. Philippe Jaccottet. Paris: Seuil, 1957.

Naaman, Antoine, and Louis Painchaud, eds. *Le roman contemporain d'expression française*. Sherbrooke: CELEF, 1971.

Nadaud, Alain. *Malaise dans la littérature*. Seysell: Champ Vallon, 1993.

———. "Pour un nouvel imaginaire." *Infini* 19 (1987): 3–12.

Nadeau, Maurice. "L'état des lieux." *Quinzaine Littéraire* 532 (1989): 3–4.

———. *Le roman français depuis la guerre*. Paris: Gallimard, 1970.

Narcejac, Thomas. *Le roman policier, une machine à lire*. Paris: Denoël, 1975.

Natoli, Joseph. *Mots d'ordre: Disorder in Literary Worlds*. Albany: SUNY P, 1992.

Nemer, Monique. "L'éditeur et le dilemne de la valeur." *Page des Libraires* 44 (1997): 40–41.

Nerval, Gérard de. *Les nuits d'octobre*. Paris: Garnier, 1985.

———. *Paris et ses alentours*. Paris: Encre, 1984.

Noguez, Dominique. "Structure du langage humoristique." *Revue d'esthétique* 22 (1959): 37–54.

Noiret, Gérard. "Une aventure d'écriture, une aventure de sens." Rev. of *Limite*, by François Bon. *Quinzaine Littéraire* 449 (1985): 32–33.

———. "Le cri de la banlieue." Rev. of *Décor ciment*, by François Bon. *Quinzaine Littéraire* 522 (1988): 14–15.

———. "Pulsions internes et vacarmes extérieurs." Rev. of *Temps-Machine*, by François Bon. *Quinzaine Littéraire* 522 (1993): 9–10.

Noiville, Florence. "Minuit: Savoir attendre." *Monde* 27 Jan. 1995: 4.

Nora, Pierre. *Les lieux de mémoire.* 3 vols. Paris: Gallimard, 1992.

———. "La ruée vers le passé." *Magazine Littéraire* Hors-Série (1995): 58–70.

Nowoselsky-Müler, Sonia. "Aus der Küche geplaudert: Ein Gespräch mit François Bon" [Kitchen talk: An interview with François Bon]. *Extreme Gegenwart* [Contemporary writers]. Ed. Christiane Baumann and Gisela Lerch. Bremen: Manholt, 1989. 135–42.

Ollier, Claude. *Fuzzy sets.* Paris: Union Générale d'Editions, 1975.

Oppenheim, Lois, ed. *Three Decades of the French New Novel.* Chicago: U of Illinois P, 1985.

Oster, Christian. *Les rendez-vous.* Paris: Minuit, 2003.

Otchakovsky-Laurens, Paul. "Interview." *Magazine Littéraire* 459 (1985): 35.

Otten, Anna. "Innovation in Modern French Fiction." *Antioch Review* 45 (1987): 255–74.

Oulipo: Atlas de littérature potentielle. Paris: Gallimard, 1988.

Ovid. *The Metamorphoses.* Ed. Horace Gregory. New York: New American Library, 1958.

P., J. "La cheville de Chevillard." Rev. of *Palafox*, by Eric Chevillard. *Libération* 22 Nov. 1990: 27.

Padis, Marc-Olivier. "Une littérature de l'enfermement: Rollin, Darley, Chevillard, Bon, Boyer." *Esprit* 205 (1994): 114–25.

Pascal, Blaise. *Les pensées.* Paris: Mercure de France, 1975.

———. *Pensées.* Trans. A. J. Krailsheimer. London: Penguin, 1955.

Patocka, Jan. *L'écrivain, son "objet."* Trans. Erika Abrams. Paris: POL, 1990.

"Le patrimoine. Les groupes, les écoles. La situation actuelle." *Roman* 25 (1989): 9–24.

Paulson, William. "Literature, Complexity, Interdisciplinarity." Hayles 37–53.

Pécheur, Jacques. Rev. of *L'appareil-photo*, by Jean-Philippe Toussaint. *Français dans le Monde* 229 (1989): 22.

———. "Identités." Rev. of *Candy Story*, by Marie Redonnet. *Français dans le Monde* 255 (1993): 13.

———. "Morte saison des certitudes." Rev. of *La réticence*, by Jean-Philippe Toussaint. *Français dans le Monde* 245 (1991): 12–13.

———. Rev. of *Silsie*, by Marie Redonnet. *Français dans le Monde* 238 (1991): 17–18.

Perec, Georges. *L'infra-ordinaire.* Paris: Seuil, 1989.

———. "Pour une littérature réaliste." *L. G.: Une aventure des années 50*. Paris: Seuil, 1992. 47–55.

Péret, Benjamin. *Le déshonneur des poètes*. Paris: Mille et Une Nuits, 1995.

Pessoa, Fernando. *Oeuvres complètes I: Proses publiées du vivant de l'auteur*. Ed. Joaquim Vital. Paris: La Différence, 1988.

———. *Ultimatum*. Paris: Mille et Une Nuits, 1989.

Pétillon, Monique. "Une bête faramineuse." Rev. of *Palafox*, by Eric Chevillard. *Monde des Livres* 7 Dec. 1990: 29.

———. "Le gardien enfermé." Rev. of *Préhistoire*, by Eric Chevillard. *Monde des Livres* 14 Nov. 1994: 3.

Picard, Anne-Marie. "Arrêts sur image: Identité et altérité dans *Le désert mauve* de Nicole Brossard et *Rose Mélie Rose* de Marie Redonnet." *Dalhousie French Studies* 32 (1995): 101–12.

———. "Dans le paysage, une figure presque féminine: Le triptyque de Marie Redonnet." *Australian Journal of French Studies* 31.2 (1994): 228–40.

Pinget, Robert. *Taches d'encre*. Paris: Minuit, 1997.

Pivin-Ziegel, Jaqueline. "A French Intellectual in the 1980s." *Antioch Review* 45 (1987): 280–82.

Pleynet, Marcelin. "Les problèmes de l'avant-garde." *Tel Quel* 25 (1955): 77–85.

Poirot-Delpech, Bertrand. "Chiendent." Rev. of *Le crime de Buzon*, by François Bon. *Monde des Livres* 19 Sept. 1985: 15+.

Poletti, Marie-Laure. "Redonnet: Un auteur contemporain pour la classe." *Français dans le Monde* 275 (1995): 53–51.

Poovey, Mary. "Feminism and Deconstruction." *Feminist Studies* 14.1 (1988): 51–55.

Porter, Charles A. *After the Age of Suspicion: The French Novel Today*. New Haven: Yale UP, 1988.

Porush, David. "Literature as Dissipative Structure: Prigogine's Theory and the Postmodern 'Chaos' Machine." *Literature and Technology*. Research in Technology Studies 5. Ed. Mark L. Greenberg and Lance Schachterle. Bethelehem PA: Lehigh UP, 1992.

Prévost, Claude. "Au-delà du soupçon." *Quinzaine Littéraire* 532 (1989): 25.

Prigent, Michel. *A quoi bon encore des poètes?* Paris: POL, 1995.

———. *Ceux qui merdRent*. Paris: POL, 1991.

———. *La langue et ses monstres*. N.p.: Cadex, 1989.

———. "L'ordre alphabétique des sciences humaines." *Magazine Littéraire* Hors-Série (1995): 75–79.

Prigogine, Ilya. *La fin des certitudes*. Paris: Odile Jacob, 1995.

Prigogine, Ilya, and Isabelle Stengers. *Order out of Chaos: Man's New Dialogue with Nature*. New York: Bantam: 1984.

Prince, Gerald. "L'appareil récit de Jean-Philippe Toussaint." Henry 109–14.

———. *Narratology: The Form and Functioning of Narrative*. Berlin: Mouton, 1982.

Propp, Vladimir. *Morphologie du conte*. Trans. Marguerite Derrida, Tzvetan Todorov, and Claude Kahn. Paris: Seuil, 1955.

Queneau, Raymond. *Bâtons, chiffres et lettres*. Paris: Gallimard, 1955.

Quignard, Pascal. *Une gêne technique à l'égard des fragments*. Montpellier: Fata Morgana, 1985.

———. "Le mot contemporain." *Français Aujourd'hui* 75 (1985): 93–95.

———. *Les ombres errantes*. Paris: Grasset, 2002.

Raaphorst-Rousseau, Madeleine. "L'année littéraire 1981." *French Review* 55.5 (1982): 859–81.

———. "L'année littéraire 1982." *French Review* 55.5 (1983): 904–15.

———. "L'année littéraire 1983." *French Review* 57.5 (1984): 843–55.

———. "L'année littéraire 1984." *French Review* 58.5 (1985): 843–58.

———. "L'année littéraire 1985." *French Review* 59.5 (1985): 942–55.

Rabaté, Dominique. *Vers une littérature de l'épuisement*. Paris: José Corti, 1985.

Rabelais, François. *Oeuvres complètes*. Paris: Seuil, 1973.

Racevskis, Karlis. "The Modernity of Moralistes and the (A)Morality of Postmodernists." *Antioch Review* 45 (1987): 275–79.

Raillard, Georges. "La chimère et l'élégance de Marie Redonnet." Rev. of *Silsie*, by Marie Redonnet. *Quinzaine Littéraire* 555 (1990): 11.

Raimond, Michel. *La crise du roman*. Paris: Corti, 1957.

Rambures, Jean-Louis de. *Comment travaillent les écrivains*. Paris: Flammarion, 1978.

Rascevskis, Karlis. Rev. of *Décor ciment*, by François Bon. *World Literature Today* 53.4 (1989): 549–50.

Reboux, Jean-Jacques. "Le polar français." Interview with Jean-Christophe Millois. *Prétexte* 12 (1997): 57–59.

Redonnet, Marie. *L'accord de paix*. Paris: Grasset, 2000.

———. *Candy Story*. Paris: Gallimard, 1992.

———. *Candy Story*. Trans. Alexandra Quinn. Lincoln: U of Nebraska P, 1995.

———. *Le cirque Pandor* and *Fort Gambo*. Paris: POL, 1994.

————. *Dead Man & Company*. Trans. Gilbert Alter-Gilbert. San Jose: Leaping Dog Press, 2004.

————. *Doublures*. Paris: POL, 1985.

————. "Entretien avec Marie Redonnet." Interview with Pascale Hassoun and Chantal Maillet. *Patio/Psychanalyse* 10 (1988): 135–43.

————. *Forever Valley*. Paris: Minuit, 1987.

————. *Forever Valley*. Trans. Jordan Stump. Lincoln: U of Nebraska P, 1994.

————. *Hôtel Splendid*. Trans. Jordan Stump. Lincoln: U of Nebraska P, 1994.

————. *Jean Genet, le poète travesti*. Paris: Grasset, 2000.

————. Letter to the author. 15 May 1994.

————. *Mobie-Diq*. Paris: Minuit, 1989.

————. *Mobie-Diq*. Dir. Alain Françon. With Francine Bergé and Jean-Claude Jay. Théâtre de la Bastille, Paris. 17 Jan.–12 Feb. 1989.

————. *Le mort & Cie*. Paris: POL, 1985.

————. *Nevermore*. Paris: Gallimard, 1994.

————. Personal interview. 27 Jan. 1995.

————. "Portraiture." *Les Lettres Françaises* 3 (1990): 12.

————. "Redonne après maldonne." *Infini* 19 (1987): 150–53.

————. "Redonnet, Marie." *Dictionnaire de littérature française contemporaine*. Ed. Jérôme Garcin. Paris: François Bourin, 1988.

————. "Rencontre avec Marie Redonnet: Ecrire entre énigme et secret." Interview with Olivier Schmitt. *Monde des Livres* 13 July 1988: 12.

————. "Réponses pour une question brouillée." *Quai Voltaire 2: La question de la postérité*. Paris: Quai Voltaire, 1991. 45–48.

————. *Rose Mélie Rose*. Paris: Minuit, 1987.

————. *Rose Mellie Rose*. Trans. Jordan Stump. Lincoln: U of Nebraska P, 1994.

————. *Seaside*. Paris: Minuit, 1992.

————. *Seaside*. Dir. Gilles Gleize. Chapelle Sainte-Claire/Théâtre des Halles, Festival d'Avignon. 1992.

————. "Un secret inavouable." *Public: Journal du Théâtre National de la Colline* 4 (1988–89): n.p.

————. "Seulement un trou avec n'importe quoi autour." *Europe* 808–9 (1995): 48–55.

————. *Silsie*. Paris: Gallimard, 1990.

————. *Splendid Hôtel*. Paris: Minuit, 1985.

———. "Le théâtre de Jean Genet." Course. Université de Paris III, 1995–97.

———. *Tir & Lir*. Paris: Minuit, 1988.

———. *Tir et Lir*. Dir. Alain Françon. Théâtre National de la Colline, Paris. 2 Dec. 1988–7 Jan. 1989.

———. *Villa Rosa*. Charenton: Flohic, 1995.

Redonnet, Marie, and Alain Françon. "Marie Redonnet: *Tir et Lir* et *Mobie-Diq* mis en scène par Alain Françon." Interview with Irène Sadowska-Guillon. *Acteurs* 51–53 (1988): 121–24.

Reeves, Hubert, Joël de Rosnay, Yves Coppens, and Dominique Simonnet. *La plus belle histoire du monde: Le secret de nos origines*. Paris: Seuil, 1995.

Reyes, Alina. *Nus devant les fantômes: Franz Kafka et Milena Jensesca*. Paris: Editions 1, 2000.

Ribaupierre, Claire de. "Postmoderne: Généalogie d'un concept en crise." *Etudes de Lettres* (1995): 53–77.

Ricardou, Jean. *Nouveau roman: Hier, aujourd'hui: Pratiques*. Paris: Plon, 1972.

———. *Le nouveau roman*. Paris: Seuil, 1973.

———. *Pour une théorie du nouveau roman*. Paris: Seuil, 1971.

Ricardou, Jean, and Françoise Rossum-Guyon, eds. *Nouveau roman: Hier, aujourd'hui: Problèmes généraux*. Paris: Plon, 1972.

Richard, Jean-Pierre. *L'état des choses: Etudes sur huit écrivains d'aujourd'hui*. Paris: Gallimard, 1990.

———. *Poésie et profondeur*. Paris: Seuil, 1955.

———. *Terrains de lecture*. Paris: Gallimard, 1995.

Ricoeur, Paul. *Temps et récit*. 3 vols. Paris: Seuil, 1983–85.

Riebling, Barbara. "Remodeling Truth, Power and Society: Implications of Chaos Theory, Nonequilibrium Dynamics, and Systems Science for the Study of Politics and Literature." *After Poststructuralism: Interdisciplinarity and Literary Theory*. Ed. Narray Easterlin and Barbara Riebling. Evanston: Northwestern UP, 1993. 177–201.

Rimbaud, Arthur. *Illuminations*. Paris: Gallimard, 1955.

Rivière, Jean-Loup. "Le monde et la phrase." *Public: Journal du Théâtre national de la Colline* 4 (1988–89): n.p.

Robbe-Grillet, Alain. "The French New Novel." Trans. Anna Otten. *Antioch Review* 45 (1987): 253–55.

———. "The French Novel: From Nouveau to New." *Times Literary Supplement* 13 Oct. 1989: 1122+.

———. *Pour un nouveau roman*. Paris: Minuit, 1953.

Roegiers, Patrick. *L'artiste, la servante et le savant*. Paris: Seuil, 1997.

———. *Beau regard*. Paris: Seuil, 1990.

Rollin, André. *Ils écrivent, où? quand? comment?* Paris: Mazarine, 1985.

Rorty, Richard. "How Many Grains Make a Heap?" *London Review of Books* 20 Jan. 2005: 12.

Rose, Margaret A. "Parody/Postmodernism." *Poetics* 17 (1988): 49–55.

———. "Post-Modern Pastiche." *British Journal of Aesthetics* 31 (1991): 25–38.

Rosset, Clément. *Le réel, traité de l'idiotie*. Paris: Minuit, 1977.

Rosset, François. "Viendront d'autres horribles travailleurs." *Quinzaine Littéraire* 712 (1995): 9.

Rossi, Paul Louis. *Vocabulaire de la modernité littéraire*. Paris: Minerve, 1995.

Rouaud, Jean. *Les champs d'honneur*. Paris: Minuit, 1990.

Roudiez, Léon S. *French Fiction Revisited*. 2nd ed. Elmwood Park: Dalkey Archive, 1991.

Rousset, Jean. *Forme et signification: Essai sur les structures littéraires de Corneille à Claudel*. Paris: Corti, 1952.

Roy, Max. "Stratégies de lecture dans le roman contemporain." *Tangence* 39 (1993): 75–88.

Ruano-Borbalan, Jean-Claude. "Les peuples guerriers." *Sciences Humaines* 41 (1994): 18–21.

Ruano-Borbalan, Jean-Claude, and Nicolas Journet. "Aux sources de la guerre." *Sciences Humaines* 41 (1994): 10–13.

Rushdie, Salman. *The Ground Beneath Her Feet*. New York: Picador, 1999.

Safir, Margery Arent. *Melancholies of Knowledge*. New York: SUNY P, 1999.

Said, Edward. *Orientalism*. New York: Random House, 1979.

Salgas, Jean-Pierre. *1958–1983–1998: Romans mode d'emploi*. Proceedings of Exhibit on Contemporary French Literature. 12–15 Mar. 1997. Salon du Livre, Paris. Paris: ADPF, 1997.

Sallenave, Danièle, Alain Finkielkraut, and Alain Nadaud. "Où en est la littérature?" *Infini* 23 (1988): 90–104.

Salvayre, Lydie. *La puissance des mouches*. Paris: Seuil, 1997.

Sandbank, Shimon. *After Kafka: The Influence of Kafka's Fiction*. Athens: U of Georgia P, 1989.

Sarraute, Nathalie. "Conférence de Milan." *Nathalie Sarraute: Portrait d'un écrivain.* Paris: Bibliothèque Nationale de France, 1995. 19–24.

———. *L'ère du soupçon: Essais sur le roman.* Paris: Gallimard, 1955.

Sartorius, Joachim. "François Bon, ein Nomade, der den ganz anderen Tourismus praktiziert" [François Bon: A nomad for another kind of tourism]. *World Literature Today* 53.4 (1989): 130–34.

Sartre, Jean-Paul. *Critiques littéraires: Situations, I.* Paris: Gallimard, 1947.

———. *Literary Essays.* Trans. Annette Michelson. New York: Citadel, 1955.

———. *Les mots.* Paris: Gallimard, 1954.

———. *Qu'est-ce que la littérature?* Paris: Gallimard, 1948.

———. *Situations I: Essais critiques.* Paris: Gallimard, 1958.

———. *What Is Literature?* Cambridge: Harvard UP, 1988.

Savigneau, Josyane. "La peur de Volodine." Rev. of *Alto solo*, by Antoine Volodine. *Monde des Livres* 20 Sept. 1991: 19.

———. "*Silsie* ou le rêve englouti." Rev. of *Silsie*, by Marie Redonnet. *Monde des Livres* 9 Nov. 1990: 27.

———. "Une vie et une vallée perdues." Rev. of *Forever Valley*, by Marie Redonnet. *Monde des Livres* 27 Feb. 1987: 13.

Scanlan, Margaret. "Literature at the Margins: The Terrorist as the Novelist in Antoine Volodine's *Lisbonne dernière marge.*" *New Novel Review* 3.1 (1995): 57–81.

Schmitt, Olivier. "Les chants de la peur." Rev. of *Tir et Lir*, by Marie Redonnet. Cloitre de la Collégiale de Villeneuve. *Monde* 18 July 1988: 7.

———. "Qui a tué la baleine blanche?" Rev. of *Mobie Diq*, by Marie Redonnet. Théâtre de la Bastille. *Monde des Livres* 28 Jan. 1989: 19.

———. "Les vestiges de la cruauté." Rev. of *Seaside*, by Gilles Gleize. Chapelle Sainte-Claire/Théâtre des Halles, Festival d'Avignon. *Monde des Livres* 15 July 1992: 11.

Schoots, Fieke. "L'écriture minimaliste." Ammouche-Kremers and Hillenaar, *Jeunes auteurs* 127–44.

Sciscery-Ronay, Istvan. "Modeling the Chaosphere: Stanislaw Lem's Alien Communications. Hayles 244–52.

Segalen, Victor. *Essai sur l'exotisme.* Paris: Fata Morgana, 1978.

Serres, Michel. *Atlas.* Paris: Flammarion, 1995.

———. *Hermes: Literature, Science, Philosophy.* Ed. and trans. Josué Harari and David F. Bell. Baltimore: Johns Hopkins UP, 1982.

———. *Hermès III: La traduction*. Paris: Minuit, 1974.

———. *Hermès IV: La distribution*. Paris: Minuit, 1977.

———. *La naissance de la physique dans le texte de Lucrèce: Fleuves et turbulences*. Paris: Minuit, 1977.

———. *Le parasite*. Paris: Grasset, 1980.

Servier, Jean. *Histoire de l'utopie*. Paris: Gallimard, 1991.

Shakespeare, William. *The Complete Works*. Oxford: Oxford UP, 1955.

Sherzer, Dina. *Representation in Contemporary French Fiction*. Lincoln: U of Nebraska P, 1985.

Siclier, Jacques. "Entre Keaton et Tati: 'Monsieur,' premier film de Jean-Philippe Toussaint." Rev. of *Monsieur*, by Jean-Philippe Toussaint. *Monde* 24 Jan. 1990: 15.

Silverman, Kaja. *The Subject of Semiotics*. Oxford: Oxford UP, 1983.

Simon, Claude. *Discours de Stockholm*. Paris: Minuit, 1985.

Simonin, Anne. *Les éditions de Minuit (1942–1955): Le devoir d'insoumission*. Paris: IMEC, 1994.

———. "La guerre des Editions de Minuit." *Histoire* 150 (1992): 78–80.

———. Interview with Laure Adler. *Le cercle de Minuit*. France 2. 14 Nov. 1994.

Sinnassamy, Evelyne. "Je parle d'une ville qui a disparu: *Calvaire des chiens* de François Bon." *Lendemains* 52 (1991): 93–95.

Smith, Paul J. "François Bon: Rabelaisien." Ammouche-Kremers and Hillenaar, *Jeunes auteurs* 103–15.

Sollers, Philippe. *L'écriture et l'expérience des limites*. Paris: Seuil, 1958.

———. *Logiques*. Paris: Seuil, 1958.

———. Interview with Carole Vantroys. *Lire* 253 (1997): 32–37.

———. Interview with P. Werner. *Le témoin du temps qui change*. France Culture. 8 Aug. 1997.

Sorin, Raphaël. "François Bon: Terra dolorosa." Rev. of *L'enterrement*, by François Bon. *Express* 14 Feb. 1992: 53.

Spilka, Marc, and Caroline McCracken-Flesher, eds. *Why the Novel Matters: A Postmodern Perplex*. Bloomington: Indiana UP, 1990.

Sroka, Ewa. "L'écriture fragmentaire ou la discontinuité de la pensée après 1958." Henry 171–81.

Starre, Evert van der. "Marie Redonnet." Ammouche-Kremers and Hillenaar, *Jeunes auteurs* 53–58.

Stendhal. *Vie de Henry Brulard*. Paris: Gallimard, 1955.

Stewart, Garrett. "Signing Off: Dickens and Thackeray, Woolf and Beckett." *Philosophical Approaches to Literature: New Essays in*

Nineteenth- and Twentieth-Century Texts. Ed. William Cain. Lewisburg PA: Bucknell UP, 1984. 117–39.

Strand, John. "An Interview with Jean Baudrillard." *Art International* 12 (1990): 55–55.

Strougatski, Arkadi, and Boris Strougatski. *L'auberge de l'alpiniste mort*. Trans. Antoine Volodine. Paris: Denoël, 1988.

Stump, Jordan. "L'eau qui s'efface, l'eau qui s'anime: Du triptyque de Marie Redonnet." *L'eau: Source d'une écriture dans les littératures féminines francophones*. Ed. Yolande Helm. New York: Lang, 1995. 103–11.

———. "Separation and Permeability in Marie Redonnet's Triptych." *French Forum* 20.1 (1995): 105–19.

Sun Tzu. *L'art de la guerre*. Trans. Le père Amiot. Paris: Mille et Une Nuits, 1995.

Tadié, Jean-Yves. *Le roman au XXe siècle*. Paris: Belfond, 1990.

Tahourdin, Adrian. "Atlantis Transplanted." *Times Literary Supplement* 4 (1991): 28.

Tailleux, Dominique. *L'espace nervalien*. Paris: Nizet, 1975.

Taminiaux, Pierre. "Images de la dépossession: Jean-Philippe Toussaint et Christian Boltanski." *Dalhousie French Studies* 32 (1995): 87–100.

Taylor, John. Rev. of *Décor ciment*, by François Bon. *Review of Contemporary Fiction* 9.3 (1989): 218–19.

———. Rev. of *Monsieur*, by Jean-Philippe Toussaint. *Review of Contemporary Fiction* 7.2 (1987): 193–95.

Thody, Philip. "New Writing in France." *Critical Quarterly* 28.3 (1985): 97–101.

Thom, René. *Paraboles et catastrophes*. Paris: Flammarion, 1983.

Tilby, Michael, ed. *Beyond the Nouveau Roman: Essays on the Contemporary French Novel*. New York: Berg, 1990.

Tison, Jean-Pierre. "M. Toussaint boude l'écran." Rev. of *La télévision*, by Jean-Philippe Toussaint. *Lire* 253 (1997): 50.

Todd, Emmanuel. *L'invention de l'Europe*. Paris: Seuil, 1995.

Todorov, Tzvetan. *Les genres du discours*. Paris: Seuil, 1978.

———. *Genres in Discourse*. Trans. Catherine Porter. Cambridge: Cambridge UP, 1990.

———. *Introduction à la littérature fantastique*. Paris: Seuil, 1970.

———. "Typologie du roman policier." *Poétique de la prose choix* suivi de *Nouvelles recherches sur le récit*. Paris: Seuil, 1978. 9–19.

Torgovnick, Marianna. *Closure in the Novel*. Princeton: Princeton UP, 1981.

Torrekens, Michel. Rev. of *Monsieur*, by Jean-Philippe Toussaint. *Marginales* 219 (1987): 45–47.

———. Rev. of *La salle de bain*, by Jean-Philippe Toussaint. *Marginales* 215 (1985): 44–45.

Touraine, Alain. *Critique de la modernité*. Paris: Fayard, 1992.

Toussaint, Jean-Philippe. *L'appareil-photo*. Paris: Minuit, 1988.

———. *Autoportrait (à l'étranger)*. Paris: Minuit, 2000.

———. *The Bathroom*. Trans. Nancy Amphoux and Paul De Angelis. New York: E. P. Dutton, 1990.

———. *Faire l'amour*. Paris: Minuit, 2003.

———. Interview. France Inter. 28 Feb. 1997.

———. Interview with Bernard Rapp. *Jamais sans mon livre*. France 3. 28 Feb. 1993.

———. Interview with Marc Toesca. *Lumière: Magazine du Cinéma*. France 2. 1 May 1992.

———. *Making Love*. Trans. Linda Coverdale. New York: New Press, 2002.

———. *Monsieur*. Paris: Minuit, 1985.

———. *Monsieur*. Trans. John Lambert. New York: Marion Boyars, 1991.

———. Personal interview. 31 May 1997.

———. *La réticence*. Paris: Minuit, 1991.

———. *La salle de bain*. Paris: Minuit, 1985.

———. *La télévision*. Paris: Minuit, 1997.

———. "Toussaint, Jean-Philippe." *Dictionnaire de littérature française contemporaine*. Ed. Jérôme Garcin. Paris: François Bourin, 1988. 422.

———. "The Writer." Interview. *Contemporanea* 3.4 (1990): 85.

Toussaint, Jean-Philippe, and John Lvoff, screenwriters. *La salle de bain*. Dir. John Lvoff. With Tom Novembre and Gunilla Karisen. Paradis Films/Générale d'Images, 1989.

Troaino, Maureen DiLonardo. *New Physics and the Modern French Novel: An Investigation of Interdisciplinary Discourse*. New York: Lang, 1995.

Tye, Michael. "Fuzzy Realism and the Problem of the Many." *Philosophical Studies* 81.2–3 (1995): 215–25.

Uhalde, Antoine. "Un désert blanc." Rev. of *Seaside*, by Marie Redonnet. *Magazine Littéraire* 299 (1992): 74–75.

Vaillant, Alain. *Le rire*. Paris: Quinquette, 1991.

Van Renterghem, Marion. "Bourgois: Au présent." *Monde* 27 Jan. 1995: 5.

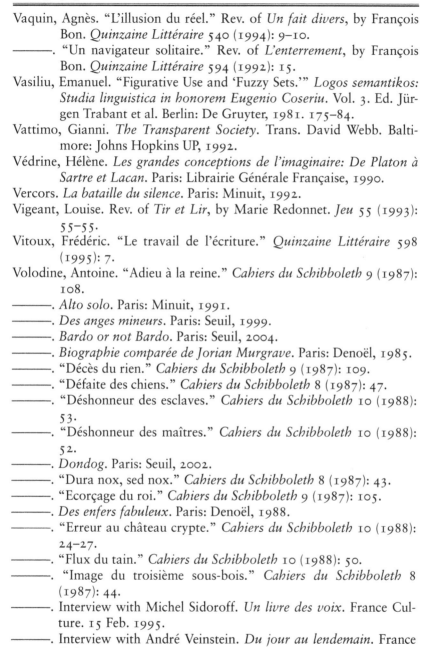

———. "Justice est fête." *Cahiers du Schibboleth* 10 (1988): 54.

———. Letter to the author. 5 May 1994.

———. Letter to the author. 9 Sept. 1994.

———. Letter to the author. 12 Sept. 1994.

———. Letter to the author. 3 Nov. 1995.

———. Letter to the author. 25 Nov. 1995.

———. Letter to the author. 2 Dec. 1995.

———. *Lisbonne, dernière marge*. Paris: Minuit, 1990.

———. *Minor Angels*. Trans. Jordan Stump. Lincoln: U of Nebraska P, 2004.

———. *Naming the Jungle*. Trans. Linda Coverdale. New York: New P, 1995.

———. *Un navire de nulle part*. Paris: Denoël, 1985.

———. *Le nom des singes*. Paris: Minuit, 1994.

———. *Nuit blanche en Balkhyrie*. Paris: Gallimard, 1997.

———. Personal interview. 28 Nov. 1995.

———. *Le port intérieur*. Paris: Minuit, 1995.

———. *Le post-exotisme en dix leçons: Leçon onze*. Paris: Gallimard, 1998.

———. *Une recette pour ne pas vieillir*. N.p.: Agir, 1994.

———. "Reflux du tain." *Cahiers du Schibboleth* 10 (1988): 51.

———. "Quatre propositions pour un rai." *Cahiers du Schibboleth* 9 (1987): 107.

———. *Rituel du mépris: Variante Moldscher*. Paris: Denoël, 1985.

———. "Spectre du deuxième sous-bois." *Cahiers du Schibboleth* 8 (1987): 45.

———. "Victoire des chiens." *Cahiers du Schibboleth* 8 (1987): 45.

———. *Vue sur l'ossuaire*. Paris: Gallimard. 1998.

———, trans. *L'auberge de l'alpiniste mort*. By Arkadi Strougatski and Boris Strougatski. Paris: Denoël, 1988.

———, trans. *Le chat sur la route*. By Viktoria Tokareva. Paris: Flammarion, 1992.

———, trans. *La grande époque*. By Edouard Limonov. Paris: Flammarion, 1989.

———, trans. *Happy End*. By Viktoria Tokareva. Paris: Flammarion, 1995.

———, trans. *Opération Faust*. By Fridrikh Neznanski. Paris: Denoël, 1988.

———, trans. *Roulette russe*. By Guennadi Botcharov. Paris: Denoël, 1990.

Vonnegut, Kurt. *Galapagos*. New York: Doubleday, 1985.
———. *Timequake*. New York: Berkley, 1998.
Vullierme, Jean-Louis. "Individu et complexité." *Magazine Littéraire* 254 (1989): 90–92.
Wajsbrot, Cécile. "Détruire, disent-elles." *Page des Libraires* 44 (1997): 28–29.
Watt, Ian. "Réalisme et forme romanesque." *Littérature et réalité*. Paris: Seuil, 1982. 11–45.
Waugh, Patricia. *Postmodernism: A Reader*. London: Arnold, 1992.
Weitzmann, Marc, and Sylvain Bourmeau. Foreword. *Dix: Virginie Despentes, Lorette Nobécourt, Michel Houellebecq, Caroline Lamarche, Eric Faye, Marie NDiaye, Lydie Salvayre, Stéphane Zagdanski, Dominique Meens, Marie Darrieusecq*. Paris: Grasset, 1997.
Went-Daoust, Yvette. "Ecrire le conte de fées: L'oeuvre de Marie Redonnet." *Neophilologus* 77 (1993): 387–94.
Werth, Nicolas. "La prise du pouvoir par les Bolcheviks." *Histoire* 205 (1997): 24–35.
Westphal, Bertrand. "Le quadrillage de l'arène: Temps et histoire chez Jean-Philippe Toussaint." *Versants: Revue Suisse des Littératures Romanes* 25 (1994): 117–30.
White, Eric. "Negentropy, Noise and Emancipatory Thought." Hayles 253–77.
———. "Serres' Revaluation of Chaos." *New Orleans Review* 18.1 (1991): 94–99.
White, Hayden. *Tropics of Discourse*. Baltimore: Johns Hopkins UP, 1978.
Williams, Raymond Leslie. *The Postmodern Novel in Latin America*. New York: St. Martin's, 1995.
———. "Western Truth Claims in the Context of the Modern and the Postmodern Latin American Novel." *Readerly/Writerly Texts* 1.1 (1993): 39–54.
Wingrove, David. "Thinking in Fuzzy Sets: The Recent SF of Brian W. Aldiss." *Pacific Quarterly* 4 (1979): 288–94.
Wright, Joanne. *Terrorist Propaganda: The Red Army Fraction and the Provisional IRA, 1958–1985*. New York: St. Martin's, 1991.
Zamyatin, Evgeny. "On Literature, Revolution and Entropy." *Dissonant Voices in Soviet Literature*. Ed. Patricia Hayward and Max Hayward. New York: Pantheon, 1952. 12–19.
———. "On Literature, Revolution, Entropy and Other Matters." *A So-*

viet Heretic: Essays by Yevgeny Zamyatin. Ed. Mirra Grinsburg. Chicago: U of Chicago P, 1970. 107–12.

Zeltner, Gerda. *Aesthetik der Abweichung: Aufsätze zum alternativen Erzählen in Frankreich* [The aesthetics of deviation: Essays on alternative fiction in France]. Mainz: Hase, 1995.

———. "François Bon." *Der Roman der Seitenstrassen: Neue Strukturen in der französischen Epik* [Marginal novels: New structures in the French epic]. Mainz: Akademie der Wissenschaften und der Literatur, 1991. 18–23.

———. *La grande aventure du roman français au XXe siècle*. Trans. Christine Kubler. Paris: Gonthier, 1957.

———. "Ein Selbsporträt ohne mich: Jean-Philippe Toussaint" [Self-portrait without me]. *Aesthetik der Abweichung* 240–47.

———. "Die unverbrauchte Kraft des alten Traums: François Bon" [The undying vigor of the old dream: François Bon]. *Aesthetik der Abweichung* 220–230.

———. "Wörter mit zu grossen Wurzeln: Marie Redonnet" [Words with oversized roots: Marie Redonnet]. *Aesthetik der Abweichung* 211–19.

Zurbrugg, Nicholas. "Postmodernity, Métaphore Manquée, and the Myth of the Trans-Avant-Garde." *Leonardo* 21 (1988): 51–70.

Index

In the Stages Series

Volume 1
The Rushdie Letters: Freedom to Speak, Freedom to Write
Edited by Steve MacDonogh in association with Article 19

Volume 2
Mimologics
By Gérard Genette
Edited and translated by Thaïs Morgan

Volume 3
Playtexts: Ludics in Contemporary Literature
By Warren Motte

Volume 4
*New Novel, New Wave, New Politics: Fiction and the Represen-
tation of History in Postwar France*
By Lynn A. Higgins

Volume 5
*Art for Art's Sake and Literary Life: How Politics and Markets Helped
Shape the Ideology and Culture of Aestheticism, 1790–1990*
By Gene H. Bell-Villada

Volume 6
Semiotic Investigations: Towards an Effective Semiotics
By Alec McHoul

Volume 7
Rue Ordener, Rue Labat
By Sarah Kofman
Translated by Ann Smock

Volume 8
Palimpsests: Literature in the Second Degree
By Gérard Genette
Translated by Channa Newman and Claude Doubinsky

Lightning Source UK Ltd.
Milton Keynes UK
UKHW012248280822
407869UK00010B/144